HISTORIC
MAR... , ...

Presented

By

Martin Woman's Club

2015

The Little Town of Martin, a historic village in Northeast
Georgia, located in Stephens
County, near Interstate 85 and Lake Hartwell. While small, it is
a town very much traditional
with progressive, cultured and hospitable people.

Table of Contents

CHAPTER ONE
From the Mayor

I am excited to share some good things through the publishing of this Martin History book. I am very proud of our community and hope that you will enjoy Martin as a visitor, tourist, resident or business owner.

Martin is considered by many as one of the most beautiful historical towns in Georgia boasting an exceptional "quality of life" for its citizens and visitors. We are committed to the preservation and protection of our historic structures, our clean and healthy environment and the safety of our residents.

Our Community takes pride in our services, our recreation facilities, our park, our water system, our fire department and other programs and services.
Some of the major events enjoyed by many visitors include the "Martin Fall Festival", "Martin Spring Festival," "Martin Lions Club - Chicken-que", "Martin Woman's Club Tour of Homes" and the beautiful Christmas lights and decorations.

The Town of Martin is a caring community where neighbors support each other and where families grow and prosper in a safe and healthy environment. It is my hope you will enjoy this "Historic Ramblings of Martin, Georgia".

Don Foster, Mayor.

Others who have served as mayor are; Robert Garner (1907), R. M. Freeman (great grandfather of Danny Sue White), Cliff Mitchell (son of Pink Mitchell), L. V. Matheson, M. C. Jarrett, Pope Yow, (son of T.R. Yow), Elmer Freeman, J. F. Taylor, R. T. Littleton, W. H. Swaim,

J. E. Brown, J. H. Chappelear, G. W. Walters, G. W. Hayes, J. A. Burruss, Dr. J. H. Crawford, C. T. Fisher, M. P. Carter, E. A. Blackwell, Doyle Land, Richard B. Dean, (son of Richard Arthur Dean), F. M. Massey, Thomas Russell Yow Williams (grandson of T. R. Yow), Thomas Looney (relative of J. M. Looney), R. R. Dick Yow (grandson of T. R. Yow), Mose Thomas (son of Anderson Thomas), Mike Cole (former husband of Diane Yow Cole White) and current mayor Donald Foster.

Those who have served as councilmen, J. B. McMurry, H. T. Mitchell, R. M. Freeman, G. W. Hayes, P. D. Landrum, J. T. Farmer, Cliff Mitchell, W. J. Mitchell, R. T. Littleton, R. C. Land, R. M. Freeman, R. A. Seyne, H. H. Bagwell, Lloyd Brown, J. H. Clodfelter, Richard Dean, H. C. Verner, Ralph Clodfelter, L. F. Taylor, B. J. Price, W. B. Price, L. B. Thomas, J. T. Turner, Ivan Thomas, Robert (Bob) Mitchell, Lee Yow, E. A. Blackwell, J. T. McCall, R. C. Land, J. H. Chappelear, Pope Yow, A. L. Harrison, Mrs. Lee Yow, Mrs. Lloyd Brown, Claude Mitchell, Dante Freeman, Miller Stovall, John Goodwin, Ralph Dean, Dan Mathews, George H. Dean, J. H. Burress, Thomas G. Walters, D. A. Garner, W. R. Odell, Elmer Freeman, T. S. Seagers, T. C. Stovall, Robert A.Dean, L. C. Stovall, B. N. Walters, Harold Vandiver, Fred Holland, Mrs. Clarence Stovall, Pete McCall, Mildred Crawford, Sarah Stovall, Mose Thomas, Vera Bagwell, Mrs. Grady Bell, Dick Yow, Donald Foster, Bruce Thomas, R. Brown Dean, Mike Cole, Mark Gearhart, Jimmy Turner, Roy Walters,.Harold Walters, Mrs. Gerry Stovall, Tom Williams, Doyle Combs, James R. (Dickey) Turner, Chester Brock, Swain Looney, Harold Thomas, Harold Alexander, Johnnie Hornick, Sandy Stovall, Bob Stovall, Roger Looney.

The Mayors and Councilmen have put into place numerous ordinances for the town of Martin over the years. Some of these are:

1. No one is permitted to build a wooden structure in town.
2. In 1911, street tax ordinance was $3.00 or 4 days work on the roads for a year.
3. In 1910 the (Street Gang Ordinance) was enacted; Anyone who violated the ordinance had to work on the streets, sidewalks, or alleys, under the supervision of the Marshall.
4. No one was to hitch a horse, mule or ox, or any other animal to a shade tree, fence, or railing, other than their own property. They would be fined .50 cents to $1.00 or to be confined to the calaboose (jail) for one to five hours.
5. No one was to jump or get on a railroad train while in motion, or be fined .50 cents to $5.00.
6. Anyone turning horses, mules, or other stock loose in town shall pay for damage and be fined .25s cents to $1.00 or put in the calaboose (jail) for 1 to 5 hours.
7. All residents and owners of property in the town of Martin are required to keep their premises in a clean and healthy condition; anyone failing to remove nuisance when requested to do so by the Mayor is subject is subject to a fine of .50 cents to $5.00, together for cost of removing same.
8. In 1918 an ordinance was passed to prevent dogs from running at large without being muzzled; these dogs would be killed by the Marshall or any person so offended.
9. Lloyd Brown, G. W. Hayes and J. T. McCall were elected Tax Assessors of property for taxation in 1918.
10. On April 12, 1921, was set for a general clean up day in Martin to make the town clean and healthy.
11. In 1923 a law was passed by the Mayor and Council that all life insurance companies pay $10.

12. In 1923 a motion was passed by Mayor and Council to provide lemonade for highway tourists and the Mayor was given the power to prevent boys from loitering and loafing on the streets of Martin after 9 P.M. and he was to use his own discretion of punishment of those who violated the regulation.

13. In January, 1924 a "night watchman" was hired by the Mayor and Council; the salary being $75 per month. He was unemployed by June, 1924.

14. In June, 1924 a public water closet (toilet) was moved to a gully behind the courthouse.

15. In the '20's Napolean Belcher was paid $7.50 to clean off the Martin cemetery.

16. In May of 1922 R. M. Freeman, G. H. Dean, R. D. Clodfelter and Andrew Thomas asked the Bank of Toccoa to borrow money to pay teachers' salaries.

17. By the '30's Martin had street lights.

18. In September, 1933, Martin asked the State Highway Board for funds to pave the downtown section of Martin (2 1/2 miles).

19. Also in September, 1933 a motion was carried to pay $10 to help get the Ty Cobb Highway paved.

20. In 1935, a tax was $5 to those who sold beer and wine in Martin. This was repealed in January, 1936. On December 23, 1935, an election was held to see if they wanted to do away with the school system.

21. In February, 1936, W. J. Burgess was hired to put up 12 hitching posts in Martin.

22. In February, 1937, it was voted to leave on the two street lights.

23. In May, 1937, two open wells were on the property of the Woman's Club and Mrs. Bess Dean.

24. In January, 1939, it was voted that the two street lights be turned off.

25. In 1940 a yearly tax of $10 was due from oil companies, $7.50 from Coca Cola Company and .50 cents for other bottling companies. Candy companies were charged $2.00.

26. In 1941 speed limit signs were installed in the school zones.

27. In 1942 the Mayor and Clerk were to see what they could get for the Calaboose and lot.

28. In 1950, Council and Mayor voted to not keep a street light at the school, since the school closed in 1949.

29. In 1952, no more pool playing was allowed in Martin on Sunday.

30. In 1953, a vote was taken to keep beer out of Martin.

31. In 1954, Council voted to ask voters to abolish the school system.

32. In 1954, the Martin school system merged with the Stephens County school system.

33. In the '60's the water system was put in the town of Martin.

34. In 1966, an ordinance was passed that no one was to post advertisements in public places or streets, poles, buildings or trees in town limits.

35. The Mayor and Council told Glenn Mosely to not park his car on the sidewalk.

36. In October, 1967, Council met with Representative Dan Moore and Commissioner Chuck Gaines to discuss street pavement in Martin.

37. In 1968, the Council made available the Community Center field for baseball players.

38. In 1969, the Council purchased Walkie Talkies for the police force.

39. In 1970, the Barbecue Shed was built behind the Martin Community Center and the Boy Scouts were paid .50 cents an hour to clean Martin streets.

40. In the 1970's a new fire truck was purchased.

41. In 1972, Mrs. Leon Harrison became the town clerk.

From 1912 through 1956 the following men served as marshals: J. H. Kelley, Ben Watson, M. D. Phillips, J. H. Balt, J. P. Miller, J. D. Hatchett, W. J. Elrod, T. M. Collins, Grady Haley, J. H. Hambey and Claude LeCroy.

In 1956, fines were issued to R. Pinkston (disorderly conduct $10), H. Arthur (disorderly conduct and no license $10), L. Carter (speeding $14), J. Bond ($10 speeding), M. C. Robertson (speeding $12), W. R. Howard (speeding $12), W. Brown (Carnesville GA, speeding $10), G. C. Rogers, Lavonia (speeding $10), Harold Barmore (speeding $45), T. Reese (speeding $45), N. Etheridge ($5) and B. Davis (speeding $10).

CHAPTER TWO
DEDICATION

The Martin Woman's Club is happy to dedicate this history to the people of Martin who have made this town known throughout the state and nation as a friendly, progressive, and delightful place in which to live. The history should have nationwide interest because so many families are descended from the original Martin family settlers.

In assembling all the material which has gone into the writing of this history, mistakes are sure to have been made but they have not been intentional. It has also been necessary to delete parts of the information received to keep the size of the book within salable bounds. It is hoped the errors and omissions will be understood by the good people of Martin.

The time span of this history is from the early 1800s with the first recorded settler and the first Railroad Depot agent. It covers the periods when this area was a part of Indian Territory, Franklin County and later Stephens County. The history of the town begins around the 1870's, it was chartered September 7, 1891. It includes all phases of the town, surrounding areas and the people. Martin area includes by our definition, the Martin Post Office routes: Avalon, Clarkes Creek, Fairview, Lyons, Mullins Ford, Toms Creek, Gumlog and Pleasant Hill.

Proceeds from the sale of this book will go for projects to promote and encourage the beautification, promotion and improvement of the Martin Township and the Martin area.

No one who worked on the Martin History Book had more enthusiasm and fun than Jody Freeman, age 92 and J. C. Farrow, age 89. They reminisced about school days, Saturday 'night life' in Martin and numerous funny happenings.

CHAPTER THREE
FORWARD

The place of Martin, Georgia, is unique in Georgia history because of its creation when the railroad was built. Martin was originally a part of Franklin County and became a hub for farm distribution. To those of us whose ancestors lived in Martin, we owe a debt of gratitude to the many compilers of this history who have worked faithfully and long to complete this volume as a resource document. The problems were compounded by the long span of 125 years.

This Martin History couldn't have come together without the help of many people. First, a special thanks to the Martin Woman's Club, who have believed in the need for a written history and have worked to get this book written and published.

Also thanks to the people in the Martin community who have contributed stories of happenings over the past years and the surrounding communities that now consist of mail deliveries with the Martin address.

Many people should be interested to own and to read this history because, it presents glimpses of their own ancestors in places and by events now unfamiliar in today's culture. We appreciate the work in which the contributors have shared with us for today and with others for tomorrow. Of course, the greatest thanks go to the Lord God Almighty, the most wonderful Author of all - the Author of life.
Rebecca Dean Kennemur.

CHAPTER FOUR
INTRODUCTION

Town of Martin History is a collection of family stories, church, school and community histories, reminiscences and photographs. This book tells many stories of the hardships and joys that have confronted our people. Throughout the history of Martin, its people have contributed much to the history and development of this great county, state and country. This book is by no means a complete genealogy or history, but rather a collection of articles submitted by and about Martin.

The Martin Woman's Club and/or committee are not responsible for any information that may be incorrect or omitted.

Pictured above the Woman's Club at a Book work meeting!

Seated L-R: Mildred Thomas, Kay Martz, Mary Jo Easley, and Rebecca Kennemur. Standing L-R: Barbara Sheppard, Carolyn Williams, Barbara Freeman, Sue Morgan, Diane Cole, Linda Dean, and Louise Wilson. Not pictured are Dannie Sue White, Polly Earle, Laura Turner, Margie Williams, and Andrea Pair.

CHAPTER FIVE
ACKNOWLEDGEMENTS

To acknowledge everyone who helped in compiling this history, would be almost impossible. It is our hope that no one will be omitted from the list below, but if so it will be from human error and we ask for understanding and forgiveness.

First we would like to acknowledge the help and cooperation of the Martin Woman's Club committee who so diligently worked to gather, research, write, and type this history. Special thanks to Dr. Joe White for his time spent in the creation of this Historical Rambling.

The Martin Woman's Club is the publisher of this history. The committee in charge of sales and promotion was: Mary Camp, Diane Cole, Linda Dean, Barbara Freeman, Rebekah Gonzalez, Cynthia Hilliard, Martha Jo Hunt, Rebecca Kennemur, Kay Martz, Sue Shore, Sue Morgan, Dannie Sue White, Carolyn Williams, Cindy Rondeau, Mary McNeff, Ann Mills, Sandra Oliver, Ruth Pless, Bonita Sherman, Margie Williams, Dawn McCall, Polly Earle, Laura Turner, Andrea Pair and Jeraldine Hayes.

We wish to thank the Mayor and Town Council and Clerk for their contribution; Don Foster, Harold Alexander, Mark Gearhart, Johnny Hornick, Sandi Stovall, Bob Stovall, Roger Looney and Attorney Don Tabor.

Much history of the Toccoa/Stephens County area has been recorded through "The Toccoa Record", "Toccoa Shopping News," Anderson Independent Mail, The Lavonia Times, Kathern Trogden in her book, "History of Stephens County," and "Stephens County and its People" published by the Toccoa Woman's Club.

Others who have contributed to this book include: Brian Stovall, Nancy White, Dannie Sue White, Mary Jo Easley, Diane Yow Cole, Katheryn Bradford, Cynthia Hilliard, Diane Carpenter, James "Spec" Landrum, J. W. Farrow, Jody Freeman, Wenferd and Leona Shedd, Pauline Keels Walker, George Knox, Loyd & Linda Melton, Mary Frances Bryan, Susan Watson, Kay Martz, Lamar Davis, Tom Williams, Evelyn Davis, Don Foster, Nadine Foster, Brown Dean, Jo Evelyn Dean, Linda Dean, Jayne Pressley, Terry Edmonds, Max Freeman, Barbara Freeman, David Mitchell, Ann Mitchell, Jean Thomas, Walter Fox, Andrea Pair, Dawn McCall, Dean Terrell, Marcille Sorrells, Grady Goodwin, Jack Bell, Loretta Moody, Jerry Poole, Jan Brown, Joy Mitchell, Claude Childs, Bruce Adams, Jewel Clark, Ray Ward, Connie Tabor, Sue Morgan, Charles Fagan, Geneva Pitts, Laverne Cheek, Jim Phillips, Lamar Davis, Eleanor Denman, Betty Farr, Miriam Purdy, Alma Teasley, Bob Stovall, Eugene Teasley, Ernelle Combs, Rebecca Kennemur, Ram Ramey, Stan Freeman, Ann Turner Young, David Medlin, Raymond Medlin, Phillip Eidson, Swain Looney, Mary Dean Oxford, Bryan Stovall, Tom Law (Toccoa Record), Judge Glenda Ernest and all the families.

CHAPTER SIX
EARLY MAPS, TRAILS AND TRANSPORTATION

Map of the Cherokee Nation with the names of the Tugalue River and Old Estoloe

CHAPTER SIX (1)
RED HOLLOW ROAD

The Historical Marker "Red Hollow Road" can be seen in the front of the Martin Community Center. This marker outlines a history of the road and its origins from Oglethorpe's creation of River Road which ran from Savannah to Augusta and then joined with the upper Cherokee Path. Red Hollow Road holds a place in history as part of a complex pioneer road system.

The earliest information known of the Martin area is of a trail that followed a ridge that divides the southwest water runoff into the Broad River and the northeast water runoff into the Tugalo River. This trail was first used by the Cherokee Indians as they took their furs, pottery, etc. to trade with settlers around the ports of Savannah. There were no hard to maneuver places on the trail until about 20 miles south of Elberton at Fort Monroe and Petersburg near where the Broad River intersects with the Savannah River.

Later the portion of the trail in the now Martin area became known as the Red Hollow Road. This trail has been a vital path since as early as 1700 (before James Oglethorpe came to Georgia). This road derived its name from a red hollow stump near the road.

Later the Elberton Railroad laid its tracks on the ridge known as Red Hollow Road. The Red Hollow Road continued alongside of the railroad tracks crossing the tracks several times.

Participating in the dedication of the Red Hollow Road historical marker are (from left) Martin Mayor Thomas Looney, Stephens County Historical Society President Ray Ward, Martin Woman's Club President Jean Goodwin, Mrs. Richard Dean, Martin Lions Club President Larry Whitesell and Richard Dean.
This photo is from *Toccoa Shopping News*, Tuesday, August 11, 1987.

CHAPTER SIX (2)
MULLINS FORD ROAD

There doesn't seem to be a record of another trail possibly from Pendleton, SC to Athens, GA. There most likely was a road as Mullins Ford community was named for a ford in the Tugalo River and the Jenkins Ferry area was named for a ferry that was operated by the Jenkins family. There was also a Perkins Ferry on the Tugalo River south of Mullins Ford. Because of these three crossings on the river there was a road that traversed through the Martin area and on to Athens.

According to several, including Brown Dean and Tom Jones, who remember the area, the original Franklin County Courthouse was located near the mouth of the Eastanollee Creek where it runs into the Tugalo River. Later when Stephens County was formed from Habersham and Franklin County, the Franklin County Courthouse was moved to Carnesville.

A plat surveyed by Thomas A. Yow, County Surveyor for Franklin County Georgia has been located. These 1287 acres of land was given as a wedding dowry to Russell Dean. This land was bordered by the Tugalo River east, had two creeks running through it: Flat Creek and Mill Creek, a road from Mullins Ford to Carnesville and another road from Jenkins Ferry south along the river called "River Road". It bordered lands owned by the Jenkins, Swift, Akins, Davis, McDaniel and Crawford families in Georgia. The original owners of the land were Walter Richardson, John Mullins and Drucilla Hackett, widow of William Hackett

CHAPTER SIX (3)
RIVER ROAD

There was a road that traversed alongside of the Tugaloo River (originally Tugalo River) called the River Road. Parts of this road still exist, however much of it was swallowed up by Lake Hartwell. Mullins Road, parts of Hardy Road and parts of Holcomb Drive and Seven Forks Road travel along the old River Road. Fording Mill Creek just below the Dean Home Place was a special treat for Sunday afternoon car rides in the 1950s.

This barn was built in the early 1800s and is located in Dean's Pointe on Lake Hartwell.

CHAPTER SEVEN
THE BEGINNING OF MARTIN
THE EARLY YEARS

In order to reach Fort Moore, the Cherokees had to backpack their goods through what was then the Creek Nation. A great deal of hostility existed between the two tribes and the journey was a perilous one for the Cherokees. Yet another peril was the crossing of any major body of water. In order to cross a large stream or river, the bearers were forced to construct makeshift rafts of skins and saplings to get their goods to the opposite side. The necessity of having a good trail to follow with as few obstacles as possible was evident and led to the establishment of what was to become the Red Hollow Road. With settlements in the area, it was soon to become Franklin County and later Stephens County, struggling to establish commerce, the need for a road system was met in every aspect of daily life. In 1792, the Georgia General Assembly passed a law that every lower court would be responsible for laying out a road system in their county. Every free man between the ages of 16 and 50 was required by law to bring tools, one good gun or a pair of pistols and work on the roads for twelve days out of every year. They needed a very wide area for the size of the wagons necessary to transport large cargos such as bales of cotton, or hogsheads of tobacco.

These wagons, pulled by teams of four to six horses, were driven by a peculiar breed of men. John Lambert, a widely traveled Englishman, wrote in 1814: 'These waggoneers are familiarly called "crackers" (from the cracking of their whips, we think). They were said to have often been rude and insolent to strangers and people of the towns, whom they met on the road.

The Waggoner constantly rode on one of the shaft horses and with a long whip, guided the leading horses. Their long legs, lank figures, and mean countenances, sometimes had a curious appearance when this mounted, especially if a string of them happened to pass along the road. Red Hollow Road, which began as a path made by Indians to carry trade goods to Fort Moore, evolved into a wagon road used to transport trade goods to shipping points along the rivers and on to the port of Savannah. Though the complete location of "Red Hollow," as a parcel of property, has been lost in the passage of time, a deed for 2,700 acres (called the Red Hollow tract,) located on Clarkes Creek, near Martin, Georgia, was established and dated in 1779. Though somewhat changed by time and the building of the railroad, the road still shows signs of its beginnings. The winding manner, in which it runs, evidences avoidance of obstacles such as hills, groups of trees, rocks, etc., as it laces back and forth across the stretch of rail that runs from Toccoa through Martin. Martin was an agricultural countryside, until the establishment of a depot. In 1877, the railroad was completed from Toccoa to Elberton. Approximately 12 miles south of Toccoa, where the much traveled Red Hollow Road, crossed the Airline Railroad, a station was built around 1875.

Around this station Martin, Georgia became a town. Practically all the land "round about what is known now as Martin" was owned by Martin and Herd, of Elberton, GA. Martin was named for I.J. Martin according to The Toccoa Record, September 17, 1925. Other accounts state that Martin was named for Governor John Martin, who served as Governor from January 1782 to January 1783.

 The establishment of the railroad station caused the marketing of cotton to far away textile centers such as Atlanta, Charlotte and Greenville to be an economic feasibility for area growers.

Landowners who raised cotton in the surrounding region profited financially from the sale of cotton. People brought in their cotton from miles away to be ginned at the Martin Gin Company, up to 40 bales a day. Officers were E. K. Matthews, T. M. Looney, W. H. Whiten, T. H. Knox, R. B. Harrison and W. B. Mitchell.

According to "Glimpses of Martin" in the Toccoa Record, Sept 26, 1907, Henry C. Black was the first depot agent and first settler in the community, however, according to "Journals of Flora Yow Williams," O. G. Childs was the first settler in Martin. He married Elizabeth Brock and lived in the vicinity of the former LeRoy Yow House, presently owned by Mr. and Mrs. Mark Gearhart. The Childs' store, located where the present post office is, was also used for the depot. Flora wrote, "At the store in Martin at various times, a clerk was hired because the train ticket office was in the Childs' store as well as the post office."

Shortly after the founding of the railroad, a great portion of the land around Martin was bought by Mr. H. C. Black for the sum of $3.00 per acre. He built the first dwelling on a lot where the T. R. Yow House (now owned by the Cynthia Williams Hilliard estate) stands. The first store on the corner where Hunt's Home Store building is located was built by Mr. H. C. Black. He was also Martin's first postmaster and the first railroad depot agent in 1880. Mr. O. G. Childs moved to Martin and built its second store on the lot where Randy Shirley's house now stands. In 1881, Mr. I. R. Randall built the third store and dwelling. Mr. T. R. Yow came one year later, building the block of brick stores.

The most prosperous business enterprise in Martin near the turn if the century consisted of a cotton gin (The Martin Gin Company) and a cotton seed oil mill, operated by Curtis McCall and Henry Price. The Farmers Cotton Seed Oil Company was founded in 1902. The original cornerstone is in the possession of the Cynthia Hilliard estate and reads; "T. R. Yow, Pres., S. B. Yow, Sec., Directors: S. Bruce, E. K. Mathews, T. W. McAlister, J. S. Crawford, and S. B. Yow." At the bottom of the cornerstone reads "D.A. Tomkins Co. Engineers 1902."

Neither of these buildings still exists. The brick buildings, which compose the present historic core of Martin, served various functions including general merchandise stores, drug store, Masonic Hall, post office, millinery shop, funeral home, several schools, two black smith shops, livery stable, leather goods and buggy shop, and the Bank of Martin. The farmers provided fresh produce, the fair and horse swapping convention were highlights during the year. Early business establishments were owned by O.G. Childs, I. W. Randall, W. A. Mitchell, T. R. Yow, W. B. Mitchell, J. C. Watkins and I. V. Matheson. The town grew and prospered.

Martin was referred to as "this splendid little business center," and the town's citizens as "so peaceful and law-abiding that it had no need of a town marshal or police, since there was nothing for them to do.

Landowners and business owners constructed large, high style houses along the railroad to reflect their new prosperity.

Most of the houses in Martin were built between 1882 and 1920. They have changed very little in their outward appearance. Martin has been called "a town frozen in time."

The oldest house is still standing and is owned by Dawn McCall. It was built by her great grandfather, Dr. James D. Ketcherside, Martin's first doctor. Two noted contractors that were given credit for building houses in Martin were J. M. Looney and Farmer Land. Martin was incorporated and received its charter, September 7, 1891.

CHAPTER SEVEN (1)
EARLY RESIDENTS

Adams, Acree, Addison, Ayers, Arthur, Alexander, Allen, Bailey, Burkette, Bond, Black, Brock, Brown, Bryant, Bruce, Burton, Barrett, Bussey, Burgess, Bagwell, Burress, Breazel, Baker, Camp, Cason, Childs, Chaffin, Cheek, Clark, Cleveland, Clodfelter, Combs, Coe, Cooper, Crawford, Crenshaw, Chapplear, Carnog, Carter, Collier, Collins, Chandler, Carpender, Crump, Dance, Davis, Dean, Daniel, Defoor, Edwards, Eskew, Edmonds, Elrod, Fowler, Fricks, Freen, Freeman, Farrow, Farmer, Fagan, Fulbright, Ford, Fischer, Freiman, Guinn, Garner, Grant, Goode, Gober, Griffith, Harrison, Holland, Hayes, Hodson, Herndon, Hulsey, Henson, Haden, Hardy, Hembree, Henry, Herron, Hoitt, Holcomb, Higgins, Haynie, Hilliyer, Ivester, Isbell, Knox, Johnson, Jones, Jame, Jordan, Jarretts, Ketcherside, Kay, Kennedy, King, Keith, Lyon, Land, Landrum, Landcaster, Lanier, Liles, Littleton, Looney, Mason, Matheson, Mitchell, Mathews, McAvoy, Mosley, Moss, Martin, McMurry, Mills, McCurdy, McCall, McAlister, Medlin, Montgomery, McCart, McCarb, Masey, Nelms, Nemmons, Norris, Oglesby,Owens, Outz, Pulliam, Perteet, Perkins, Price, Paybee, Pinkston, Pitts, Pruitt, Palmer, Payne, Porter, Poullmun, Reese, Rumsey, Randall, Rumsay, Rothell, Ropon, Rudeseal, Stephenson, Stovall, Stowe, Stancil, Swaim, Swilling, Schackleford, Smith, Sisk, Sanders, Skelton, Simpson, Simmons, Shirley, Spearman, Shaeffer, Stone, South, Thomas, Thompson, Turner, Teasley, Telford, Terrell, Thornton, Tribble, Vandiver, Verner, Voyles, Walters, Watkins, Whiten, Westmore, Williams, Woodall, Wheeler, Wilson, Whitworth, Westbrook, Watson, Whitlock, West, Young and Yow.

CHAPTER EIGHT
MARTIN HISTORICAL DISTRICT CELEBRATION

Thirty homes and buildings were named to the National Register of Historic Places, July 7, 1995, as the Martin Historic District. A walking/driving tour followed a celebration held on March 24, 1996 to commemorate this honor along with a display of memorabilia. The district includes 21 houses, the former railroad depot, the school building, business buildings, a gas station, and a former cotton warehouse. The historic residences in Martin are a mix of Queen Anne and Colonial Revival, and Craftsman elements. The commercial buildings are examples of Romanesque Revival architecture.

The Martin Historical District Celebration was held from 2:00 p.m. until 5:00 p.m. The program opened with special music by The Toccoa Brass Band followed by the presentation and posting of the colors by the Georgia Army National Guard. The national anthem was sung by the audience of over 500 who attended the celebration. Rev. Clarence Davis of Martin gave the invocation and choral music was presented by Martin's Greater Hope Baptist Choir.

Martha Mathews Hunt made remarks on the behalf of the Celebration Committee and Martin's Mayor Mike Cole extended a welcome to those in attendance.

The Stephens County Historical Society was represented by Mrs. Ben Cheek II. Brief remarks were made by Brockington and Associates' Scott Butler, an architectural historian and archaeologist who completed the nomination for the Town of Martin's placement on the National Register of Historic Places. A certificate was presented to Mayor Cole by Leslie Sharp, the State of Georgia's coordinator of the National Registry.

Former Governor Ernest Vandiver made remarks at this special occasion followed by guest speaker Representative Jeanette Jamieson of Toccoa who presented a framed copy of the Resolution passed by the Georgia House of Representatives recognizing the Town of Martin as an addition to the National Register. Mayor Cole received the Resolution and invited all those in attendance at the celebration to view displays that had been put in place inside the Martin Community Center (one of the Historic Places) and to also partake of the available refreshments.

All of the historic buildings are within the original 1891 map of the Town of Martin which was determined by an area of one-half mile in every direction from the railroad depot.

Open for the Celebration Tour were the Miller-Stovall house, the Martin Community Center, the Walters-Alexander, Mitchell-Mills, and Yow-Gearhart houses, a circa 1882 brick store building, a circa 1890 brick store building, the Dean, Yow, Yow-Brown-Eddy home and the Pope Yow houses.

The following picture along with a write-up about the celebration was found in the Anderson Independent-Mail, Tuesday, April 9, 1996.

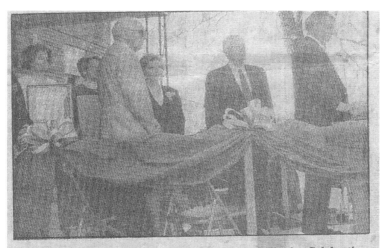

Participants in the Town of Martin's Historical District Celebration, left to right, are: Leslie Sharp, coordinator of the National Registry for the State of Georgia; Martha Hunt of the Celebration Committee; Clarence Davis, who gave the invocation; Rep. Jeanette Jamieson, who presented a resolution from the House of Representatives, Gov. Ernest Vandiver, and Martin's Mayor Mike Cole.

The committee members responsible for the celebration were Harold Alexander, Diane Cole, Evelyn Davis, Max Freeman, Walter Fox, Mark Gearhart, Kip Herring, Cynthia Hilliard, Martha Hunt, Rebecca Kennemur, Sue Morgan, Gerry Stovall and Sandy Stovall.

As a part of the Celebration, the Town of Martin Council approved the erection and agreed to purchase three signs that will communicate this historical honor to visitors traveling through Martin. Signs were placed on the North, South and East entries into the Town of Martin. The signs are approximately 4' x 4' with an arched top, cream color background and hunter green trim with wording in hunter green and will be "*Martin*" in bold letters at the top and "*est. September 7, 1891*" in smaller letters near the center of the sign and "*National Registry of Historic Places*" near the bottom of the sign.

Welcome sign for Martin

Cynthia Hilliard & Rebecca Kennemur

CHAPTER EIGHT (1)
MARTIN HISTORIC HOMES AND OTHER SIGNIFICANT STRUCTURES

The Martin Historic District was placed on the *National Registry of Historic Sites* on July 7, 1995. Listing in the National Register helps preserve historic properties. It provides recognition of a property's architectural, historical, or archeological significance. A listing in the National Register automatically puts properties on the Georgia Register of Historic Places.

A total of 26 historic resources were identified within the Martin Town Limits during the Stephens County Historical comprehensive survey conducted in 1989. The twenty-six structures have been listed within the Historical District. The structures are known somewhat by the residents who aboded there or the type of activity conducted in the structure.

A plaque was placed on each of the structures identified for entry into the National Register. The plaques were provided by the Martin Woman's Club to the property owners. The plaque reads **"MARTIN HISTORIC DISTRICT** – This property has been placed on the National Register of Historical Places of the United States Department of the Interior". The date or approximate date the structure was constructed is placed on the plaque.

The Martin Community Center, Highway 17 South was formally a private school called "Martin Institute". Built of brick in 1902 with additions c.1980; originally three rooms, a large room in the middle with 2 smaller rooms on each end. It has a hip roof with a large front gable. The windows are topped with lintels. There were ten grades and after 1934, upper grade students were sent to Eastanollee. The school closed in 1946. The building was given to the Town of Martin in the late 1940's and serves as the community center and the town offices. The hardwood floor has been preserved.

The Stovall-Griffith-Land Home, Highway 17 South, built 1890, an I-house with a front portico and second story balcony. The Interior consists of entry hall, living, dining, two bedrooms, kitchen & bath. 6/6 windows. George Stovall built the house for his daughter Virginia who never lived in the house due to her death in 1902. The house is owned and being restored by Robert Zmud & Susan Batka.

The Stovall-Morgan House, Highway 17 South c. 1920, a high-style Craftsman and Colonial Revival Stylistic elements, consists of brick foundation, yellow brick exterior, 8/1 windows and more than 4200 square feet of heated space. The house is two stories with a basement including nine rooms and two baths. The house was built for Thomas Henry Stovall and has always been occupied by the Stovall family. The property is owned and was restored by Ferrell and Sue (Stovall) Morgan.

The Alexander-Walters-Davis Home, Highway 17 South, 1905; high-style Queen Anne house with 1/1 windows. Interior features a spindle railing staircase and a circular landing. An upstairs parlor features a diamond-shaped window seen from the front of the house. The center chimney with five original fireplaces gives the appearance that the house was built around it. The house has more than 2700 square feet of heated space. The House was originally built for Dr. Robert M. Alexander. Present owners are Clarence and Evelyn Davis who added three rooms in 1993.

The Walters – Alexander Home, Walters Road. 1904; a high-style Queen Anne house with 16 rooms, 1/1 windows, and high gable pressed metal shingle roof and more than 5300 square feet heated. The house has floors of pine and original chair railing and wainscoting with a spindle staircase to the upper level. There are five original fireplaces with mantles intact. All of the timbers of native pine and oak were hand-cut and milled on the property. A sun porch, bath, and laundry room has been added. The original summer porch was converted to a kitchen. The house was built for Robert M. Walters and has been restored by present owner Harold L. Alexander.

The Yow-Gearhart Home, Highway 17 South (Main Street), Built for Lee Yow in 1911 by Tom Young. It is an eclectic high-style house with neoclassical, Queen Anne, and Colonial Revival stylistic elements. The residence has leaded and beveled glass windows with a porch that extends across the front and side with double columns as support and bannisters between the columns. Some windows are diamond shaped over single pane. The home has four unique mantles, pocket doors and floors of heart pine. The house was restored by current owners Mark and Tammy (Looney) Gearhart.

The Ketchersid – Crawford - McCall Home, Banks Street, 1882. It was the first home built in Martin. Dr. James Douglas Ketchersid was Martin's first physician. Built by W.B. Mitchell, this home has four rooms on the first floor, and four on the second. A hall runs the length of the house on both floors. 6/6 windows and gables are interesting features of the house. The front features a central two-story portico. The home was restored to its original condition with an added screened porch to the rear of the house by present owner Dawn McCall, great-granddaughter of Dr. Ketchersid.

The Garner – Hayes – Mitchell – Crawford - Pair Home, Banks Street, 1895, a Queen Anne gable ell cottage. It features 6/6 windows, a cupola on the front porch, high gables and boxed returns. The house was built for Bob Garner by W.A. Mitchell. It was originally a four room house with two additions over time and has an enclosed porch containing a well. The house has been restored by current owners Tom and Andrea (McCall) Pair.

The Mitchell – Crawford – McCall – Medlin - Love House, Banks Street, 1890 is a vernacular Queen Anne cottage. The residence consists of 2/2 windows, six rooms, an entry hall and a bath that was added in 1953. Present owners are Kevin and Lori Love.

Hunt's Store, Highway 17 North (Main Street), 1890; Built as the Bank of Martin and contains the original bank vault. It is a brick building exhibiting Romanesque stylistic elements. It has a brick foundation, brick exterior, and an asphalt shingle roof. *The Greater Faith Fellowship Church* currently uses the building for their services. The building is owned by Bill and Martha Jo (Matthews) Hunt.

The Clodfelter – Mitchell – Stephenson - Watson Home, Highway 17 North (Main Street), 1890, a high-style Queen Anne House designed with a center hall from front to back with leaded glass windows and multiple fireplaces. The house was built by William Alexander Mitchell and consists of eleven rooms, two halls, and 3 baths with3300 sq. ft. heated. There are several gables with cornice and boxed returns, a wraparound porch and a two-story bay. The house was once used as a private school and has been restored to its original condition by current owner Susan Blakley Watson.

The Lloyd Brown - Shirley House, Highway 17 North, 1925; a simple Colonial Revival house built by Farmer Land. The residence is built of brick and clapboard siding. Present owners are Randy and Cheryl Shirley.

The Martin Baptist Church was constituted in 1886 and called "The Red Hollow Church". The name was changed in 1886. The first pastor was Dr. P. F. Crawford. The church is a member of the Tugalo Association. The structure is not in the National Register but is significant to the Town of Martin.

The Pope Yow House, Red Hollow Road was built in 1921 and was designed by Leila Ross Wilburn, an early 20th-century architect, one of the first women in Georgia to enter that profession. The Craftsman American Bungalow with 16 rooms and includes a 44' long hall down the center of the house. The dormer windows and the latticework are typical of this style. The stone columns are built from Elberton granite. The interior is original with 1920 furnishings. Current owner is granddaughter Diane Yow Cole-White.

The Yow-Brown-Foster Home, Red Hollow Road, 1895 is a high style Colonial Revival Home. The original portion of this house was built for Herbert Yow by Tom Young. Additions were made to the house in 1908 and 1923, when the second story was added. The home has two central monumental porticos with six columns of the Tuscan order, the gables on the portico and on the sides of the house. The interior features massive wood trim, solid oak floors and a *"Gone with the Wind"* staircase. The lighted stone and iron fence were added by present owners, Martin Mayor Don and Nadean Foster.

The T.R. Yow – Williams - Hilliard House, Red Hollow Road, a 4000 heated square foot house constructed 1895 for $3,500. This grand house is a vernacular center hall Victorian house. The house has fancy scroll-work over the unusually wide wraparound porch, very tall chimneys, and a small second story balcony. Presently owned by T.R. Yow's great granddaughter.

The Yow – Dean House, c. 1880, Red Hollow Road, is a vernacular two – story center hall cottage with three gabled dormers. The house, which is said to be the second oldest in Martin, was built for T. R. Yow and sold to R. Arthur Dean in 1885. The house has 6/6 windows, a small front porch with boxed columns, boxed cornices and returns. Present owner is R. Brown Dean.

The Dean House. Red Hollow Road, c. 1904, an eclectic high style with Colonial Revival, Neoclassical, and Queen Anne stylistic elements. The two-story quadrangle with cone shaped roofs on each end of the house has 15 rooms and basement. The house was built for R. Arthur Dean by John Looney. It was remodeled c.1932 by Farmer Land who added two tall white columns that support the recessed entry and has a trabeated doorway to the balcony and main entry. Present owner is R. Brown Dean.

The Mitchell-Mills House, Childs Street built c.1908 for Pink Mitchell during the time of great prosperity in Martin is a high-style Queen Anne house. This large double-gabled house features two large gables over the two bay windows on the upper floor, and a large wraparound porch. The porch has three smaller gables, which complement the roof gables. Present owners are David & Ann Mills.

The Mitchell–Gibson House, Childs Street, c. 1883. The outstanding features of this house are the three front gables with boxed cornices and returns, the original house had a shed front porch with six brick pillars, and square posts supporting the roof. Windows are 4/4. The present owners are Leon & Blanche Gibson.

The Bagwell House, Knox Street, c. 1890. Was built for Jerry Dickson and is a one story structure of clapboard siding with a brick foundation. The Henry Bagwell Family were former residents and the present owner is Roger Looney.

The Jarrett House, Knox Street, c. 1890 was built for Max Jarrett who was the Depot agent for the railroad. The house is currently owned by Swain and Jean Looney.

Martin Train Depot, Highway 17 (Main Street) c. 1875 is a frame building with no stylist elements. The building was modified in 1970 into a business. Except for modern siding, the structure retains most of its integrity. The train depot consists of a brick pier foundation, modern corrugated metal exterior, and a V-crimp roof. The building is currently owned by Mountain Air.

Additional houses / structures on the National Register include:

The Mitchell-Morgan House, Childs Street, c. 1900 is a gable ell cottage. The residence consists of a rock pier foundation, weatherboard exterior, 6/6 windows, and a V-crimp metal roof. For many years two families lived in the house at the same time. The current owner is Charles Morgan.

Gas Station / Garage, Highway 17 South, c. 1940 exhibits some Streamline Modern stylistic elements. The building consists of a poured concrete foundation, stuccoed concrete block exterior, and a flat, tar and gravel roof. Formerly Glenn Moseley's Service Station, the Town of Martin presently owns it.

Palmer-Medlin House, Red Hollow Road, c. 1890, is a Colonial revival cottage house. The house was built for the Palmer family. Mrs. Palmer was Maggie Brown. Clarence Palmer was born in the house around 1902. The present owner is Susan Watson.

CHAPTER NINE
INSTITUTIONS

CHAPTER NINE (1)
TRAIN STATION

This was the railroad depot at Martin sometime early in the 19th century. There is no date on the photograph, but note the style of dress of the boys seated against the building and the adult man standing. Note, also, the separate waiting rooms for white and black train passengers.

The sign above the doors details the distance to Toccoa (12 miles) and the distance to Elberton (38 miles). Photo submitted by Randy Shirley.

The former Southern Railway depot was built around 1875. Renovated for business use in the 60's and 70's, it is now occupied by Mountain Air, a local heating and air conditioning company. The tracks are still used by the Hartwell Railroad.

The Depot included a passenger waiting room, the Depot agents' office, and a freight room. The original waiting room contained benches and a pot-bellied stove. The agents' office has a bump out desk area where the agent could look up and down the tracks.

The original Depots offered no indoor bathrooms. Privies (outhouses) were used as noted in 1917 Southern Railway documents.

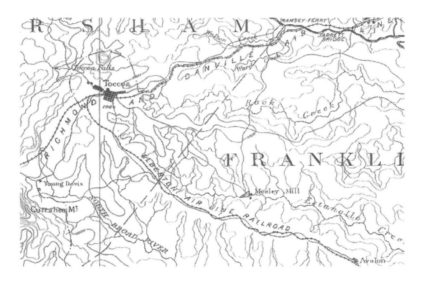

Martin - The Railroad and Depot Agents

The Elberton to Toccoa line running through Martin was built by the Elberton Air-Line Railroad, chartered in December 1871 to build a connecting road from Elberton to the Atlanta and Richmond Air-Line Railroad. The 51-mile 3- foot or narrow gauge (the rails were three feet apart or 20.5 inches narrower than standard gauge) tracks line from Elberton to Toccoa was completed in late 1878.

ELBERTON AIR-LINE RAILROAD.

Acc.	Mls	May 1, 1882.		Mls	Acc.	
A.M.		LEAVE]	[ARRIVE		P.M.	G. J. FOREACRE,
9 30	0	.......Toccoa[1]......		51	6 30	Gen. Manager,
10 18	12	.......Martin's........		39	5 35	Atlanta, Ga
11 12	24	....Bowersville[2]...		27	4 35	
11 21	26	...West Bowersville...		25	4 17	CONNECTIONS,
12 14	39	.......Bowman.......		12	3 24	[1] With Atlan.& Charl
100	51	......Elberton......		0	+2 35	Div. Rich. & Dan. R. R
P.M.		ARRIVE]	[LEAVE		P.M.	[2] With Hartwell R.R.

The railroad was controlled by the Atlanta and Charlotte from 1878 to 1881 and was part of the Richmond and Danville Railroad system from 1881 to 1894. After 1894 it was controlled by Southern Railway and was later absorbed into the Southern who converted the line to standard gauge in 1905.

A station was established at the crossroads of the Red Hollow Road and the railroad, which was to become the City of Martin. The railroad station brought into existence one of the most prominent figures in the social life of the country - the station agent. The agent was the local representative of the railroad in all of its dealings with the public. The life of a station agent at a small station like Martin would have been interesting and sometimes exciting, but never boring. Life revolved around the activities of the railroad along with those of the post office. Almost everyone in the community sooner or later did some type of business with the depot agent.

Typical qualifications for employment were a high school diploma, be 18 years of age, be able to telegraph at least 15 words per minute, and be proficient in the Uniform Code of Operating Rules.

The typical small town station agent opened the depot at 7:00am or 8:00am, daily except Sunday. The agent took care of everything and was highly versatile: after letting the dispatcher know he was in, the agent then cleaned the depot and greeted any passengers waiting for trains. If the weather was cold, the agent would build a fire in one or more pot-bellied stoves to heat the depot. Every time the agent left the depot, the agent had to obtain permission from the dispatcher - if his station was a train order station and most of them were in the early part of the 1900s.

At 10:59 each day, the telegraph sounder started clicking once per second until there was a pause and the final click denoted 11:00 am sharp. The correct time signal came from the U.S. Bureau of Standards in Washington D.C. All railroad personnel present were expected to reset their pocket watches. No wrist watches allowed. Precise time was essential for safety and smooth operation. It was the railroads that established time zones in the United States in 1892 to bring order out of the chaotic local time systems.

The station agent had other duties, such as making out freight reports, way bills, bills of lading, selling tickets, making reports, copying Western Union telegrams in Morse code, and processing package express shipments for Wells Fargo & Co. Express. People in those days shipped and received almost everything by rail: farm animals, tools, milk and cream, produce, dried fruit, gravel, automobiles, fertilizer, and dry goods.

Vivian Crawford McCall remembers bread being delivered from Elberton in baskets via the train. (Vivian has one of the original baskets. It belonged to one of the merchants in town. When her father, Dr James H. Crawford asked to buy one of the baskets; the store owner gave it to him.)

Customers were constantly in and out of the depots. Travel was by rail except for the shortest of trips that were made by personal transportation. In 1877, Henry C. Black was appointed as the first agent for the railroad and thereby became the town's first settler. Mr. Black built several houses at the station and established the first stores, in addition to his position as agent. The 1880 census shows Mr. Black as single, age 28.

The 1900 census identifies Orv R. Randal, age 26 who lived in Martin with his wife Norah and 4-year-old son Edwin as the depot Agent. In 1910, Jarrett McAlister, age 29 was the depot agent followed by Sterlang Thornton, age 56 who is identified as the Martin Depot Agent in 1920.

Thorton had a wife Victoria, age 48, and a daughter age 22. Other agents were Hollis Tollison and Paul Cooper.There were four individuals identified as railroad laborers in the 1920 census (John Sisk, age 43; Jimmy Martin, age 53; Charles South, age 27; and Guss Keith age 26 and Johnny Williams, black fireman.

In the 1940's, John Goodwin worked as a railway agent.

CHAPTER NINE (2)
SCHOOLS

Most people remember the Martin Institute, built about 1902, however, there is evidence that several other schools existed in Martin. There was an early school, where the Pope Yow property is now located. The teacher was Mr. T. B. Belcher. After that, there was a private school in the Clodfelter-Stephenson house with only 6 pupils.

Shortly after that, the Martin Institute (a private school) was built. Another school "Yow Academy" was in the area. Very little information is available about the school, however, several teachers are listed as having taught there around the turn of the century; Ada Acree, J. C. Addison, T. B. Harrison and C. K. Westmore and Ruth Crawford, according to an article in the Toccoa Record. In 1923, C. F. Fischer was the superintendent.

Several local citizens provided funds ($1,000 each) to O. G. Childs to purchase land to build the Martin School. They were R. A Dean, T. R. Yow, J. M. Looney, W. B. Mitchell, Mrs. Sally Randall, J. C. Watson, Reeves Randall, W. B. Mitchell, Fannie Fricks and others.

This was the first brick school in Franklin County (later Stephens County). Rush Burton was hired as the principal. Some of the teachers were; Lucille Roark Dean, Sarah Dean Jones, E. D. Mitchell, Joseph Eskew, Dr. Bailey, Julia Bell Clodfelter, Mrs. Hubert Yow, Richard Carpenter, Rev. Bussey, Mrs. Acree, C. F. Fischer, Mary Mitchell, Miss West, Rossie Harrison, Donnah Williford Yow, Madge Land, Sam Crawford, Harold Higgins, Ethel Haynie, Tom McCall, Vera Bagwell, Ben Burkette, Ruth Crawford, Herschel Crump and Professor F. W. Freyman (1907 Principal).

Martin Institute about 1904. Teacher Dr. Bailey.
Flora Yow, second from right, middle row

Martin School about 1910. Front row L-R Grace Yow Age 11,
Beulah Dean. Back Row. Yow Dean, Henry Price.

Pupils who were known to attend; Mildred Crawford, Estelle Bagwell, Vera Bagwell, Lillian Bagwell, Ethel Farrow, Brisdon Pitts, Ollie Thomas, Lallie Price, Alice Sisk, Ruth Yow, Clarence Stovall, Bernard McCall, Billy Burkett, Minnie Dean, Lottie Ruth Price, Harold Waycaster, Mildred Brown, Katherine Thomas, Edna Dean, Abief Bagwell, Gearldine Freeman, Bobby Craven, Donald Craven, Royce Craven, Dasey Lee Craven, Bonnie Sue Cheek, Cerelle Freeman, Celeste Freeman, F. M. Freeman, Harold Freeman, Eleanor Freeman, Dan Freeman, Joe Freeman, Elmer Freeman, Owen Freeman, Max Freeman, Danny Sue Freeman, Gwenelle Freeman, Phillip Edson, Ronnie Land, Harold Blackwell, Betty Jean Sale, Lyman Sale, Jr., Marjorie Mitchell, Louie Mitchell, Louise Mitchell, Royce Mitchell, Elizabeth Mitchell, Catherine Mitchell, Weldon Tolison, J. O. Garrett, Charles Graves, Catherine Graves, Ralph (Buck) McCall and sister, Geneva Vaughn, James Vaughn, Betty Jean Cheek, Jack Hubbard, Fred Dean, Henry Richard (Dick) Dean, Frank Phillip Dean, Hoyt Chandler Dean, Willie Washington (Bill) Dean, Mary Faith Dean, Lulye Harrell Dean, George (Andrew Jackson) Dean (Jack), Minnie Lee Dean, Jule Howard (Tootsie) Dean, Billy Turner, Joe Dean, Richard Dean, Clarence Stephenson, Herbert (Pete) Brown, Jr., Blandia Thomas, Harold Walters, Estelle Dean, Dick Brown, Gerald Walters, J. C. Farrow, Margaret Walters, Ben Stephenson, Evie Matt Thomas, Mallie Thomas, Sue Farrow, Vivian Crawford, Mary Cannie Stephenson, Grace Price, Miller Stovall, Reece Farrow, Pete McCall, Sarah Stephenson, Lamarr Addison, Jack Dean, Willie Norton, Christine Stovall, Joe Freeman, Doyle Land, Zetus McCall, Zach Thomas, England Sisk, Estelle McCall, Nellie Thomas, Merle Freeman, Mary Franklin Thomas, Dorothy Brown, Ethen Guinn, Yow Dean, Grace Yow, Fred Farrow, Beulah Dean, Dorothy Dean, Bernard McCall, Mildred Brown, Jim Crawford, Vannon Brock, Flora Yow, Henry Price, Ollie

Sisk, Tom Williams, Bob Stovall, Sue Stovall, Kell Mitchell, Jr., Richard Dean, Jody Pitts, Curt Pitts, Lee Price, Daisy Pearman, Fay Price, Lorene Price, Norman Price, Henry Stovall and Elizabeth Stovall

The Martin School had a newspaper, and the paper was "Margachat". The purpose of the paper was to create an interest in the school, to bring closer cooperation between the school and patrons, to furnish local news and to train for literary ability. The paper was first published December 7, 1928, bi-monthly. According to the "Margachat" school paper, one of the highlights of the pupils was conducting plays. The play, "A Silver Lining", given at the schoolhouse last Friday night was attended by a good crowd, Proceeds to be used for school equipment. This is a quote from "Martin Local News" in the Toccoa Record, December 12, 1929. The school closed in the 1940's due to lack of pupils.

Hurricane Grove was an early black school founded before the Civil War. There were only 6 students. Those associated with the school were Will Burress, Major Westbrooks and G. W. Norris. Later the school was replaced by Martin Grove Baptist Church. The Teasley family was very important to this church and its development.

TIMES HAVE CHANGED

Recently while looking through some old papers. I found a teacher's contract that existed in Maysville in 1920·s. It stated: This person agrees:

1. Not to get married. This contract becomes null and void immediately if the teacher marries.
2. Not to have company with men.

3. To be home between the hours of 8 p.m. to 6 a.m. unless in attendance at a school function.
4. Not to loiter downtown in ice cream stores.
5. Not to leave town at any time without the permission of the chairman of the trustees.
6. Not to smoke cigarettes. This contract becomes null and void immediately if the teacher is found smoking.

7. Not to drink beer, wine or whiskey. This contract becomes null and void if the teacher is found drinking beer, wine or whiskey.
8. Not to ride in a carriage or automobile with any man except her brother or father.
9. Not to dress in bright colors.
10. Not to dye her hair.
11. To wear at least two petticoats.
12. Not to wear dresses more than two inches above the ankles.

13. To keep the classroom clean:
       a. To sweep the classroom floor at least once daily.
       b. To scrub the classroom floor at least once weekly with soap and hot water.
       c. To clean the blackboard once daily.
       a. To start the fire at 7 AM., so that the room will be warm at 8 am when the children arrive.
14. Not to wear face powder. Mascara or to paint the lips. The pay was $30 per month. Times have certainly changed! Would you say for the better or worse?

CHAPTER NINE (3)
BANK

The Bank of Martin opened October 1, 1907 with a capital of $25,000. W. C. Mason, W. A. Mitchell, P. D. Landrum, George Stovall, W. B. Mitchell were the organizers. Herbert Brown was appointed director since he had the most money on deposit.

Some of the presidents who served were; T. H. Stovall, G. N. Stovall, and Dave Landrum. Other officers and directors were; Cashiers, H. S. Brown, T. H. Stovall, F. C. Gross. Directors were George G. Allen, C. H. Dance, H. S. Brown, Pope Yow, W. A. Mitchell, G. N. Stovall, T. A. Stovall, M. P. Sewell, C. C. Knox, Hubert Yow and R. A. P. Dean. The bank closed during the Crash of 1929.

The story of the attempted robbery of the Bank of Martin in the mid 1920's by a not-so-bright person: An elderly man entered Hunt's Home Store during 1999 and related a story his father had told him as a child. He said that a man with the intention of robbing the Bank of Martin entered the Bank before noon and hid behind some furniture. When the bank employees went to lunch and locked the bank, the robber climbed on the top of the vault. Later in the afternoon, employees heard someone snoring. Upon investigating the source of the snoring, the bank employees discovered the would be robber sleeping on the top of the vault. The Sheriff was called and the robber was arrested.

CHAPTER NINE (4)
CHURCHES

TOM'S CREEK BAPTIST CHURCH

The People of Tom's Creek Community met for Sunday school for several years in what had once been a schoolhouse located on the lower section of what is now the church cemetery. Interest in starting a church arose and, on Friday, October 17, 1913, a meeting was called for this purpose. There were seven (7) pastors from the Eastanollee, Mullins Ford, Lavonia and Bowersville area present. Three of the pastors were appointed as a committee to examine the 76 letters presented for membership. Those presented were: Liberty 1, Broad River 22, Eastanollee 3, New Hope 1, Liberty Hill 34, Clarks Creek 10, Pleasant Hill 1, and Providence 1. The Church Covenant and the Articles of Faith were read and unanimously adopted. The new church was pronounced TOM'S CREEK MISSIONARY BAPTIST CHURCH and was charged to emphasize a daily walk, family worship, church worship, keeping the house of worship, maintenance of church worship, and the Great Commission. Seven deacons were selected: J.V. Jordan, A.J. Watson, E.K. Matthews, W.L. Collins, J.I. Adams, A.L. Herron, and E.L. Matthews.

J.F. Goode	February 1918 to December 1918 (part-time)
C.T. Burgess	March 1919 to December 1920 (part-time
E.H. Collins	January 1921 to November 1923 (part-time)
J.R. Lancaster	December 1923 to December 1927 (part-time)
G.H. Collins	February 1928 to October 1930 (part-time)
J.K. Williams	December 1930 to March 1931 (part-time)
G.H. Collins	June 1931 to October 1935 (second term)

John Wren	March 1936 to August 1936 (part-time)
G.R. Fuller	March 1937 to November 1941
B.F. Turner	January 1942 to November 1954 (part-time)
V.A. Merck	1955 to April 1961
D.W. Satterfield	May 1961 to Sept.1965
Elton Lane	March 1966 to April 1972
Kenneth Moon	February 1973 to May 1975
Michael Dellinger	December 1975 to May 1980
Bill Humphries	October 1980 to August 1981
Don Harper	May 1982 to January 1987
Clack Stubbs	August 1987 to February 1998
Wayne Marcus	November 1998 to present

The People of Tom's Creek Community met for Sunday school for several years in what had once been a schoolhouse located on the lower section of what is now the church cemetery. The first Church building was dedicated in August 1916 On May 13, 1939 the original building was completely destroyed by fire. The second church building was finished and dedicated by the end of 1939 In 2006 the sanctuary was expanded by 700 seats and the front of the church remodeled. The first service held in the new sanctuary was Sept. 3, 2006

1914 Tom's Creek Baptist Church   1939 Tom's Creek Baptist Church

CONFIDENCE UNITED METHODIST CHURCH

Located on Highway 17 South in Avalon, eight miles from Toccoa, stands Confidence United Methodist Church (UMC) and, adjacent its cemetery. Confidence UMC is in the Gainesville District of the North Georgia Conference of the Methodist Church.

In the years preceding the Civil War, a small group of Methodists had for their meeting house a small one room log building located along the old Jarrett's Bridge Road which ran through the Eastanollee community, from Carnesville, Georgia, by way of Jarrett's Bridge, a covered span over into South Carolina, to the other side of the Tugalo River. The name of the log building which was used for a church and school was Mount Carmel.

The war took its toll and the few remaining Methodists located to another log schoolhouse known as Post Oak and Seven Oaks, located on the Old Red Hollow Road which ran from Toccoa to Lavonia. The building was located about a half of a mile north of the present location of Confidence.

Confidence UMC was organized in 1870, and in the early 1880's a campaign began to build a new church building. On October 14, 1882, a committee was appointed to solicit funds for the purpose of erecting a suitable church building on the Red Hollow Road one half mile south of the Seven Oaks School.

The location was in Franklin County until 1905 when this part of Franklin County and a part of Habersham County were granted to create Stephens County. The church building erected in the early 1880's served the congregation until the present building was erected in 1956, just north of the old building on the same lot.

In 1970, the church celebrated its centennial and an historical marble marker was erected on the original site of the white framed building. Confidence was a member of the Toccoa Methodist Circuit Church until the early 1970's. Fu" time programming has continued to the present, with outreach to the community ever present. In 2006, a long awaited cemetery grounds renovation project was completed with an arbor, fencing and an updated landscape.

MULLINS FORD BAPTIST CHURCH

Information in this section was obtained from family descendants in the community, Church records, deeds, and maps.

Mullins Ford Community encompasses the area of land down Brookhaven Circle from Jenkins Ferry Road to Eastanollee Creek. The land was first inhabited by Indians along Tugalo River until pioneers began to settle this part of Georgia. There was a ford in the river between land later owned by Russell Dean and where George and Claude Hardy, brothers, became landowners. A Mullins family owned land on the north side of the river and the ford was named Mullins Ford. According to Ray Ward, Mullins Ford was part of one of the main roadways going from the southeast to the northwest of an expanding nation.

Later a Jenkins family on the north side of the river and a Perkins family on the south side of the river put in a ferry. It is believed that the ferry was first called Perkins Ferry and became Jenkins Ferry when one of the Perkins girls married into the Jenkins family. The ferry became the most used method of crossing the river by travelers rather than fording the river.

Mullins Ford was sparsely populated with each family owning large tracts of land. Children went to school in a one-room log cabin not far down Dean Road on the left hand side. This school was called Mullins Ford School.

The families drove their wagons, buggies, or horses over to Tugalo Baptist Church for worship services on a road along the river. Traveling over rough roads to Tugalo Church was a hardship on the families due to the distance. It was decided by the community to organize its own Church.

A meeting was held in the Mullins Ford School and as told in the first minutes of the Church, Mullins Ford Baptist Church came into being. Its first meetings were held in the school until the Church was built.

There were two known schools on Holcomb Road. The Davis School and the Bruce Academy School. It isn't known when they were built. Later all of these schools were closed. The Fairview School was built at the corner of Brookhaven Circle and Bruce Road to accommodate more children since the community was changing and growing with new families. More information is given in my letter from Jerry Russell. It was told that Rev. Walter James (one of the former pastors of Mullins Ford Baptist Church) gave an acre of land on Jenkins Ferry to the school to plant a garden. The students worked this garden to raise vegetables for the school. The school deeded this acre back to Rev. James when he sold all his land on Jenkins Ferry to Julian Stancil. Mr. Stancil's daughter's home now stands on this garden plot. The school was built on land given by Marion David Payne whose home was right next to the school. Trustees for the school were: William Burton Payne, George Elrod, and Jack Fulbright. The Hugh Thomas home now stands on the school property.

Mrs. Payne ran a country store from her home. Later a country store was built on the land where Deman McFalin now has his garden which was across the street from the school.

Mrs. Christine Whitlock prepared lunches for the students and brought them to the school since there were no facilities at the school-only a water pump close to the road. The lunches were sandwiches of some type, fruit or a baked sweet potato.

Much of the land is still owned by the descendants of the original families but much has changed since the building of Lake Hartwell. Quite a bit of the land has been sold to people outside of the Franklin-Stephens County area, many families moving down from the North and the Atlanta or Athens areas.

Following are the names of families who have lived or still live in the Community:

ORIGINAL FAMILIES

William Hembree, John Ropon, Thomas A Yow, Russell Dean, Charlie Elrod, L. C. Perkins, Sloan Bruce, and others.

DESCENDANTS AND FAMILIES

Arthur Dean, Jasper Hembree, John Cheek, Henry Cheek, Jule Brock, John Brock, Hannible Isabell, George Hardy, Claude Hardy, Charlie Holcomb W. B. Harrison, Bob Harrison.Clyde Outz, Terrell Clark, Clam Clark, Joe Cheek, T. C. Burrus, Cecil, Poullmum, Morris DeFoor, George Bruce, Rev. Walter Jame, James F. Porter, J. S. Rudeseal, J. J. Liles, J. S. Edmonds, J. Turner Perkins, Clinton Fulbright. R. R. Voyles, Georgia Nelms, Joseph Whitlock, Julian Stancil, Harrison Turner, Marion David Payne, William Burton Payne, the Wilson family, Lanier family, Massey family, Alexander family, and Medlin family.

Mullins Ford Baptist Church

Mullins Ford Baptist Church

1940

1980

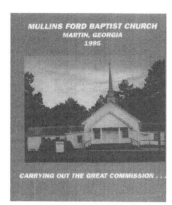

Rev. James F. Porter, Center

PLEASANT HILL BAPTIST CHURCH

The Pleasant Hill Baptist Church is situated in Franklin County, Martin, Georgia, about two miles north of Lavonia and about one-mile north of the Elberton railroad. It was formerly constituted October 18, 1872 by the following Presbytery: Rev. Jesse Brown and deacons: R.C. Burgess of Clarks Creek Baptist Church; L.A. Tribble and Hezekiah Hughes of Pleasant Grove Baptist church; B.P. Vandiver of Broad River Baptist Church; A.J. York of Poplar Springs Baptist Church; and W.M. Baldwin of Corinth Baptist Church.

Now the church being organized, Rev. Jesse Brown was elected pastor. The same day and hour the door of the church was opened for membership. Those joining were Rev. Jesse Brown and wife; Solomon Gillespie, Elizabeth G. Gillespie, Mary E. Gillespie, Nancy L. Gillespie, Louise Cassann Gillespie, Henry Pierce and wife, John Pierce, Nancy Pierce, Sarah Ann Thomas, W.W. Thomas, Mary F. Thomas, Alford Gunyon, wife and daughter, Ann Guinn, Sabre Guinn, Margarette Crawford and A.L. Stephenson.

PLEASANT HILL BAPTIST CHURCH: TIMELINE OF BUILDING EVENTS

Oct. 18, 1872	Pleasant Hill Baptist Church was established;
	Rev. Jesse Brown, pastor
1920	Recognized need for new church building
1931	Building Committee; see Cornerstone
March 16, 1932	First service in 2nd sanctuary
1934	Donated lumber for floor and benches
1935	Ceiling
1938	Electricity
1944	Gas and heat

1951	Finished sanctuary and classrooms
Sept. 13, 1964	Ground-breaking for 3 story building
Jan. 31, 1965	Open House!
April 15, 1973	New pastorium: Rev. Walker and family.
April 1, 1979	Ground-breaking for Multi-Purpose Building & Gym
Oct. 26, 2008	Ground-breaking for new church building!
Feb. 26, 2012	First service in new building: Worship Center
March 25, 2012	Dedication Service for Worship Center (Bottom floor unfinished)

MARTIN BAPTIST CHURCH

On Thursday, September 16, 1886 the Tugalo Association received Red Hollow Church as a constitutional member. Delegates to the association were I,W. Randall and W.B. Mitchell. The association meeting was held at Poplar Springs Baptist Church with T.G. Underwood as moderator. P.F. Crawford was the first pastor and served as such until December, 1889.

The name of the church was changed to Martin Baptist Church in 1896. The early records of the church were destroyed by fire in 1920 when J. Blanton McMurry's house burned. Information obtained prior to 1920 is exclusively from memory of current church members and from The History of the Tugalo Association published by Rev. J.F. Goode in 1924.

To quote Rev. Goode, "This church has always been a liberal contributor to every religious enterprise fostered by the association and is composed of a body of enterprising men and a band of noble Christian women."

The love of God and community is evident in that the members since the 1800's have continued to strive to keep the needs of each other in mind as they worked together to keep the church maintained and men of God to lead them during these days of striving to seek and serve God.

Martin Baptist Church has been blessed to have had fifty-one great ministers starting with Rev. P.F. Crawford as the first pastor and currently, Dr. Roddy Turner. The church has a resident membership of 228 and a total membership of 272. The church supports the programs fostered by the Southern Baptist Convention and the Tugalo Baptist Association.

Five ministers have been ordained by the church. Howard Walters, our own native son, was ordained in March 1942, Truman Brown Jr. was ordained in 1958, Roy Smith was ordained in 1961, Rob Stovall was ordained on Dec. 21, 1997 and Kyle Caudell was ordained in Nov. 2004.

According to Rev. J.B. Goode, the following named brethren served the church as deacons up to 1924: M.M. McMurry, B.J. Cleveland, G.L. Nelms, (J.L. Brown, W.A. Mitchell, E.M. Holland were ordained to the deaconship by this church May 3, 1908). W.T. Alexander was received into the church by letter as a deacon. R.M. Freeman, W.J. Mitchell and P.O. Landrum were ordained as deacons July 15, 1916. C.P. Mitchell, R.A.P. Dean, Herbert Brown and Elmer Freeman were ordained in April 1922. Active and inactive deacons who are living in 2014 are: Claude Childs, Clarence Davis, Brown Dean, Jerry DeFoor, Donald Foster, Gerald Freeman, Harold Freeman, Max Freeman, Darrell Harper, Paul Juday III, Gary Lowen, Loyd Melton, Alan Mitchell, David A. Mitchell, Charles Morgan, James Pless, Shane Roberson, Jimmy Shore, Bob Stovall, Bob Stowe, Mike Stowe, Bruce Thomas, Harold Thomas, Tommy Whitfield and Wes Whitfield. In the 1920's Sunday School classes met in the church auditorium, scattered about in small groups. To meet the needs, curtained off spaces in the auditorium were provided for some of the classes.

In 1934, the church began to see the need for a larger church building to take care of the additional growth. The church adopted "A One Acre Cotton Plan" and other projects to raise funds for a church annex. On November 27, 1934 a committee composed of E.F. Land, B.N. Walters and R.M. Freeman Sr. was appointed to make plans for building the annex.

The committee submitted the plans to the church on March 23, 1935 to build a wing sixteen feet square on each corner and a Sunday School Plant sixteen feet across the back of the auditorium to be divided into six classrooms and a restroom. The church accepted this plan and the annex was soon constructed.

In 1936, the steeple and bell tower were damaged in a storm. The same building committee was delegated the task of building a new church steeple and bell tower. The building and grounds committee undertook the task of landscaping the grounds with very little money with which to work.

In 1945, a movement was started to install a gas heating system, memorial windows and new pews.

In 1946, the church felt it was ready for a full time pastor and wanted the pastor to live adjacent to the church. A movement was started to build a pastorium. Most of the work was done by local people. The pastorium, located adjacent to the church on the south side was dedicated on November 23, 1950.

On December 23, 1951, land was donated by the family of W.A. Mitchell, with the stipulation that the land be sold and funds be used to rebuild a church steeple in honor of the donor's parents. The $2,000 proceeds from the sale of the land along with gifts from other church members were used to pay for the steeple.

In 1952, the road in front of the church and pastorium (Red Hollow Road) was paved. The church paid fifty cents per foot to get the road from the railroad to the church building paved. An electric Hammond Organ was purchased as a memorial to Rev. A.W. Bussey, a beloved former pastor and teacher at Martin High School.

The organ was dedicated in a home coming celebration on June 14, 1953. On June 17, 1956, a piano given by the family of Mrs. Lee Yow as a memorial to Mr. Lee Yow, was accepted and dedicated.

This piano is currently (2014) being used in the choir room.

Rev. Herbert Doud and his lovely wife, Sue recall the baptistery being made of brick and leaking. They also recall that their boys would play in the baptistery pool. Preacher Doud was privileged to baptize fifty-one people during his four years as pastor. Rev. Doud (currently age 91) continues to play the organ every week at Liberty Hill Baptist Church.

In 1957, the sanctuary was remodeled including heating of the baptistery, providing choir space, sheet rocking the walls, tiling the floor, painting the sanctuary and adjoining classrooms. Storage cabinets were placed in all classrooms. To protect the rugs and the tile, the walkways were poured in concrete. Most of the funds for this project were raised during the time the work was being done. A small loan was obtained and paid back by July 1958. The boost of the renovated auditorium gave the church a desire for an education building.

The Sunday School was overly crowded, new classes needed to be organized, but no space was available. Some of the classes were meeting in the auditorium and others in the pastorium. On May 11, 1958, the church accepted the recommendation from the board of deacons, that a Sunday School program be worked out for the purpose of drawing up plans for an education building.

This called for a great deal of work and much discussion before a plan was adopted. At that time, the church decided to continue giving the fourth Sunday offering to the building fund.

Chimes were installed and dedicated in memory of Mr. and Mrs. Arthur Dean and family. The chimes were given by Mr. and Mrs. Fred Terrell and family.

On October 29, 1961 the church accepted the following report presented by the building committee, "that we build an adequate educational building back of the present building and that a new auditorium be constructed as soon after the educational building is completed as circumstances will permit."

On Sunday, April 22, 1962, the church voted to start the educational building immediately without waiting for a greater increase in the building fund. Again, local people contributed many hours of hard labor. Much of the work was done at night by laymen who were willing to donate their time. The educational building was completed at a cost of $35,057. The building fund increased monthly during this time, but some funds were borrowed to complete this project. The first service in the new educational building was held on January 6, 1963. It soon became evident that the current auditorium was too small to take care of the additional growth in attendance. A campaign was started to raise funds for the building of the sanctuary.

This campaign was successful and in a short time the committee reported that numerous details had been worked out and sufficient finances were in sight to start the sanctuary.

On April 30, 1964 the work of demolishing the old sanctuary began. In December, the sanctuary was completed and paid for. This was accomplished through local subscriptions and with the help of many church friends. The estimated cost of the sanctuary was $40,000, but because of many free hours of labor by members and friends, the building was completed at a cost of $25,000. The building committee for this project was Mr. Joe Freeman, Mr. Mose Thomas and Mr. Horace Pruitt.

The first service was held in the new sanctuary on December 20, 1964 and that same afternoon, Linda Stowe and Edward Carter took their wedding vows in the new sanctuary. The first ordinance of baptism in the new baptistery was administered on March 7, 1965. The candidates were Debbie Pruitt, Tammie Dean and Linda Cox. Pastor, Rev. Virgil Merck elected to proceed with the dedication service for the new sanctuary on April 11, 1965 although the sanctuary's 45 foot steeple was yet to be put in place. Former pastor, Rev. Roy Melton preached the dedication sermon and former pastor, Rev. D.W. Satterfield gave the invocation. Former minister of music, Ray Whiten sang. The steeple was erected in the early summer of 1965.

In April of 1966, the church voted to construct a new pastorium since the old pastorium had termites in the foundation. The building committee was headed by the late Mr. Joe Freeman, who had dedicated himself to the task of improving the church property. After his passing, Mr. Bob Stovall became the building chairman and together, the men of the church constructed the pastorium located in a lovely wooded area north of the church.

Open house for the new pastorium was held on Sunday, December 22, 1968 and the lovely communion service on the table was one of the earliest used in the church. It was more than 65 years old at that time and had been in storage at the home of Mrs. Lee Yow. The silver service was to be kept on display at the home. The church borrowed $18,000 in November, 1967 to help with expenses of the building projects. The debt was paid in full in November of 1973. The church celebrated their debt retirement in 1974 by having a note burning ceremony in the morning worship service. Rev. George Dowd, pastor held an urn as Tom Morgan and Dan Freeman, co-chairmen of the original building committee, burned the note.

On August 3, 1975, a special service was held to dedicate new pulpit furniture in memory of the Freeman family. New pews were purchased in 1976. This pulpit furniture and pews are still being used in 2014. A study for the pastor, a bedroom and a bathroom were completed in the basement of the pastorium in 1980.

Central heating and air conditioning was installed in the pastorium in 1984.

The church raised over $14,000 to purchase the property of Elijah Collier located on the opposite corner of Red Hollow Road and Church Street adjacent to the cemetery. This property is to be used for future building sites and parking. David Doud was called as minister of music in 1980 and served faithfully leading in worship and directing multiple choirs until July 2000.
In April 1993, the church installed a state of the art PA system, including hearing-impaired devices, cassette and CD recorders/players and speakers. The cost was $12,000.

In the spring of 1993, the grounds of the pastorium were landscaped by members of the church under the direction of Gerry Stovall. The landscaping included new shrubbery in the front as well as two islands containing various flowers and trees in the front yard.

In July 1999, Diane Yow Cole and Mildred Thomas donated the land directly behind the church property with the stipulation that a 20' easement be given to Diane for a road if ever needed.

In 2001, the church voted on a three-phase plan: Number one being the construction of a fellowship hall with a kitchen and restrooms; the next project was to convert what was the kitchen in the old fellowship hall to restrooms; the final project was a multi-use facility with gymnasium.

Beginning the first phase, Building Project Coordinator, Claude Childs and the fellowship committee presented plans to the church on March 10, 2002. The plans were approved. A building fund drive was started with a goal $125,000. $53,000 was given that first Sunday.

The money was raised and construction was ready to begin. On March 17, 2002, a groundbreaking ceremony was held. After the building (50' x 70') was purchased and erected, the church family and friends took over the task of completing the inside. The goal was to have the first meal in the new Fellowship Hall for Thanksgiving.

After many long hours of hard work, dedication, and sacrifices, the Fellowship Hall was completed in the fall of 2002, one month ahead of schedule, under budget and debt free! The final cost of the fellowship hall and playground was $119,000.

On Oct. 27, 2002 the dedication service was held. The second phase of converting the kitchen in old fellowship hall to restrooms was completed on Oct. 19, 2005 at the cost of $13,595. Groundbreaking for the third phase which was a multi-use facility with gymnasium was held on January 15, 2006. A building fund goal of $225,000 was set. Facility team members were: Claude Childs, Chairman, Tommy Slaton, Len Stovall, Alan Mitchell, Bob Stowe, Chairman of Deacons and Kyle Caudell, Pastor.

On March 19, 2006, the church held a building fund march in the Sunday morning service. $25,405.14 in gifts were given and $24,594.86 in pledges were raised. On February 4, 2007, the building fund goal was met and exceeded, $230,031.

In the summer of 2007, the multi-use facility, currently known as the Family Life Center, was completed at a value of $500,000 without incurring any debt. The gym was used for the first time that summer for Vacation Bible School. The theme was Game Day Central - Where Heroes Are Made.

In August of 2007, Ray Whiten was called as full-time Minister of Music after serving as interim for several years. The dedication service for the Family Life Center was held on January 6, 2008. Pastors taking part in the program were Ken Hubbard, interim pastor; Kyle Caudell, former pastor; Roy Rogers, former pastor; Jerry Stowe, former interim pastor; and Clarence Davis, former interim pastor and current member.

Ray Whiten resigned as Minister of Music in July 2010. The church honored Ray and his lovely wife, Betty with a Song Fest and Homemade Ice Cream Supper on Sunday evening,

July 25, 2010. Rev. Steve Reibsome accepted the position as interim minister of music in the summer of 2010. Rev. Reibsome served faithfully until May of 2012 when he went home to be with the Lord.

On Sunday, March 13,2011 a "2011 Sanctuary Renovation Committee" comprised of the house and grounds committee (Max Freeman, Billy Garmon, Ken Marz and James Pless), Claude Childs, Evelyn Davis, Alan Mitchell, Joy Mitchell, Charles Morgan, Len Stovall and Mike Stowe was elected. On Sunday morning, May 8, 2011 the church voted to begin a sanctuary renovation project for an estimated cost of $55,000. The project included painting and repairing walls in the sanctuary, replacing the ceiling, new carpet in the sanctuary and downstairs in the education building, enhancing the lighting, new pew cushions, upholster and refinish pulpit furniture, new baptismal pool and baptismal curtains and new choir chairs.

Work began immediately on Monday, May 9, 2011 and was completed by the middle of June and under budget. The first service was held in the beautiful newly renovated sanctuary on Sunday, June 26, 2011.

On October 23, 2011, the church celebrated its 125th Anniversary. Dr. Norman Waldrip, pastor from 1978 - 1987 was the guest speaker with current and former members sharing testimonies and music.

In the summer of 2013, current pastor, Dr. Roddy Turner saw a need for a stronger children's program and asked the church to remodel some of the classrooms upstairs to make a children's theatre. The men of the church pitched in and did all the remodeling and electrical work to complete the theatre debt free in about six weeks.

Ministers who have served Martin Baptist Church:

1886 - Rev. Hilliyer
1887 -1888 - P.F. Crawford
Dec. 1889 - Jan. 1890 - E.P. Stone
Jan. 1893 - Dec. 1896 - J.F. Goode
Jan. 1897 - Dec. 1898 - D.W. Hiott
Jan. 1899 - Dec. 1905 - P.F. Crawford
Jan. 1906 - Dec. 1906 - E.L. Sisk
Jan. 1907 - Dec. 1908 - O.L. Spearman
Jan. 1909 - Dec. 1917 - A.W. Bussey
Jan. 1918 - Dec. 1919 - G.W. Bussey
Jan. 1920 - Dec. 1920 - R.P. Ford
Dec. 1920 - Mar. 1922 - J.M. Skelton
Dec. 1920 - Mar. 1922 - J.M. Skelton
1922 - 1923 - S.J. Baker
1924 - 1937 - A.W. Bussey
1937 -1945 - L.P. Glass
1946 - 1947 - D.W. Satterfield
1947 -1949 - M.L. Coleman
1950 - 1952 - Robert Scruton
1952 - 1956 - Herbert Doud
1956 -1960 - Truman Brown, Sr.
1960 - 1961 - Roy Smith, Interim
1961 - 1963 - Roy Melton
1963-1964 - Harold Burrell, Interim
1964 - 1966 - Virgil Merck
1967 - 1971 - Arnold Mount

1967 - 1971 - Arnold Mount
Aug., 1992 - 1995 - Deryl R. Odom
1996 - 1997 - Clarence Davis, Interim
1997 - Feb. 16, 2000 - Roy Rogers
Apr. 2000 - Jan. 2001 - Wayne Edwards
2001 - Jerry Stowe, Interim
Oct. 10, 2004 - Aug. 5, 2007 - Kyle Caudell
Dec. 2007 - June 2008 - Ken Hubbard, Interim
June 2008 - June 2012 - David Edgar
July 2012 - March 2013 - Roddy Turner, Interim
April 2013 - Present - Roddy Turner

This is a summary of the principal events in the life and growth of the Martin Baptist Church from her beginning up to the present day. Undoubtedly there are items that may have been overlooked, or omitted because of insufficient information. It is hoped however, that these facts will prove to be of some value in preserving the history of Martin Baptist Church. The beauty of any permanent institution of benevolence or religion is that its work flows on from day to day and year to year through the generations.

GA's of Martin Baptist Church   RA's Basketball team Martin Baptist

Congregation of Martin Baptist Church   Linda Melton, Barbara
Freeman, Mildred
Crawford

MARTIN GROVE BAPTIST CHURCH
(MARTIN FULL GOSPEL CHURCH)

In 1895 with land purchased from Mr. W.A. Mitchell of Martin. The land had three buildings on it, one was used as a school house. In 1966 under the leadership of Pastor E.J. Hardy, the church of today was built by Morgan Contractors of Avalon on land purchased from the Stephens County Board of Education. Pastor Hardy served the church for 53 years.

Martin Grove Baptist Church has had eleven pastors and with the assistance of Deacons, Church clerks and a finance committee has progressed. In 1972 a fellowship hall was added, in 1978 the church was paneled and furniture added, 1979 the outside of the church was bricked, 1989 saw the addition of central heating and air conditioning, plus a new roof. Stained glass windows were installed in 1991, in 1993 a new steeple was added. 2006 restrooms, a front porch & walkway. The year of 2007 the church changed its name to Martin Full Gospel Church. The church purchased additional land adjoining the church property.

Bishop Bardel Summerhour serves as the church's leader today (2015) On October 21, 1990 a plaque was presented to the church so its history may be preserved.

Martin Grove Baptist Church has had 11 pastors; Rev. Rice, Rev. Brown, Rev. Matthis, Rev. Burress, Rev. Hosea O'Bryant, Rev. Ray, Rev. Norman, Rev. E. J. Hardy and Rev. W. Young. Two associate pastors; Rev. Obie Duncan and Minister Katie Cummings.

Five Deacons: Turner Teasley, Will Pulliam, Jim Grant, L. Wilkinson and Rosevelt Teasley. Under the leadership of Pastor E. J. Hardy: Deacon Hugh D. Teasley, Velvet Teasley, Robert Teasley, Eugene Teasley, Marvin C. Teasley, Henry Burton, Elsie Carter, L. C. Carter, Mannie N. Brown, Curtis Crawford, Jr., William Teasley, David Ramsey, Phillip Teasley and Anthony Teasley.

Church clerks: Bro. Otto Teasley, Sister Rosie Wilkinson, Sister Burruss, Sister Ida Frusher, Sister Christine Teasley Staggers, Sister Lucy Faye Carter, Sister Priscilla Brown Harrison, Sister Earlene Brown Scott, Sister Mary Lou Teasley Oglesby, Sister Belinda Smith, Sister Tammy Teasley, Sister Annie E. Teasley.

Church Finance Committee: Deacon Mannie Brown, Sister Tammy Teasley, Sister Gloria Blackwell, Sister Mary L. Oglesby, Brother Joseph B. Teasley, Sister Shirley Perry, Deacon David Ramsay. At this present time, Pastor Richard L. Town is our leader. December 2005 the church name was changed to the Full Gospel Baptist Church.

Presently serving as ministers: Minister Ann Y. Johnson, Minister Mary A. Town and Minister Chris Mayweather.

Deacons are: Eugene Teasley, Michael Teasley, chairman and Rodney Hill.

Clerk: Sister Sharon Thompson. Finance Officers and Trustee: Deacon Michael Teasley, Deacon Eugene Teasley, Deacon Rodney Hill, Sister Delencia Teasley, Sister Jennifer Hicks and Brother David Merritt.

On October 21, 1990 a plaque was presented to the church so that our history may be preserved. It bears the names of all deacons past and present, who have served at Martin Grove Baptist Church.

History is today, tomorrow and yesterday. Things that are remembered as well as written down, Martin Full Gospel Baptist Church is a place to serve and worship our Lord. There is a lot we need to remember, but also enjoy. Philippians 3:14 says," We should continue to press toward the mark for the prize of the high calling of Christ Jesus."

ADDITIONS TO THE CHURCH ARE AS FOLLOWS:

1972 – Fellowship hall was added.
1978 – The church was paneled and pulpit furniture was added.
1979 – The church was bricked
1989 – A complete central heating Air system was installed and a new roof was also added.
1991 – Stained glass windows were added.
1993 –A new steeple was installed
1994 – The choir presented new chairs to the church
2006 – Restrooms were added to the front of the church, a front porch and walkway was added, new tables and chairs were replaced in the   fellowship hall.
2007 – The name martin grove was changed to full gospel baptist church.
2009 – Under the leadership of bishop Bardel Summerour the food bank and van ministry were added.
2011 – A new aluminum roof was added

2012 – On august 17, 2012, full gospel purchased the adjoining 2 acres of property, which included, 3 bedrooms and 2 full baths. This property has been prophesied for many years to us and it also lines up with the vision our bishop has for full gospel. Our God is awesome!

Several other additions have been added to enhance the church including renovations to the pastor's study and secretarial office. Other items such as office equipment, office furniture and musical instruments were also purchased.

GREATER HOPE BAPTIST CHURCH

In the year of 1874, two former slaves, the late Robert Shackleford and Jacob Knox; who were baptized members of the white Clarke Creek Baptist Church of this community saw the need for a Black Church for their people to worship. They presented themselves to Mr. Mac McCowans to ask for some land on which to build a church. He gave it freely. The land was deeded in 1874 in Franklin County, Georgia. Bro. Shackleford, Knox, Officers of the Clarke Creek Baptist Church and others met to organize the church.

The first church was a brush harbor, then a log building. It was given the name, Little Hope, so named because from little beginnings, greater things grow. The first pastor was Rev. Crockett Dooley. The first deacons were Robert Shackleford and Jacob Knox. The first clerk was Wes Crump from the white Clarke Creek Baptist Church.

Months later, a frame structure was built. The following pastors served in this building, Rev. Wade Knox, LA. Stovall, Dead Wiley, Walt Blackwell, Larkin Teasley, Matthew Scott, W.T. Burrus, J.H.Z. Anderson and A.A. Rice.

In 1930, a new frame building was constructed under pastorate of Rev. A.A. Rice and the church was renamed Greater Hope Baptist Church. The Deacons serving under Rev. A.A. Rice were Lee Keels, Will Barmore, Sam Isom, Henry Scott, Lee Combs and L'C. Isoin. In 1949, Rev. G.B. Strickland became Pastor. Under his leadership the church was remodeled and new pews were purchased.

Numerous fund raising projects were undertaken. On August 4, 1976, the foundation of this church was poured. This church was dedicated on May 1, 1977.

Serving as Deacons at that time were Detroit Reese, L.C. Isom, Doyle Combs, Morris Oglesby, Crawford Gober, Randy Combs, and Lamar Oglesby. Other Deacons that served under Rev. Strickland were deceased at the time of the dedication of this church.

They were Deacons Warren Washington and Roy Lee Oglesby, Sr. Rev. G.B. Strickland served as pastor for 39 years, longer than any other pastor.

Strickland became Pastor. Under his leadership the church was remodeled and new pews were purchased. Numerous fund raising projects were undertaken. On August 4, 1976, the foundation of this church was poured. This church was dedicated on May 1, 1977. Serving as Deacons at that time were Detroit Reese, L.C. Isom, Doyle Combs, Morris Oglesby, Crawford Gober, Randy Combs, and Lamar Oglesby.

Other Deacons that served under Rev. Strickland were deceased at the time of the dedication of this church. They were Deacons Warren Washington and Roy Lee Oglesby, Sr. Rev. G.B. Strickland served as pastor for 39 years, longer than any other pastor.

In 1988, Rev. Larry Norman became pastor. Under his leadership, the front of the church was remodeled and the church pews were padded. Deacons serving under Rev. Norman were L.C. Isom, Doyle Combs, Morris Oglesby, Crawford Gober, Randy Combs, Calvin Combs, Howard Barmore, and Byron Barmore. Rev Norman served as pastor for 7 years.

In 1996, Rev. J. Michael Johnson was elected Interim pastor and served until December of that year, and was elected pastor of the Greater Hope Baptist Church. Under his leadership, the youth department was reorganized and established second Sunday in each month as Youth Sunday. He began Bible study classes twice a month at the church. Later, the Bible Study was increased to each Wednesday in the month. Rev. Johnson reorganized the Senior Missionary Society and it now meets regularly. The church kitchen and church basement were renovated with new kitchen cabinets, a drop ceiling and vinyl tile was installed on the floor. In 2005, under Rev. Johnson leadership, the church purchased 2 acres of land across the road from the cemetery. After 10 years of service, Rev. Johnson resigned, effective December 31, 2006.

The year 2007, Rev. Michael Sullivan ordained three new deacons, Sis. Shirley Combs was ordained as Evangelist. Also, the church received a new roof and windows were installed.

Few members have been able to trace the history of their church past two or three decades. However, we have faith in the future of this church and pray that it will live and flourish in the hearts of the youth. We hope it will continue to meet the spiritual and educational needs of its members.

CLEVELAND CHRISTIAN METHODIST EPISCOPAL CHURCH HISTORY
From 1830 to 2011

The Cleveland C.M.E. Church began in the Bridgett House. It was established in the time of slavery under the direction of Mrs. Artie Randall.

A brush harbor was established: Randall Tentlman, along with Mrs. Harriet Burton and others began the work. Later a Church was built and Reverend Bill Payne, a former slave was the Pastor at this time. The exact date is unknown, but this church and church records were destroyed by fire.

Later a beautiful church was built. The members than were the Richies, Smiths, Sewells, Earls and many others. This church had a beautiful altar, lovely pews, and lamps swinging from the ceiling. Later an organ was purchased and placed in the church.

In the twenties, most of the members moved to a town near Toccoa, In August 1930 this Church was destroyed by fire along with the church records. T. L. Durden was Pastor at this time and Reverend Ernest Norton a Baptist Preacher delivered the last sermon.

Church Services were conducted in various other churches, until another was built. The Richie, Burton, Johnson, along with Brother Henry Arthor families and the community were very instrumental in the process of building a new church. The Pastor

at this time was the Reverend L. H. Whelchel.

In the early forties, Reverend T. C. Simmons was the pastor. Under his leadership renovation began under the existing edifice. Many pastored the church during this time. Sheetrock, tin roofing material, flooring, and brick siding were purchased.

Finally in 1973, Mrs. Annie Graham and Mr. Henry Richie were the front runners in getting the present building started. Reverend Allen was Pastor at this time. During the time of Reverend Jones, an altar was built. Later a door was added, rest room, ceiling fan, gas heater, central air, piano, electric piano, sound system and new front doors.

In 2004, Reverend James E. Boggan III was appointed Pastor. The church dream was to have a fellowship hall added to the church. In August 2005, Reverend Boggan spearheaded the driving force, of raising fund for the Fellowship Hall. All proceeds raised started the foundation and erecting the building walls. Curtis Scott worked diligently to have the land survey, the deed certified and work with Northeast Georgia Bank to secure a loan for Cleveland church, along with Thomas R. Richie Sr., Thomas R. Richie Jr., Roy L. Richie Jr., and Walter C. Richie Sr., to finalize the loan. Reverend Boggan, the church pastor, was the contractor to finish the facility. In June 2006, the fellowship hall was complete.

On October 15, 2006, the Fellowship Hall was dedicated back to God. Our Presiding Prelate did dedication service for the Fellowship: Bishop Othal Hawthorne Lakey, our 44th Bishop, and Presiding Prelate Bishop of Sixth Episcopal District Christian Methodist Episcopal Church of Georgia.

In 2007 Reverend Walter C. Richie Sr., appointed as Pastor of Cleveland C.M.E Church. Under his Leadership, over 45 new members have joined or dedicated their life back to God. Reverend Richie started the first Bible Study on 2nd and 4th Saturday, which was later changed to every Wednesday night.

Our Youth Department by God's Grace has blossomed. In December 2009, our youth had their very first shut-in, follow by a youth program include praise-dancing, skits, and singing our youth was truly inspired by God.

In 2009, Brother George Thompson Jr., donated a family van to the church. In 2010 Sister Geraldine Gober and Brother Thomas R. Richie Jr., on behalf of the Stewart, Stewardesses, Missionary Society and Trustees Board, replaced the old altar set with a new traditional altar set. In September 2010 an Organ were donated to the church.

Pastor Richie often says, "God is good," this is a special day to give God all the praise and celebrate. Reverend Melvin Powers says the church has been there 184 years. At present, there are about 25 members and about 15 come every Sunday.

THE HURRICANE GROVE BAPTIST CHURCH

The Hurricane Baptist Church, which was formerly known as Poplar Springs Baptist Church was established in 1877. It is said to be the oldest Black Church in Stephens County. The church was reorganized by Rev. Houston McGarity. Numerous Pastors served the church. In 1951 Rev. G.B. Strickland was called as Pastor. Under his leadership new pulpit furniture was purchased, dining room furniture. May 28, 1972, dedication services were held for the new

Church. Rev. W.M. Garrison delivered the dedicatory sermon. In October 1980, a mortgage burning ceremony was held. Working to improve the church has been an ongoing task: a lunchroom was added ad the choir area enlarged, central air and paneling was later installed.

Rev. Ronald Gantt was called to serve as pastor. Under his leadership the church continued to move forward. A new piano, (Clavinola), a van, comfortable pews. Mr. Swell is said to have donated the tree that was used to make the pews. Members purchased the pews and one was donated to the "Stephens County Historical Society.

Rev. Ronald Gautt

Sandra Scott Moore and Family

Always Remembered

Mrs. Willie Beatrice McCode

Mrs. Callie Barnes Ramsey

Annielee Oglesby and Cordie Shackelford

Deacon Benjamin Derich and daughter, Verlina Derich

Inside view of church

der Hurricane Grove Baptist Church

Deacon Jessie Roy Hall and Will Oglesby

Roy Clemmons, Will Oglesby, and others

Rev. G. B. Strickland and Deacon Will Oglesb

Rev. Ronald Gautt and Sister Annielee Oglesby

New church - 19

REACH-OUT TIME ORIGINAL FREEWILL BAPTIST CHURCH

The Reach-Out Time, original Freewill Baptist Church was founded on January 14, 1979, because of a vision the Lord showed the late founder Pastor, Willie Bernard Hayes. The basement of the home of Deacon L. C. Hayes of Martin, Georgia. They worshiped there for six years. As Pastor Hayes sought God for direction on building a church, a spot of land caught his attention. Mr. Tommy Williams, the Mayor of Martin owned the land at the time. Mr. Williams donated this land for the Church. With much labor of love the Church that is now located on Price Road in Martin, Georgia was completed. The dedication service was held on July 27, 1984.

Our founding pastor, Elder Willie Bernard Hayes was suddenly called home on October 16, 1991.

Bishop A. C. Speakman served as interim pastor from November 20, 1991 until June 1, 1992, when Rev. Aubrey T. Hall was appointed pastor. Rev. Aubrey T. Hall served for five years. Minister Douglas Ealey was appointed pastor of Reach Out Time in the month of October, 1991 and served until June, 1998.

On October 4, 1998 Rev. Alton B. Evett was appointed pastor of Reach Out Time. Since that time Rev. Ray Morris and Rev. Ricky Town served as pastors.

The first deacons of the church were Deacon Jerry Swilling and Deacon L. C. Hayes. The first Mothers of the church were Mother Blanche Hayes, Mother Bertha Brock and Mother Geraldine Hayes. The Reach Out Time Church was built on nothing more than faith, hope and love.

God in His sovereignty chose to call Mother Blanche E. Hayes from labor to rest. Mother Blanche E. Hayes, daughter of John and Alice Elam, was born on January 5, 1942 in Vance County, NC. She departed this life on August 10, 2004.

On Wednesday, September 7, 2005, 7:00 PM, Eldeer Jonathan Bernard Hayes (son of the founding pastor Hayes & Mother Hayes) was installed as pastor.

Through it all, God has been nothing but good to us and we are yet standing on His Word. And *I say also unto thee, That thou art Peter, and upon this rock I will build my church and the gates of hell shall not prevail against it. Matthew 16:18*

CHAPTER NINE (5)
MARTIN DOCTORS

In 1876, Dr. James Douglas Ketcherside, age 52 came to Martin from Ducktown, Tennessee where he had practiced for 28 years. He was married to Maude Anna (Brown) from Tennessee. Dr. Ketcherside is said to have built the first house in Martin in 1882 and was the father of Dr. John W. Ketcherside, Dr. Thomas Lyon Ketcherside (a dentist), Maude and Blanche. This was his second marriage. He remained in Martin until his death in 1895 and is buried in the Martin Baptist Cemetery along with his wife Anna, who remained in Martin until her death in 1928.

Dr. Thomas Lyon also came to Martin from Ducktown, Tennessee. He graduated from Atlanta Medical College in 1882 and came to Martin to train under Dr. James Douglas Ketcherside, whose sister was Dr. Lyon's mother. The 1900 census shows Dr. Thomas Lyon at age 46 living with his wife Emah, age 34, a niece Pearl Thomas, his Mother, Elizabeth Lyon, age 72 and Doris Crawford, age 19, a cook.

The 1900 census also shows a Dr. Robert M. Alexander, age 28, boarding with the Randals.

Dr. John W. Ketchersid, age 22, son of Dr. James Douglas Ketcherside, was living with his wife Hattie Nee Morgan, age 19 in Martin in 1900.

Dr. Ketchersid received his first educational advantages in the public schools of Georgia, completing the course in the high school and subsequently entering Vanderbilt University in Nashville, Tennessee, where he pursued the full course in medicine and was graduated M.D. April 1, 1898. His first practice was at his old homestead in Martin, Georgia, where he remained for six years. Moving to the west, he first located at McAlester, Texas, in Indian Territory, where he remained for three years and from there to Dallas, Texas in 1906 and a year later relocated to El Paso. There he raised ten children and had a successful practice. NOTE: Dr. John Ketchersid is credited with dropping the "e" from the family name. The siblings followed suit.

Dr. Thomas Lyon Ketchersid, age 19 in 1900, the second son of Dr. James Doulglas Ketcheside, lived with his mother Anna and sister Blanche in the Ketchersid home. He was the brother of Dr. John W. Ketchersid. Dr. Thomas Lyon Ketchersid, later practiced dentistry in Eatonton, Georgia and then in Sarasota, Florida, where he died at the age of 97. He was married to "Tommie" Augusta Cochran and had 2 daughters.

The census of 1910 shows Dr. James Harrison Crawford, age 37, who married Blanche Ketchersid in 1909, practicing in Martin. Also listed as a physician in Martin in 1910 was Dr. Willie L. Bond, age 36, who lived with the Garner family.

In 1920 Dr. James Harrison Crawford was age 47 and a practicing physician in Martin. Dr. James Harrison Crawford died in 1923 with a ruptured appendix. A Dr. Emory Chaffin, age 32, lived with in-laws Hugh and Mary Verner, his wife Mable (30) and son Verner (1). Dr. Chaffin died in Hall County in 1957 at the age of 71 while living in Stephens County. His wife Mable died in 1977 and is buried in Martin Baptist Church Cemetery.

The only physician showing in the 1930 census is Dr. William H. Swaim, who lived and practiced in the house across the street from the Ketchersid house. Dr. Swaim graduated in 1917 from the Georgia College of Eclectic Medicine and Surgery in Atlanta. Dr. Swaim died in 1945 and is buried along with his wife Frankie in the Confidence Methodist Church Cemetery.

We can find no record of any physicians in Martin after 1945. Stephens County Hospital in Toccoa was established in 1937 and is believed that most of the physicians lived in Toccoa after that time.

CHAPTER NINE (6)
MARTIN FIRE DEPARTMENT

The town of Martin had no fire truck until the city council voted to establish a volunteer fire department in September 1966. Martin's first ambulance was purchased by the Martin Lions Club in 1966. The first fire truck was purchased in Pennsylvania and had to be brought in on a trailer. This truck was purchased and once again the City Council voted in 1968, to help by purchasing all the equipment that was needed for the truck. An ambulance was also purchased to be used by the fire department volunteers. In 1975, another truck was purchased with help from the citizens of Avalon.

The Martin Lions Club raised funds to build an addition to the Martin Community Center. This addition became the Martin Fire Department, all the volunteer firemen helped maintain the trucks and building. In the corner of the addition is a manual alarm that is still visible today. When there was a fire called in, the first volunteer to reach the Fire Department sounded the alarm to notify others. Finally, in 1980, Ty Cawthon installed a siren that could be heard by everyone in the community.

In 2006, a brush truck was purchased that would enable the volunteers to travel on many of the unpaved roads in the Martin area. In 2008, plans were made to purchase a more modern fire truck. It took 3 years before the Martin Fire Department received this new fire truck in 2011.

In 1999, the fire department built a new Fire Department building, near the Martin City Park. This allowed the City of Martin to have a permanent place for our water department to be located.

From 1966, until today, all of the Martin firemen are volunteers. Johnny Hornick was the first fire chief. He served in that capacity until 1977. Stan Brown was chief from 1977 / 1979; Thomas Looney served as chief from 1980/83; Harold Thomas served from 1983/2012; Len Stovall became chief in 2012 and is currently still chief.

Stan Brown accepting a donation from Bill Rumsey, of Avalon. Standing in front of Fire Truck, L to R, Johnny Hornick, Bruce Thomas, John Goodwin, Stan Brown, Richard Dean

L to R: Stan Brown, Johnny Hornick, Tommy Williams, John Goodwin, Charles Morgan, Dick Yow, Bruce Thomas, Roy Walters.

CHAPTER NINE (7)
TOWN OF MARTIN WATER DEPARTMENT

Home owners in Martin were glad when the Martin City Commissioners announced that the Martin Water system would begin construction in 1967. A dedication was held on June 27, 1967, with several of the men responsible for the development of this system present. A plaque was placed on the water tower located at the Martin Community Center.

Once the water system was up and running, 1968, it would serve about 103 homes, businesses, and public institutions in the Northeast Georgia farming and residential community of Martin. Mayor Richard Dean stated that the new water system would not only will bring an adequate supply of water to the homes, but it will also provide fire protection and make the community more attractive to industries seeking rural locations.

In 2015, the Town of Martin serves over 600 homes and businesses with water. The following were appointed to serve as the **Town of Martin Water Clerks**: This Water Clerks list is short because they did such impeccable jobs that they were asked to stay year after year until they decided to leave the job.

Miller Stovall, Gerry Stovall, Ruby Harrison, Jean Thomas, and Bob Stovall. We apologize if any name was omitted. We were unable to find a clear list of all Councilmen, so names were pulled from the Council minutes.

PICTURE IN FRONT OF WATER TOWER BASE AT DEDICATION JUNE 27, 1967.
L to R – Martin Councilman Miller Stovall, Mr. Stevenson (USDA Engineer) Clyde Cash (contractor), Stephens County Commissioner Jimmy Turner, Martin Councilman John Goodwin, Martin Mayor Richard Dean, Martin Councilman Roy Walters, Jimmy Pendleton (USDA Engineer).

CHAPTER NINE (8)
POST OFFICE AND MAIL ROUTES

In the early years the post office was located in the old wooden store building belonging to O. C. Childs and later T. R. Yow.

The mail was brought to Martin by train, a lock box was on the left side of the depot, if the agent was not there when the train went by and the mail was placed in the lock box. The agent would flag down the train if he had freight mail.

Later came the Star Routes. A man with a contract would pick up the mail and would deliver it to Post Offices along the way from Toccoa to Elberton. The Star Route driver owned his own vehicle. Two men who worked the star routes were Rip Borroughs and Hansel Miller.

POSTMASTERS

H. C. Black	Late 1870's
Richard A. Dean	Late 1880's
Hugh C. Verner	1915
Rossie Harrison	1937 – 1939
William F. Brown	1958
Ollie C. Elrod	1959
Jesse L. Garland	1963 – 1965
Martha L. Bristol	1981
Lenward L. Collier	1982
Jerry Elrod	1989
David McClure	1989
Cynthia J. Benfield	2002
Ima Thresa Kennedy	2003
Sheryl D. Franko	2004
Breann S. Ferguson	2009
Paula J. Price-Thomas	2013

Rural routes: Lloyd Brown, Herbert Brown and Grady Bell.

DEDICATION CEREMONY

UNITED STATES POST OFFICE

MARTIN, GEORGIA

May 3rd, 1964

There o'clock

Jesse L. Garland, Acting Postmaster

Post Office Dedication Program

CHAPTER TEN

ORGANIZATIONS

CHAPTER TEN (1)
MARTIN LIONS CLUB

Charter night for the Martin Lions Club was held May 23, 1957, at Avalon School sponsored by Lavonia and Toccoa Clubs. Ed Dyer, District Governor, presented the club's Charter to John F. Dillon, President of the new club. Gong and gavel were presented to Lion Tamer, Robert Stovall. Other charter members were J. Edwin Stowe, First Vice President; Grady J. Bell, Second Vice President; John O. Goodwin, Third Vice President; Paul Cooper, Secretary; Robert Slack, Treasurer; R. R. Yow, Tail Twister; Directors: Ray Stowe, H. S. Brown, Dan McCall and Miller Stovall. Other charter members were Reverend J. Truman Brown, Richard Dean, Cliff Mitchell, L. Clarence Stovall, Jimmy E. Turner, Mose W. Thomas, J. E. Day, Joe Freeman, Harold Freeman, Jones Kellar, Kell Mitchell, Dan Smith, Floyd J. Stowe, Freeman Whitworth, Joel R. Whitworth. At this time, the only remaining charter member is Robert "Bob" Stovall.

From their beginning in 1957, to today, the Martin Lions Club has focused on raising monies for various vision programs in the community and local schools, eye glasses for the needy, food banks, Love- light tree at Stephens County Hospital, Volunteer Fire Department, Community projects; such as landscaping for the park area and Community Center.

On May 19, 2007, the Martin Lions Club held an Anniversary Charter Night. The Martin Lions Club members and their wives from Martin attended the charter banquet. Special recognition was given to Mr. Robert 'Bob' Stovall, for being the only remaining charter member.

In 58 years the membership has grown from 27 to 127. During this time the following men have served as President: R. R. "Dick" Yow, John Goodwin, Max Freeman, Joe Freeman, Bruce Thomas, Grady Bell, Willard Burgess, Richard Dean, John Dillon, Jr., Edwin Stowe, Charles Morgan, Thomas R. Williams, Donald Foster, Robert Stovall, James T. Franklin, Darrell Harper, Jimmy Shore, Terry Moss, Harold Thomas, Herman Mooney, Ray Stowe, Charles Graves, Jeff Freeman, Walter Fox, Larry Whiteside, Mose Thomas, John Guest, and Doug Williams.

The Martin Lions Club and the Martin Woman's Club (originally called Young Matrons Working Club) continue to work together and accomplish many tasks along with the Town Council's assistance.

Seated left to right: John Dillion, Edwin Stowe, Grady Bell, John Goodwin; Standing left to right: Bob Stovall, Paul Cooper, Dick Yow, Bob Slack, Ray Stowe, H. S. Brown, Truman Brown, Miller Stovall, Clarence Stovall and Dan McCall.

CHAPTER TEN (2)
THE MARTIN WOMAN'S CLUB

In February, 1914, four ladies of the town of Martin met at the home of Mrs. Ed West to organize a club. In attendance were Mrs. Lee Yow, Mrs. Van Matheson, and Mrs. T.C. Clodfelter. They chose the name of the club to be the "Young Matron's Working Club. The name was inspired by the first letter of the family names of the organizers. Many members of the club today are descendants of these original four ladies.

They chose: "Look forward and not backwards" and "lend a hand" as the Club motto. The Aim was mutual helpfulness promoting educational, social, and moral advancement of the community. Green and gold were chosen for Club colors, and the Chrysanthemum was chosen for the Club flower.

The club was federated in 1920 as a member of the State Federation of Woman's Clubs and continued with that relationship for many years. It was during the time of federation that the name was changed to the Martin Woman's Club.

Today the stated mission of the Martin Women's Club is to promote civic interest in the town of Martin and to encourage interest in beautification, promotion and improvement of the Martin Township and the Martin area.

The club has been active through the years providing help in schools and churches, supporting drives for the Red Cross, Heart, and Cancer funds. The Club adopted Banks Street for cleanup.

Each fall, the Martin Woman's Club sponsors the Martin Fall Festival which takes place on the last Saturday in October. Bi-annually the Club sponsors the Christmas Tour of Historical Homes.

The Club meets monthly at the Martin Community Center or in a member's home.
The officers of the Club per its Constitution are a President, a 1 st Vice President (President- Elect), 2nd Vice President (External Vice President), Secretary, Treasurer, and the Immediate Past President who serves as the Parliamentarian. The Club elects officers for a term of one year. The officers are installed at the June meeting of the Club. The Club year begins in June and ends in May.

In 1971, the Club selected "Wisdom, Justice, Moderation" as their Motto, keeping green and gold as their colors and the Chrysanthemum as the Club flower.

Martin's Woman Club 1917.

Mrs. Newton Telford, Mrs. Jennie Crenshaw, Mrs. Lloyd Brown, Mrs. Bob Mitchell, Mrs. Dave Landrum, Mrs. H. C. Verner, Mrs. Joe Stovall, Mrs. William Palmer, Mrs. Van Matheson, Miss Iris Telford, Mrs. R. A. Dean, Miss Jessie Martin, Mrs. E. F. Chaffin, Mrs. H. S. Brown, Miss Ollie Hayes, Mrs. Lee Yow, Mrs. A. W. Bussey, Mrs. Tom Stovall, Mrs. Pink Mitchell, Miss Mittie Garner, Mrs. Madge Clodfelter, Mrs. Northan Walters, Mrs. Terrell Farmer, Miss Effie Garner.

Christmas Party

Back Row: Rebecca Kennemur, Louise Wilson, Martha Jo Hunt, Rebekah Gonzalez, Barbara Freeman, Diane Yow Cole, Carolyn Williams, Carolyn Grubbs, Mary Camp, Sue Shore.Front Row: Kaye Martz, Mary Jo Easley, Pam Euliss, Danny Sue White, Polly Earle, Mary McNeff   Not Pictured: Laura Turner, Andrea Pair, Dawn McCall, Bonita Sherman, Kathy Maner, Sandra Oliver, Margie Williams, Carrie Albrecht, Cyndy Rondau, Jan Britte, Cynthia Hilliard, Ann Mills, Sue Morgan, Ruth Pless, Brenda Thomas, Sandy Rhodes and Pat Garmon.

The Martin Woman's Club has always had a membership of local women who are dedicated to promoting educational, social, and moral advancement of the community. As this historical document goes to press, the current membership meets the criteria that have shaped the Martin Woman's Club since1914. The current membership consists of:

Jan Britt (Jimmy) – Jan retired in 2013 as a Cafeteria Manager for the Gwinnett County (Georgia) School System, Jimmy retired as a builder and they moved to Lake Hartwell from Snellville Georgia. They have two children (Jared and Julie) and seven grandchildren. Jan is an active member of Tom's Creek Baptist Church in addition to The Martin Woman's Club.

Mary Camp (Charles) – Mary is currently the Treasurer of The Martin Woman's Club. When Charles retired, they moved from Lawrenceville Georgia to the lake where they could enjoy their love of water sports. Mary continued her career as a bookkeeper becoming self-employed and able to work from the lake. Mary has two children, son Taft and daughter Tina and four grandchildren. Boating and swimming with children and grandchildren are a big part of their lives taking Mary back to her days of being a lifeguard.

Polly Earle (Larry) – In 2005, Polly and Larry downsized form a big farm house and land to a small cabin in Martin. They spent most of their lives in Forest Park Georgia, went to the same high school and married in 1960. For thirty years, Polly and Larry had a metal fabrication business. Upon retirement, they moved to Martin. They have two daughters, one son, three granddaughters and two great grandchildren. Since moving to Martin, they attend Martin Baptist church and feel truly blessed with many friends.

Barbara Freeman (Max) – Barbara married Max in 1957 and quickly became a Martin person. They purchased the Matthews-Goodwin grocery store in Martin and operated the store for 4 years. Barbara was employed by Franklin County Department of Family and Children's Services for 32 ½ years and retired in 1991. After retiring, Barbara worked part time in the Gwinnett County Department of Family and Children Service for three years. Barbara is a member of Martin Baptist Church where she served as pianist / organist until 2005 after 58 years of serving in this capacity at several different churches. Barbara has been a member of the Martin Woman's Club since 1991. Their family consists of Major Max Freeman, who works fulltime for Georgia National Guard, his wife Melanie, a Franklin County School System nutrition director, and grandson Beau, who is employed in an Atlanta area airport.

Rebekah Gonzalez – Rebekah was born in Cuba but came to the USA at a young age, In 1995, Rebekah and her husband Gus, along with children Kristy, Gus, and Elizabeth came to Tugalo State Park for a camping trip. They saw the old Yow- Cooper Victorian house (pictured below) and fell in love with the house and the area.

Martha Jo Matthews Hunt (Bill) – As a child, Martha Jo's family moved from Toccoa to Martin and opened Matthews General Merchandise in the former Bank of Martin building. The back rooms were converted to living quarters and Martha Jo's mother joined the Martin Woman's Club. Fifty years later, she and husband Bill bought the same building and opened Hunt's Home Store and Martha Jo became a member of the Martin Woman's Club. In between those times, Martha Jo graduated from University of Georgia with a degree in education and taught all over the USA including Hawaii as she and US Army career officer Bill lived in many places. Returning to the area in 1991, the store closed in 2000. There are 4 children; daughters Tonya and Leah living in Greenville South Carolina, Son Phillip in Toccoa, and son Patrick, a physician in Columbia South Carolina. The extended family includes fifteen grandchildren and one great grandchild. Martha Jo is a member of the First Presbyterian Church in Toccoa.

Kathy Maner (Gary) – When Kathy retired as the City Clerk for the town of Lilburn Georgia, she and Gary moved to their vacation home in Martin at Lake Hartwell. Kathy is a graduate of Dekalb College and has a son Curtis and a daughter Jennifer and one grandchild. She is a member of Tom's Creek Baptist Church and for over forty years served as a pianist / organist for a church in Norcross Georgia. Kathy and Gary have a farm and love to garden. Kathy enjoys reading, sewing, and needlework.

Kay Mitchell Martz (Ken) – Kay grew up in Martin and moved to Lakeland Florida when she was twenty. She and husband Ken moved back to Martin in 2004 to the Mitchell family farm in the rural area of Martin. Kay was a stay at home mom when the children were young and then worked in Christian Education prior to moving back to Martin. Kay is the church secretary at Martin Baptist Church where she is a member. Kay and Ken have two daughters, Kassandra who lives in New England and has four children and two grandchildren; and Kelli who lives in Florida and has three children.

Dawn McCall – Dawn was born in Martin but at age three moved to Marietta Georgia where she spent her childhood. Dawn is a graduate of the Henry W. Grady School of Journalism at the University of Georgia. She spent four years in Washington with the Jimmy Carter Administration; worked with the Weather Channel in Atlanta and San Francisco and later the Discovery Channel in San Francisco and Miami Florida becoming the President of Discovery Channel International. After retiring Dawn was asked to return to government service with the US Department of State and served as the Coordinator of the Bureau of International Information Programs for three years under Madam Secretary Hillary Clinton. Dawn restored the 1882 Ketchersid-Crawford home in 2007 and spends her time between Martin, Miami Beach Florida and Provincetown Massachusetts. Dawn's mother, grandmother and aunt were long time members of The Martin Woman's Club.

Mary McNeff – In 2008, Mary retired as a Community Service Representative and looking to escape the cold of Somers Connecticut, moved to Martin. Mary is working part-time at Rite Aid as a cashier and is a member of Martin Baptist Church. Mary has five children; sons Gary, Jerry, and Larry, and daughters Carrie (Albrecht) and Mary (Caldwell) Ten grandchildren make up her family. Mary is the current President of the Martin Woman's Club.

Ann Mills (Ed) – Ann was born in West Virginia but moved often before settling in Atlanta. She is a University of Georgia graduate with a B.S.Ed. degree in Education and a Master's in Education Guidance and Counseling. Ann's 30 year counselor career was at Stephens County Junior / Middle School where she met husband Ed who went on to become the Superintendent of Schools for Stephens County. After retiring, Ann has been a mentor in the Stephens County schools. She works with the Martin Baptist Church Food Bank and belongs to the Georgia Retired Educators and Stephens County Retired Educators as well as the The Martin Woman's Club. Ed and Ann have two sons, Jonathan Edward and Matthew William.

Sue Stovall Morgan (Ferrell) – Sue was born in The Stovall House in Martin where her mother was a member of The Martin Woman's Club and attended the Martin School through fifth grade, graduating from Stephens County High School and then Georgia State College for Women (now Georgia College and State University) with a BS in General Science and a minor in Health and Physical Education. After marrying Ferrell, they lived in Fulton County Georgia where she taught at College Park High School before moving back to Stephens County in 1966. After her youngest was in fifth grade, Sue returned to teaching at Stephens County Junior High, then Stephens County High School for a total of 30 years teaching. She has three children, Scott Ferrell, John Robert, and Merideth Sue, each currently with a Martin address.

There are six grandchildren and one great grandchild. Sue is a member of First Baptist Church of Toccoa, active in many civic organizations including the Retired Teachers Association, Pilot Club of Toccoa and The Martin Woman's Club. Sue and Ferrell restored and moved back to The Stovall House in 2007.

Sandra Oliver (Jerry) – Sandra was born in Gainesville Georgia and moved to the Avalon / Martin area in 1951. She attended Avalon Grammar School and graduated from Stephens County High School. Sandra worked for 1st Franklin Financial for forty-eight (48) years until her retirement in 2012. Sandra and Jerry have two daughters and five granddaughters. She is an active member of The Martin Woman's Club and was active with the American Cancer Society Relay For Life for twenty years. Sue attends Tom's Creek Baptist Church and enjoys traveling, camping, boating, reading, sewing, and crocheting. Sandra is the current Secretary of The Martin Woman's Club.

Andrea McCall Pair (Tom) – Andrea lived in Martin the first 12 years of her life, attended Eastanollee Elementary and was baptized at Martin Baptist Church. Her grandmother, mother, and aunt were long time members of The Martin Woman's Club. The remainder of her childhood was spent in Marietta GA where she met and married Tom. Andrea is a graduate of The Woman's College of Georgia (now Georgia College & State University) and spent her career with Lockheed Martin Corporation in Information Technology, retiring as a Vice President. After retiring, she returned to college to study law. Andrea returned to Martin in 2007 and splits her time between Martin and Daytona Beach Florida. She and Tom have four children (Michele, Jason, Nicole, and Josh) and three grandsons. Andrea is an avid birder and enjoys traveling, photography and community service work. She bought and restored the 1895 Cleo Mitchell home in 2014.

Ruth Pless (James) – Ruth was born and raised in Lavonia. In 1965, after marrying James, they moved to Red Hollow Road in Martin and eventually South Yow Mill Road. After having two sons, Stephen Grant and Michael Shane, Ruth graduated from Piedmont College with a BS in Education. She also earned a Master's from North Georgia College and a specialist degree from Brenau University. Ruth taught at Stephens County Middle School until retiring in 2006. She has always been active in her church, both Poplar Springs Baptist and Martin Baptist where she is currently a member and in charge of the Food Bank. In addition to the Martin Woman's Club, she is active in Stephens County Retired Educators Association, and '62 Lunch Group. Ruth and James have four grandchildren.

Cynthia (Cindy) Rondeau (Stace) – Cindy moved to Martin in 2012 from Dublin Georgia where she was the Chief Professional Officer for local Boys and Girls Clubs. Cindy is a graduate of Georgia Regents University where she earned a Master's degree in Educational Administration and Supervision. She has taught school, worked as federal grants administrator, and helped design computer and technology curriculums for The National Headquarters of Boys and Girls Clubs and Microsoft Corporation. After retiring, Cindy pursued her Realtor License. She attend church at St. Mathias Episcopal Church. Cindy has two daughters (Allison and Katherine) and two sons (Paul and J P), and three grandchildren.

Bonita Sherman – Bonita obtained a Business degree from North Georgia Technical. She is a member of Mt Zion Baptist Church in Toccoa. Bonita enjoys acting, especially doing drama plays. She is member of the Eastern Stars and is an advocate for individuals with special needs. Bonita had two children, Tenita and Briaune.

Sue Smith Shore (James) – Sue was born in Franklin County, grew up on the family farm in Eastanollee and Toccoa and later moved to Chamblee Georgia where she graduated from Chamblee High School. She met her husband James her senior year, married, and lived in Norcross Georgia for thirty-four years before moving to the rural area of Martin in 1993. They are members of Martin Baptist Church and also active in the Martin Lions Club. Sue and James have two sons; Danny in Southlake Texas (granddaughter Heather in New York City and grandson Daniel in San Francisco California) and Jerry, wife Linda and daughter Emma are in Jacksonville, Florida. After finishing school,

Sue worked for the John H. Harland Company as an assistant to the Chief Executive Office of the company. She later held the role of assistant corporate secretary / treasurer. The Smith families (great grandfather, grandfather, and dad) all owned farms in the Avalon and Eastanollee area.

Brenda Thomas (Bobby) – Brenda moved to Martin from Lilburn Georgia where she was Personnel manager with Georgia Correctional Industries (a Division of Georgia Department of Corrections). Brenda and Bobby built a home on Lake Hartwell. She loves boating, swimming, reading, and church functions at Tom's Creek Baptist where she is a member and friends. Brenda has three children (Angela Adleman, David, and Richard) and nine grandchildren.

Laura Turner – Laura was raised in Toccoa and in 1978, she and husband Dicky who was raised in Martin built a home on the site of Dicky's grandparents' home on Red Hollow Road. Laura recently retired after working 35 years for the Stephens County School System as the secretary for Eastanollee Elementary School. She enjoys reading and gets together regularly with a group of friends from Eastanollee Elementary to discuss and exchange books. Laura enjoys working on family histories, and watching the birds and butterflies in her flower garden. She is excited to help with the Martin Woman's Club projects.

Dannie Sue Freeman White (Howard) – Dannie Sue grew up in Franklin county (just across the line from Stephens), attended Line Elementary and Lavonia High Schools. Upon graduation, Dannie Sue headed to Atlanta, met Howard, married and lived in Lawrenceville Georgia for forty plus years. In 2004, after she retired from the insurance business and Charles retired, they return to the area where her father, grandfather, and great grandfather had farmed the land and built their home.

Dannie Sue has two grandsons, Christopher and Chretien. Dannie Sue's mother Ethel was a member of the Martin Woman's Club.

Diane Yow Cole White (Joe) – Diane was born in Atlanta, lived in several locations in Georgia, North and South Carolina before moving from Murphy, North Carolina to Martin where Diane's dad was in the cotton business with her grandfather. She grew up in Martin and attended Avalon, Toccoa, and Stephens County schools. Diane graduated with a BS degree in Education from the University of Georgia where she was a cheerleader. After teaching school for three years, Diane became a "stay at home mom" and started a "mail-order antique business" while living in Marietta Georgia. For the last eighteen years, Diane has organized antique shows and estate sales. Like her grandmother and mother before her, Diane has been a long time active Martin Woman's Club member and currently serves as Vice President. .

Carolyn Williams (Ralph) – Carolyn moved from Independence, Missouri to her Lake Hartwell home in 2000 after she and her husband both retired; Carolyn was an elementary and middle school librarian and also taught elementary art. Her first job after college was at Hallmark Cards in Kansas City Missouri as a finish artist. Carolyn and Ralph attend the Community of Christ church in North Atlanta area. On a church sponsored trip to Iowa is where she met her husband Ralph. Carolyn has two children, two grandchildren, and two great-grandchildren. Daughter Sharrie is a Spanish teacher at American International Schools presently teaching in Warsaw, Poland fueling Carolyn's "travel bug". Son Steve lives in Cedar Rapids, Iowa.

Carolyn feels as if she returned "home" to Georgia as her father worked for Delta Air Lines and she graduated from Russell High School in Atlanta. Carolyn has moved back to Missouri after an extended trip to Europe.

Margie Williams (Tom) – Margie is a retired cosmetologist and became attached to the Town of Martin when she married, Tom Williams, a lifelong resident and entrepreneur of Martin.

CHAPTER TEN (4)
MARTIN WOMAN'S CLUB CONTRIBUTIONS OF THE YEARS

This is a list of most of the different donations and organizations that we have contributed to since 2002. Over the years we have raised money by the Martin Fall Festival and our Tour of Homes. Total money raised and used to help others for the past 13 years is $13,596.00.

- Boys & Girls Club of Toccoa - To pay for kids to be able to go to Summer Camp.
- Christmas for Kids - We work with the local school system to help at Christmas Dental
- Care for Kids in the local area and Eye Glasses for local kids.
- Food 2 Kids Program.
- Friends of Lavonia Library, and Stephens County Read at Home - reading programs for kids
- Reins of Life - Help them with their needs so they can help others with physical and emotional needs.
- Kick-it - Program to make funds available for woman who need mammograms.
- Relay for Life - support their cause.
- Stephens County Auxiliary - help them with needs.
- Stephens County Fire Department - help with their needs.
- Second Chance Ministries - help young people with drug addiction.
- Shepherds Hill Farm - help with their needs to summer programs.
- Stephens County FF A - help with their needs.
- Postage for the Military.
- Repairs and New Equipment -Tables, Chairs, etc. at the Martin Community Center.

CHAPTER TEN (5)
LODGES

The citizens of Martin had the opportunity to belong to several organizations and lodges.

HEPTASOPHS

The organization was originally called the "Seven Wise Men", and it may have been formed by graduates of the earlier Mystical Seven or Rainbow Society that were popular college fraternities in the South during this period. Albert Stevens noted at least a strong similarity in their rituals and nomenclature.

The Heptasophs themselves elaborated an ornate pseudohistory dating back to 1104 BC and "the first Zoroaster". Allegedly the ancient King of Persia would select six Magi who were skilled in both statecraft and occult arts and they would meet in a subterranean cavern beneath the royal palace at Ispahan. This was also how princes were trained but they were only admitted "by merit". The philosophy of these "Seven Wise Men" directed the affairs of the Persian Empire until their overthrow by Muhammad in 638 AD.

What is known is that after being "introduced" in New Orleans in April 1852, a Grand Conclave of Louisiana was set in June of that year and incorporated in 1854. A "Supreme Conclave", or organization embracing several states was organized in 1857 and had its first "communication" (convention).

The early growth of the organization was principally in the Southern states and it lost many members much of its influence during the Civil War. The group was always conservative with little effort being made to extend it into other areas.

After the Civil War the group began to grow again and during the early 1870s experienced a rapid growth in membership, reaching a high point of 4,000. The depression of the mid-1870s checked its growth and led to a movement for a general death benefit (local conclaves were allowed to create benefit options, but there were not overall benefits). When the Supreme Conclave rejected this idea the zeta Conclave of Baltimore forced a schism leading to the creation of the Improved Order of Heptasophs. There was an intense rivalry between the two groups for a few years, but this died down after the older order adopted its own benefit plan in 1880.

During the 1870s, the Order became popular among some German Americans and was said to have spread to Germany by 1877.

MASONS

A band of English colonists under the leadership of General James Edward Oglethorpe, British soldier, statesman and humanitarian, arrived on the west bank of the Savannah River on February 12, 1733. This was the birth of the English Province of Georgia, the last of the Thirteen Colonies. Georgia was the southwestern frontier of British America for many years.

In the same year, December 13, 1733, the Grand Lodge of England at its Quarterly Communication in London adopted a resolution to "collect the Charity of this Society towards enabling the Trustees (of Georgia) to send distressed Brethren to Georgia where they may be comfortably provided for ... that it be strenuously (sic) recommended by the Masters and Wardens of regular Lodges to make a generous collection amongst all their Members for that purpose ... "

Some three months later, February 21, 1734, a Lodge of Freemasons was organized at Savannah under the "old Customs" (without warrant). Noble Jones, intimate friend of James Oglethorpe, was initiated on that date, the first Freemason made in Georgia. On December 2, 1735, the lodge was warranted by the Grand lodge of England and entered on the engraved list as "The lodge at Savannah in Ye Province of Georgia". It was assigned number 139 on the register of English lodges. By 1770 its number had been reduced to No. 63 and by 1792 it was No. 46, although no longer an English lodge.

The lodge at Savannah changed its name in or prior to 1770 to Solomon's lodge. In 1774 and 1775, respectively, the Grand lodge of England warranted two more lodges in Savannah, Unity No. 465 and Grenadiers No. 481. Both lodges died an early death.

Except for that brief period, Solomon's lodge was the only lodge in Georgia from 1734 until 1785. Solomon's Lodge was the second duly constituted lodge in America, next only to a lodge in Boston warranted in 1733. Solomon's lodge is the Mother Lodge of Georgia.

Serving as Provincial Grand Masters in Georgia were: Grey Elliott, 1760 until he was succeeded in 1771 by Noble Jones. Brother Jones served until his death in 1775. Sometime during the War for independence, Samuel Elbert, American soldier and later Governor of Georgia, was "elected" Provincial Grand Master. On December 15, 1786, Brother Elbert resigned as Provincial Grand Master so that the independent Grand Lodge of Georgia might be formed.

A group of dissident Freemasons in Savannah, disapproving the workings of Solomon's Lodge,
petitioned the Grand Lodge of Pennsylvania in 1784 for a charter to organize a Lodge. Their petition was granted by Pennsylvania on March 31, 1785, the Lodge being listed on Pennsylvania's register as no. 42, to be known as Hiram Lodge, Savannah, Georgia.

In the true spirit of Freemasonry the differences between the two Lodges were soon reconciled. In the following year it is known that two additional Lodges existed in the, one at Augusta and one at Washington. It is believed these four Lodges, on December 16, 1786 met together and created the most Worshipful Grand Lodge of Free and Accepted Masons for the of Georgia.

William Stephens, Past Master of Solomon's Lodge, now NO.1, and the first U.S. Court Judge in Georgia, was elected and installed Grand Master.

The next eight Lodges in Georgia were: Columbia No.3, Augusta; St. Louis No.4, Washington; Washington No.5, Washington; St. John's No.6, Sunbury; Little River No.7, Little River; St. Patrick's No.8, Waynesboro; St. George's No.9, Kiokas; Union No. 10, Savannah.

With the exception of Solomon's No.1, all of the above Lodges are extinct. Social Lodge, originally No. 18, Augusta, Georgia, now also No.1, was chartered in December, 1799. Georgia has 451 Lodges and 72,451 members (as of October, 1997).

Freemasonry has existed continuously in Georgia since 1734. The Grand Lodge of Georgia, F. & A. M., has existed since 1786.

The Grand Lodge of Free and Accepted Masons for Georgia was incorporated with perpetual duration on February 6, 1796, by an Act of the General Assembly of Georgia passed for that purpose, and has been delivered down to the present day.

ODDFELLOWS

The Oddfellows are one of the earliest and oldest Friendly Societies, but their early history is obscure and largely undocumented. There have been legends tracing their origins back to Moses and Aaron, to the exile of the Israelites in Babylon in the sixth century BC, and claims that the order was brought to Europe by Jewish prisoners after the destruction of the temple at Jerusalem by the Roman Emperor Titus in 70 CE. Another draws on the concept of mutual support amongst soldiers of the Roman Empire, and the spread of the concept throughout Europe in the 11th century. Another states that "Although no formal records exist ... an Order of Odd Fellows was established in 1452 by knights who were said to have met at the pub named 'Boulogne-sur-Mer' in London and formed a fraternity."

Although some of these legends are at best, dubious, the evolution from the Guilds is more reliably documented. By the 13th century, the tradesmen's Guilds had become established and prosperous. During the 14th century, with the growth of trade, the guild "Masters" moved to protect their power (and wealth) by restricting access to the Guilds. In response, the less experienced (and less wealthy) "Fellows" set up their own rival Guilds.

One recurring theme is that the name Odd Fellows" arose because, in smaller towns and villages, there were too few Guild "Fellows" in the same trade to form a local Guild. The Fellows from a number of trades therefore joined together to form a local Guild of Fellows from an assortment of different trades, the Odd Fellows.

A second recurring theme explains the name as adopted "at a time when the severance into sects and classes was so wide that persons aiming at social union and mutual help were a marked exception to the general rule"

During the early centuries the idea of a common union brought a reaction from the upper classes, who saw them possibly as a source of revenue (taxes) but also as a possible threat to their power. For example, when the English King Henry VIII broke with the Roman Catholic Church, the Guilds were viewed by him as supporting the Pope, and in 1545 he confiscated all material property of the Guilds. Queen Elizabeth I took from the Guilds the responsibility for training apprentices, and by the end of her reign, most Guilds had been suppressed.

The elimination of the Trade Guilds removed an important form of social and financial support from ordinary working people. In major cities like London, some Guilds (e.g. the "Free Masons" and the Odd Fellows") survived by adapting their roles to a social support function. Both of these had their base in London, but had established branches (called 1 Lodges I) across the country.

CHAPTER TEN (6)
MARTIN COMMUNITY GROUP

The Martin Community Group was organized September 25, 2010.The members of the Martin Community Group are: Jeraldine Hayes, L. C. Hayes, Marlyn Woodruff, Pastor Walter Richie, Thomas Richie, Diane Yow Cole, Angie Wiley, Carrie Beasley, Agnes Oglesby, Betty Gober, Samuel Issac, Charlene Merritt, Oliver Dorsey. Linda Drinkard.

The purpose of the Martin Community Group is sponsor a Martin Spring Festival. The money generated from the festivals will benefit local charities.

The first Martin Spring festival was April 30, 2011 and we've made it an annual event.

Thanks to Diane Yow Cole, Mayor Don Foster, the Martin City Council, the Martin Community, numerous Vendors, and the members of the Martin Community Group the festivals have been very successful even in rainy weather.

The majority of the meeting are held at the Swift Multipurpose Center at 2215 Defoor Road in Toccoa Ga and at the gazebo in Martin. Every meeting begin and ended with prayer. All money raised has benefited The Boys and Girls Club of Toccoa, Ga. The Swift Multipurpose Center and the Black Christian Men's Association.
Article contributed by Jeraldine Hayes.

Those pictured are:
The Martin Community Group and members of the Swift Family

CHAPTER 11

BUSINESSES

Several of the early families got the future town of Martin off to a good start. These are some of those whose endeavors gave the area a boost.

James D. Ketcherside (first doctor), Willie Alexander (merchant, Bank of Martin), H. C. Black (depot agent and builder), O. G. Childs (merchant and builder), T. R. Yow (merchant, cotton broker, oil mill VP), I. W. Randall (builder, farmer, merchant).
Henry Mitchell, W. A. Mitchell, W. B. Mitchell, J. C. Watkins, I. V. Matheson (merchant),, F. J. Brock, T. H. Stovall, all of which were merchants in Martin.
As the area grew, there were many farmers, merchants and businessmen that made Martin what was to become later. Martin was chartered September 7, 1891.
Ada Acree (teacher), G. G. Allen (bank director), Dr. R. M. Alexander (Mayor), J. I. Adams, J. Addison (teacher), Willie L. Bond (doctor), John P. Bailey, R. A. Brown, Rush Burton (first principal), Jim Burton, Sloan Bruce (oil mill), Bob Bruce, Dave Brock (blacksmith), Henry Blackwell (blacksmith), John D. Brown (Mayor), John E. Brown, Lloyd Brown (mail carrier), H. S. Brown (bank cashier, mail carrier), Ben Burkette (teacher), Rev. Bussey (Martin Baptist Church Pastor), W. F. Clark, Clem T. Clark (blacksmith & farmer), J. P. Camp, Luther Clodfelter (pharmacy and funeral parlor), Randlall Cleveland, Otis Clodfelter, J. S. Crawford (oil mill), J. H. Crawford (doctor), John Crawford (drub store), W. A. Cooper (minister), W. L. Cooper (doctor), J. F. Cooper (oil mill president), Weymond Combs (assistant Veterinarian), Bob Cason (dentist), Theron Combs (Baptist minister), L. H. Coe (livery stable), Ernell Combs (teacher), Emory Chaffin

(doctor), Wallace Carnog (store clerk & doctor), T. J. Crenshaw, E. P. Cheek, Herschel Crump (teacher), Richard Carpenter (teacher), George H. Dean (merchant), C. H. Dance (building owner, bank director), R. A. Dean (postmaster), R. A. P. Dean (bank director, merchant), Russell Dean (farmer), John B. Davis, Thomas Davis, Joe McCall Dean, D. W. Edwards (merchant), J. F. Eskew (farmer), Tom Farmer, James P. Farrow (saw mill), Eady Farrow (saw mill), Fred Farrow (grocery store), Henry Farrow, F. W. Freen (school principal), Lula Fagan (farmer), F. Fricks, R. M. Freeman (mayor & farmer), F. W. Freyman (teacher and principal), Farmer (Oil Mill 1902), Owen Freeman (merchant and dry goods), W. T. Fagan (farmer), Ben Fagan (farmer), C. F. Fischer (teacher), F. C. Gross (bank cashier), Bob Garner, L. E. Guinn, George W. Hayes (merchant), R. B. Harrison (Martin Gin Company), T. B. Harrison (Yow Academy superintendent), E. M. Holland (merchant), Ethel Haynie (teacher), Isbell, Sarah Jones (teacher), Claud Kay (service station), J. J. Kay, Mack Kay (blacksmith), Joe Kay (farmer), Cyrus Kay, T. H. Knox (Martin Gin Company), C. C. Knox (bank director), Tom Knox, Will Knox (farmer), Tugalo Knox, G. M. Kennedy, Thomas Ketcherside (doctor), John W. Ketchersid (doctor), Farmer Land (builder), Phil Landrum (congressman), W. B. Land, T. M. Looney (Martin Gin Company) J. M. Looney (builder), P. D. Landrum (bank president), George Looney, Rick Mason, Fred Looney, Sr., Wiley (Jack) Mitchell (sawmill), E. R. Mathews (oil mill), W. S. McCart, E. L. Mathews, E. K. Mathews (Martin Gin Company), T. W. McAlister (oil mill), W. C. Mason (Bank of Martin & Cotton Gin), Tony Mills, M. M. McMurry, Ed McMurry, McAvoy (barber), S. L. Moss, W. T. Mosley, J. R. Martin, B. J. Martin, Kell Mitchell, Sr (service station & merchant), Russ Mitchell (corn mill), C. P. Mitchell, Eddis Mitchell (teacher), W. A. Mitchell (bank director), W. B. Mitchell (Martin Gin Company, builder & merchant), W. A.

Mitchell (Merchant, Justice of the Peace, Bank of Martin), Mose Outz, Homer Outz (oil mill workers), Will Oglesby (Farmer, Southern Railroad, Coats & Clark), Henry Pearman (merchant), T. W. Perkins, Perteet (millinary shop), Benjamin Price (lumber mill), Norman Price (lumber mill), Henry Price (cotton gin), S. T. Pulliam, S. W. Pulliam, Curtis Pitts (sawmill), Ramsey (millenary shop), Reeves Randall, E. F. Rumsay, G. F. Rumsey, M. P. Sewell (bank director), George F. Stovall (variety shop), G. N. Stovall (Martin Bank President), T. H. Stovall (pharmacy, funeral parlor, service station, oil mill, Bank of Martin President), W. B. Stovall, T. Y. Stephenson, A. A. Stowe, M. E. Stancil, W. H. Swaim (doctor), M. C. Swilling, Robert Shackleford, G. E. Smith, Hugh Dorsey Teasly (R. R. & Pope Yow truck Driver), Howard Thomas (fertilizer business & school bus driver), Charles Turner (hogs, beef and vegetable farmer). F. C. Verner, John D. Verner, Hugh C. Verner (farmer, teacher and post master), Roy Whitworth (farmer), Buck Wheeler, Lee Walters, J. C. Watkins (merchant), J. M. Walters (merchant), W. J. Whiten (Martin Gin Company) C. K. Westmore (teacher Yow Academy), Will Williams, Woodall (drugstore), Jeff Wilson, Robert Wilson, T. S. Young, T. J. Young (Oil mill superintendent), S. B. Yow (merchant, oil mill), T. A. Yow (farmer & merchant), R. D. Yow (merchant), E. M. Yow (merchant), T. R. Yow (merchant, cotton broker), T. B. Yow, Jones duBingion Yow (farmer), LeeRoy Yow (merchant), Hubert Yow (merchant), Pope Yow (merchant, cotton broker). Harold Alexander (florist), Grady Bell (mail carrier), Chester Brock (heat and air conditioning), J. E. Brown (buggies, wagons & farm equipment), Cash's Service Station, Richard B. Dean, Sr. (dairy farmer), Richard B. Dean, Jr. (dairy farmer), John O. Goodwin (railroad agent, furniture store), Harold Looney (builder), Earnest Wood (feed store), Edge Thomas (merchant), R. R. (Dick) Yow (merchant, cotton broker), Pitt Carter (drug store), Norris

Holland (furniture store), B. F. Fagan (furniture store), Dan Mathews (general store & furniture store), Bruce Thomas (mail carrier, furniture store, beef & poultry farmer), Bill & Martha Hunt (furniture store), Thomas R. Y. Williams (tire store), H. S. Brown III (tire store), Bill Burgess (trim shop), Fred Farrow (grocery store), Max Freeman (grocery store), Charles Morgan (grocery store), Clarence Stovall (service station), Miller Stovall (service station), Claude Kay (service station), Glenn Mosley (service station), Henry Bagwell (blacksmith), Willie Dean (blacksmith), Will Medlin (garage), David Medlin (mail carrier), Joe R. Medlin (small engine repair), Jake Wilson (garage), Peeler (dairy products), Diane Yow Cole (antiques), Blanch Gibson (antiques), Adam Murray (heat and air conditioning), Edna Godfrey (antiques and collectibles), Shelia Holcomb (collectibles), Laurie Welshans One Stop baby shop, William and Margarett Burke Martin Thrift Store, Tim Pierce Shorty's Flea Market, Tod Holley Martin Tire and Wholesale, Nelson Bradshaw Water Wheel ice cream shop, Stanley Johnson Back in Stanley and Margaret Johnson Back in Time classic cars, Jeff Whitlock Northeast GA recycling, Shane Wilson (transmissions, Tammie Gerhart (teacher), Mark Gerhart (car sales & repair shop), Swain Looney (farmer), Joseph Hulsey (farmer), Thomas Looney (construction), David Mitchell (beef, poultry, farmer & truck driver), Jerry Nunnaly (paint & body shop), Robert (Bob) Stovall (town clerk, water department supervisor), Sonya Stovall Town of Martin Secretary, Hugh Alexander, Water Department, Roy Whitworth (farmer), Randy Shirley (Sheriff).

HUNT'S HOME STORE/BANK OF MARTIN

Hunt's Home Store…located on Highway 17 in Martin, GA, has a very interesting history. The brick store building built around 1890 in a Romanesque style completed of a brick foundation, brick exterior and a flat roof.

Originally it housed the Bank of Martin and Apothecary, and embalming room and stored caskets.

The Bank of Martin served the community for several years, but failed during the Depression, around 1929. Vestiges of the buildings, early role are still present. The first vault became a bathroom and the newer one was used as an office for the store.

Later the building served as the Martin Post Office on the left side and a dry goods store on the right, in what had been the bank. In the intervening half century, it has changed ownership and name several times. In 1947, although the building was empty, Dan Mathews saw an opportunity. He left his job as a payroll supervisor at LeTourneau, sold his house in Toccoa and moved to Martin, with his wife Ruth and two daughters, Martha Jo and Barbara. The girls were six and eight years old at that time.

DEAN'S GROCERY

 Ralph Dean began a grocery store for the communities of Avalon and Martin in the Yow – Cooper Plantation Store, about one half mile south of the Avalon School. Due to the large sign advertising Jazz Feed on the side of the building, this location was called Jazz Town. At age 13, George began pumping gas for 19 cents per gallon.

On January 1, 1965, Ralph and George moved their store to the old Avalon School, which was built in the early 1920's. George worked the store full time after Ralph died in 1975. He worked the store for 40 years. The store was open six days a week from 8 A.M. until 9 P.M., including all holidays except Christmas Day. On January 10, 1995, the store was sold but remained, but remained Dean's Grocery.

Early Drug store in Martin

Pope & R.R. Yow
Cotton Truck

Tom Williams
Magnum Tire Company

Downtown Martin 1950's

Stovall Building in Martin

Past and present unite

The past and present owners of Goodwin and Goodwin, 1931-82; Bruce Thomas, 1958-91 Thomas were on hand Saturday to greet cus- and present owner as of April 15, 1991, Bill tomers during a weekend sale. Pictured are Hunt. Dan Matthews, original owner 1947-58, John

Hugh Dorsey Teasley
Truck Driver

Mack Kay, Blacksmith

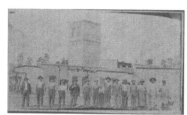

Cotton Seed Oil Mill
in Martin in 1905

Pope & Dick Yow Cotton
Warehouse in Martin

CHAPTER TWELVE
MARTIN FAMILIES

HAROLD ALEXANDER

Harold Alexander became a citizen of Martin in November, 1976. After purchasing his home on Walters Road, from Jimmy and Mary Turner.

The house was built in 1904 by Robert N. & Dora Garner Walters. It was built from material milled on the property. Harold was born in Franklin County, GA and has lived in Stephens County since 1971. He is the owner and operator of Alexander's Flowers, Gifts and Antiques in Toccoa since 1970. Harold has been on the Martin Town Council since 1985 and has served as Vice Mayor for over 20 years.

He is a graduate of American Institute of Floral Design of Baltimore, MD. He has designed in many competitions in several states. He is a member of the Martin Lions Club, an honorary member of the Toccoa Pilot Club and a member of Pleasant Hill Baptist Church.

His passion is the Christmas decorations for the Town of Martin and continues to make sure all is well and Santa is on his way. His home is usually on tour for the Martin Woman's Club. He is always eager to lend a helping hand to anyone who asks.

Finding Beauty Everywhere
Harold Alexander
By Susan Poole

Combine beautiful plants and flowers, the admiration, respect, laughter, and warmth of a close-knit family, with the joy of serving others, and you have Harold Alexander. Born and raised on the edge of Gosling, Harold was taught the values of love, life and respect as he grew up in a "happy home, filled with laughter," such that even though "you didn't have anything, you didn't know it."

Harold began a life-long affair with flowers as he began re-setting his mom's Old Pinks (chrysanthemums, for us new-timers), moving on to dahlias, zinnias, marigolds, and poppies, just for the joy of growing flowers. Though his daddy fussed when he grew a lovely border on the edge of their cotton patch, Harold kept right

Harold speaks at many club meetings throughout the year.

on planting wherever flowers he could find. Miss Lola Mae Higginbotham worked for his family, and shared her flowers with him as they grew to be friends. Church ladies came to cut and arrange Harold's flowers for church altars at Pleasant Hill Baptist and First Baptist Toomsa.

All through schooling, which a six year old Harold began at The Whitworth School with Mrs. Arthur Brown, and on to Lavenia Grammar School, and the Lavenia High School class of 1963, Harold grew flowers between chores and school work. "Walking through a garden filled with fresh grass and stumps always smells so clean and good." When there'd come in from working the fields in the sum-

Harold with three of the six dogs that he has rescued.

Robert & Dora Walters built the Alexander House

BAILEY FAMILY

John Pressley Bailey and Nancy Ida Brown were married approximately1890. He purchased a house and farm in the Clarks Creek community where they farmed and reared eight children. He valued his time caring for his family and neighbors, toiling his farmland and reaping the harvest. Their beloved Loudell Combs lived on the family farm and worked for the Baily family for many years.

Later in Mr. Bailey's life, he owned and operated a country store so his neighbors could buy their groceries without having to make a trip to Martin or Lavonia. When it was necessary for the family to go all the way to Toccoa, a neighbor, who owned a model T Ford, would provide transportation to the Martin train depot where the family would catch the train and travel on to Toccoa for their day of shopping. Mrs. Betty Farr, granddaughter, recalls as a small child, the excitement of the train ride, especially drinking water from the water fountain.

On Sundays Mr. & Mrs. Bailey would hitch up two buggies and carry their children to Clarks Creek Baptist Church where he served as deacon for many years. John P. Bailey was born 1868-died 1940. Nancy Ida Bailey was born 1874 - died 1945.

Deceased children are: Bessie Bailey South, Belle Bailey South, Virgil Bailey, Bertha Bailey Brown, Ethel Bailey Addison, Herman Bailey and Ollie Bailey Jordan. The last daughter, Inez Bailey Burgess passed away in June, 2008 at the age of 97. She lived with her only daughter, Betty Ann Burgess Farr in the Gumlog Community. Mrs. Farr's daughter, Lydia Ann Farr Ethridge and her husband, Jeff, live near Mrs. Farr. In addition to Betty Farr, the other grandchildren who are still living are Jean Addison Payne and Margaret Bailey Conwell.

Grandchildren deceased are: Mary Nell Bailey Whiten, James Bailey, Mildred Taylor Miller, Poole South, Maxine South Payne, Ray South, Travis South, Dwight South, Billy South, John Bailey, Harold and George Brown, Roy Bailey, and Deweece Addison.

The Bailey Family

Mr & Mrs Virgil Bailey

Baxter & Margaret Bailey Conwell)

GRADY AND WILMA BELL FAMILY

Grady Jackson Bell was born in Gillesville, Georgia on May 1, 1920, and Wilma Eberhardt Bell was born in Gainesville, Georgia on December 24, 1921. Grady enlisted in the United States Army January 14, 1942, and was assigned to the 17th Calvary Reconnaissance Squadron (at the time of Grady's enlistment, the 17th Calvary was a mounted cavalry but was soon converted to a mechanized cavalry). Grady was honorably discharged from military service on January 13, 1949.

Grady and Wilma were married on June 7, 1943 shortly before Grady was shipped overseas. They two met on one furlough and were married on the next! Grady was awarded the Bronze Star Medal (see attached photo). The citation reads: *"for distinguishing himself by meritorious service in connection with military operations against the enemy in France, Holland, and Germany from* 3 *August* 1944 *to* 1 *December 1944. Throughout this period he spent long hours in keeping the communications of his Squadron in continuous operation thereby contributing greatly in the successful completion of all missions assigned his organization. In performing his duty, he was often exposed to enemy artillery and mortar fire but his efficiency had not diminished. The courage, devotion to duty and disregard for personal safety displayed by Technical Sergeant Bell reflect great credit on the military service of the United States. Signed A. C. Gillem, Jr., Major General, United States Army, Commanding."* Grady also received five battle stars during his military time for meritorious service and bravery.

Back at home during the war, Wilma lived on the Eberhardt family farm in Gainesville, Georgia and worked at the Gainesville Hosiery Mill, converted to a parachute factory during the war years. It was while Grady served overseas that Wilma began her hobby as an artist by taking a correspondence course in art. Throughout her life, until she could no longer hold a paint brush, Wilma painted beautiful works of art. Her favorite scenes were old, rain washed barns. She did a series of very detailed paintings depicting the life of Christ, which she always maintained were divinely inspired.

After the war ended, Grady and Wilma moved to Albany, Georgia, where Grady worked at Dixie Dairies, owned by his Uncle Hugh Bell. While in Albany, he stood the Civil Service Test for a position in the Albany Post Office and became a substitute mail carrier. Being a mail carrier was a dream of Grady's since his childhood days when the mail carrier could deliver the mail to their rural home in Gillesville in a horse drawn wagon. The carrier would frequently have rabbits or other game he had shot while on his route, in the wagon with him. Grady always thought that would be a wonderful job. Grady loved his patrons almost as family.

On October 9, 1948, their first son Grady Jackson Bell Jr. was born while Wilma and Grady were still in Albany, Georgia. But both of them wanted to get back to North Georgia and closer to family.

Grady's first cousin John Goodwin, who was working as a railway agent at the depot in Martin, Georgia, made Grady aware of a rural mail route that was becoming available in Martin, as Mr. Lloyd Brown was approaching retirement. At that time, rural mail carriers were appointed by the district Congressional Representative, who was at that time, the Honorable Phil Landrum for the Ninth District that included Martin. Grady was awarded Route One out of the Martin Post Office and the family moved to Martin in 1951.

Moving to a new community with a young family meant searching for a place to live. An arrangement was made with Mrs. Iris Yow to rent the North side of her large house located on Highway 17. The family lived there until 1957 when the new house located on Mitchell Street was completed. They became members of the First Presbyterian Church in Toccoa shortly after moving to Martin. In 1957, Grady and Wilma's second son, Warren Stephen Bell was born.

During their years together in Martin, Grady became a charter member of the Lions Club serving as an officer in the club numerous times. The Lions were responsible for many exceptional service projects to the community such as beginning the volunteer fire department. They also began their most tasty fund raising activity that resulted in a virtual community celebration twice a year – The Martin Lions Club Chicken Que!

Wilma was an active member in the Martin Woman's Club for many years frequently hosting the meetings in the Bell home on Mitchell Street.

Grady retired from the Post Office in 1986 and shortly afterward began selling for DeVroomen Holland garden products and worked at that until he passed the torch, or bulb as it were, to his oldest son Jack in 1998. Grady went to be with the Lord on June 28, 2006. Wilma spent her married life as a dedicated mother, wife, and homemaker for her family and went to be with the Lord on April 1, 2013.

Jack retired from AT&T in 1998 with 26 years' service to take over the sales job with DeVroomen from his Dad. He and his wife Connie Chandler Bell, who retired from teaching in 2008, were married in 1969, and have two daughters, Paige Michele who is married to Dr. Brent Archer and reside in Gainesville, Georgia with their three sons, William Andrew, born in 2006, Coleman Joseph born in 2007, and Jonathan Jackson, born in 2009. Meredith Susan is married to Roger Foltynowicz and they presently reside in Berkeley Heights, New Jersey with their daughter Brinson Suzanne born in 2012.

Steve and his wife Lola Parker Bell were married in 1978 and reside in Athens, Georgia. Steve began working for the University of Georgia in 1982. He is director of UGA's Broadcast, Video and Photographic Services Unit. Lola retired from teaching in 2013. They have a son, David Stephen, born in 1985, who resides in Greenville, South Carolina with his wife Erin Roberts Bell. They have a daughter Hadley Catherine, who was born in 2013.

Steve and Lola's daughter, Susan Delane married Chase Dachenhausen in 2014 and reside in Augusta, Georgia.

Fred Bray Family

Fred Bray was born in Hart County in 1919, the son of Leon Bray and Martha Frances Shiflet Bray. Margaret Gibson Bray was born in 1925 in Oconee County South Carolina, the daughter of Ernest Lewis Gibson and Issaquena (Kizzie) Gibson.

Fred Bray met Margaret Gibson through a group of friends, and they married when Margaret was 14 years old. Their first child was born when Margaret was 16, and they had five more children, one every other year. The first two children were born in Hart County, and the other children were born in Franklin County. Fred worked at LeTourneau Company in Toccoa, and Margaret worked at Carwood Manufacturing Company in Lavonia. Even though they both worked at public jobs, they had a very large vegetable garden each year to help provide fresh vegetables for their large family.

Tragedy struck this family first in 1958 when son, Rayford was killed in an automobile accident at the age of 14. Then in the same year another son, Louie, age 16, was also killed in an automobile accident, the day before his little boy, Freddy Joe, had his first birthday. The loss of two sons in one year was just about impossible for the family to endure. Standing at the graves of his two sons, Fred Bray knew he couldn't continue living without help, and at that time surrendered his life to our heavenly Father.

He was inspired to write a heartbreaking, beautiful poem about standing on the hill at his two sons graves.
The members of the Bray family were faithful members of the Martin Baptist Church.

Fred & Margaret were remarried in the church on their 50th wedding anniversary. It was a heartfelt celebration of their first 50 years of life together. The Bray Children are: Fredrick Louie born in Hart County in 1941, married to Pat Fulghum, father of Freddy Joe Bray. Deceased at age of 16; Rayford David Bray born in Hart County on 6-5-43. Deceased at age of 14 on 2-5-58.

Clifton Crandle Bray, born in Franklin County, married to Cathy, they have two children, Cliff and Caleb, Phylis Nadean Bray, married Donald Foster. They have three children, Keith, Tracie, and Kevin, Carolyn Loretta Bray married to Tommy Moody. They have twins, Brian and Michelle. Janice Arlene Bray married Linden Roberts and they have one son, Marty.

Not only did Fred & Margaret Bray raise a family of six children, but Louie's son, Freddy Joe lived with the family from the age of 11 until he became an adult. Fred Bray passed away in 1994. Margaret Bray died in 2010.

CHESTER BROCK FAMILY

Chester B Brock. Son of Willie Grady Brock and Mildred Coe Brock of Martin, served in the US Air Force from 1-30-1946 to 12-21-1946, and then served in US Army from Oct. 16, 1950 to August 8, 1952. He received medals in both branches of service. After getting out of service, he married Mary Elizabeth Summers of Toccoa, daughter of John Isom Summers and Essie Rackley Summers, on Feb. 14, 1953. They lived in Martin where he owned a heating & air conditioning business.

Mr. & Mrs. Brock had a family of 5 children: Michael David, has one son, Zack and a daughter, Thedorah; Teresa Gail, married David Golden, and has two sons, David & Joshua. Joshua has one son, Joshua David; Connie Sue has 4 children, Branden Stevanus, Shane Stevanus, who has a daughter, Zoey, Briana Stevanus, and Jacob Stevanus .

Dale is the fourth child of the Brocks, and had a twin sister, Sarah Yvonne, who died shortly after birth. Dale is married to Angelia, and children are Damon & Shelby.

The Brock family lived directly across highway, 17 from the Martin Baptist Church where they attended church for many years during the 60s and 70s. Daughter, Connie, says they then attended Toms Creek Church where Mr. Brock taught the Men's Sunday school class for 50 years.

Mrs. Brock & Connie taught Training Union classes for many years, and they all sang in the church choir. Connie and Teresa sang solos in church for many years. Mary Brock passed away in 2003, and Chester Brock died in March, 2014.

BROCK FAMILY TREE

The Brock family began in Bozen, Aargau Switzerland with Heini Brack (1st) in 1578. Heini had a son Casper Brack, in 1612 (2nd). Casper Brack, had a son Casper Brack, II in 1646(3rd).

Casper Brack, II had a son Rudolph Brack in 1685.

Rudolph was born in Bozen, Aargau Switzerland and moved to Zweibreuken, Germany at an early age. He married Anna Maria in Germany. Rudolph and Anna Maria had a son named George Friderich Brack in 1719(5th). In 1733 Rudolph and family sailed to America on board the Ship Hope of London, which sailed from England. From the Minutes of the Provincial Council, printed in Colonial Records, Vol. III, and page 517. Not exactly sure when or why the last name was changed to Brock. The Ship Hope landed in Pennsylvania and from there the Brock family migrated from there to Virginia, to North Carolina, South Carolina and eventually to Georgia. George Brock born in Zweibreuken, Germany in 1719 and died in 1807 in Greenville, County, South Carolina, USA.

George had a son Isaac Brock in 1744(6th) in Bladen County, North Carolina and died in Brevard, Buncombe County, North Carolina in 1845. Isaac Brock married Anne and had a son Reuben Brock in 1779(7th) in Honea Path, Pendleton, South Carolina. He was married to Ann Elrod and believed to have moved to the Horseshoe area, about seven miles northeast of Brevard, in Buncombe County, North Carolina around 1815 and remaining there after the new Henderson County was formed before the 1840 census, still there for the 1850 census, age 71, and presumably dying there before 1860.

Reuben Brock married Ann Elrod had a son John R. Brock born in 1801(8th) in South Carolina and died in 1860 in Franklin County, Georgia. He married Margaret, who was born in 1796 in North Carolina (per 1850 Franklin County, Georgia census.) John R. And Margaret Brock are presumed to have married about 1821 in North Carolina. They had a son Francis J. Brock AKA John Francis Brock born October 5, 1835 (9th) in North Carolina. (At some point he became known as Frank or Franklin.) Sometime in 1837 or 1838, when Francis was 12 or 13 years old, his family moved to Georgia. The Brock 'home place' was located in an area referred to as "Smith Crossing", below Martin, Georgia off highway 1 7, (near what became known as the Coble Plant). The house was a big 2-story where Marvin lived as a boy.

Francis J. (Frank) married Sarah F. Smith born November 20 1865. F.J. BROCK in Martin GA.; married Sara F. Smith November 20, 1865 born 09/05/1848 in Franklin County, GA. Both F. J. and Sara F. Brock are buried in the Old Martin Cemetery. Mr. Brock, a prosperous land owner of 339 acres in the counties of Franklin and Stephens, known as the home place and one tract lying in the County of Franklin, adjoining lands of Mrs. J. J. Thomas and others, containing 90 acres, more or less. Mr. Brock's Military service: C.S.A. Tugalo Blues, Co. B, 15th Regiment, GA Volunteer Infantry. Private July 14, 1861. Appointed Sergeant. Wounded and captured at Gettysburg, PA, July 2, 1863.

In Memory of Mrs. Sara F. Brock

Mrs. Brock was born September 5th 1848, and departed this life September 18, 1912. Mrs. Brock's parents were Mr. And Mrs. Ezekiel Smith. She was born and reared within one and one half miles of where she died. Mrs. Brock was a devoted Christian mother and wife, and her advice and counsel will no doubt, be sadly missed by those nearest and dearest to her by the ties of nature. She united herself with Clark's Creek Baptist Church several years ago, and in church as well as in everyday life she was a model of womanhood, and now that the hand of divine Providence has removed from us our friend and mother. We are desirous of testifying our respect for her memory and expressing our earnest and affectionate sympathy for those deprived by this dispensation of their earthly head. We tenderly console with the family of the deceased in this their hour of trial and affliction, and can only devoutly commend them to the keeping of him who looks with a pitying eye upon the orphan, and while we deeply sympathize with those who were bound to her by the nearest and dearest ties of nature, we share with them the hope of a reunion in that better would where there are no more partings and bliss ineffable forbids all tears. She united herself with Clark's Creek Baptist Church several years ago, and in church as well as in everyday life she was a model of womanhood, and now that the hand of divine Providence has removed from us our friend and mother. We are desirous of testifying our respect for her memory and expressing our earnest and affectionate sympathy for those deprived by this dispensation of their earthly head.

We tenderly console with the family of the deceased in this their hour of trial and affliction, and can only devoutly commend them to the keeping of him who looks with a pitying eye upon the orphan, and while we deeply sympathize with those who were bound to her by the nearest and dearest ties of nature, we share with them the hope of a reunion in that better would where there are no more partings and bliss ineffable forbids all tears. (Obituary for Mrs. Brock in the Lavonia Times).

Children of F. J. and Sara F. Brock.
Frances "Fannie" Elizabeth Brock, b. September 2, 1866; d. February 25, 1925
Dock Franklin Brock, b. April 11, 1869; d. March 7, 1928
David Homer Brock, b. September 4, 1871; d. 1934

Henry Madison Brock, b. May 15, 1872; d. January 26, 1944
Luannah Brock, b. December 28, 1874; d. February 20, 1948
Mary Ann Brock, b. July 10, 1877; d. September 29, 1942
George Duie Brock, b. January 12, 1880; d. April 24, 1887
James Robert Brock, b. December 15, 1881; d. unknown
Daisy Brock, b. October 1, 1883; d. November 18, 1953
Colonel Albert Brock, b. September 30, 1885; d. February 21, 1964
Marvin Ramon Brock, b. September 1, 1887; d. May 18, 1958
Nancy Margarette Brock, b. November 16, 1889

Marvin Ramon Brock was born September 1, 1887 in Franklin County, Georgia near Martin and lived in them Martin area all his life. Married Rosa Cobb in 1908. Mr. Brock was a member of Pleasant Hill Baptist Church near Lavonia and was engaged in farming most of his life. He ran a small country store for a time and always had a beautiful garden. Mrs. Brock, the daughter of Reverend Samuel Roland and Susan Emma Dickson Cobb, and a devout Christian, was a member of Poplar Springs Baptist Church and had lived in the Martin Community most of her life.

Children of Marvin Ramon and Rosa Cobb Brock.
Margareet Brock, b. February 24, 1910; d. 1910
J. O. Brock, b. January 24, 1912; d. November 7, 1993
Ethel Willie Mae Brock, b. February 5, 1914; d.
Reuben Frank Brock, b. May 2, 1916; d.

J. O. Brock was born January 24, 1912 (12th) in Martin where he lived all his life and was of the Baptist faith. He was a farmer, the owner of rental properties and a country store. His favorite pass time was hunting and fishing. Married to Emma Sue Farrow, daughter of Eady and Sara "Sally" DeFoor Farrow and was a member of Martin Baptist Church. Mrs. Brock graduated from Martin Junior High School and Eastanollee High School and went on to attend Business School in Gainesville where she resided with her brother and sister-in-law, Reese and Mozelle Farrow. After business school she returned to Martin and in 1938 married J. O. Brock, and lived, in the Martin area, until her death.

Children of J. O. and Emma Sue Farrow Brock.
Romeo Brock, b. December 19, 1938; d. September 11, 2014
Baby Boy Brock, b. September 1940; d. September 1940
Jayne Marlow Brock, b. August 6, 1942
Mary Lynda Brock, b. May 3, 1944; d. October 1, 2006
Hallie Gail Brock, b. April 29, 1947

Children of Jayne and Dan:
Dan T. Pressley, Jr., Dean of Admissions at Currahee Campus Trade School, married to Tracy Pruitt and the parents of Amy. Michael Anthony Pressley, a career Army Officer, married to Maria Cabrera from Barcelona, Spain and parents of Michael, Jr. and Steven.
Laura Michelle Pressley a graduate of Georgia Southern University in Statesboro where she met and married Joey Godbee and parents of Wyatt, Zachary and Emma Jayne.Mary Lynda Brock married Tyrus Smith and had two sons, Jeffery Tyrus Smith and Lionel Gregory. Lynda divorced Tyrus Smith. Several years later she met and married Danny Spraggs, and had a daughter, Deena. Lynda and Danny lived in Stone Mountain where they both worked in the publishing business until 1999, when they moved to Lancaster, Pennsylvania. It was in Lancaster where Lynda became sick and passed away October 1, 2006.

Children of Lynda and Danny:
Jeffery Tyrus Smith, Lionel Gregory Smith Deena Renee Spraggs.

Hallie Gail Brock married Benny Beggs in 1963 and had a daughter Susan, February 21, 1965, a medical lab technician and the mother of Daniel, Jake, Amy, Hannah, Cody and Ben. Gail and Benny divorced after 12 years and she then met and married Dean Brown of Valdosta, Georgia several years later. She went to work with Jayne and Dan in January 2005 and remained with them until Dan's death in 2013. Gail still works as Assistant to the Solicitor of State Court, Stephens County, Georgia.

Child of Gail:
Susan Gayle Beggs Susan married Danny Umberhant in 1983.

Children of Susan:
Daniel Lee was born June 26, 1984.
Jake Brandon was born April 27, 1990.
Amy Cassandra was born March 25, 1992.
Susan and Danny divorced and she married Hank Yates in 1996. Hannah Cassina Gail was born July 17, 1998.

Cody Harold Dean was born March 23, 2000.
Susan and Hank separated in 2003. Susan had a son, Benjamin Brock Harris on May 2, 2007 with Tony Harris.

Children of Daniel:
Bryson Daniel, born December 5, 2012. Daniel married Chasity Hope Yearwood Bellamy on June 16, 2012. Chasity is the daughter of Cindy Pruitt Yearwood and J. D. Yearwood. Daniel and Chasity reside in Athens, Georgia where Daniel works as an electrician and Chasity is in Consumer Assistance.

Ethel Willie Mae Brock lived in the Martin area where she met and married Floyd Watkins and moved to the Mullins Ford area. They had two children, Merlon and Sara. Merlon worked in the furniture manufacturing business until his death. Sara married Roger Hemphill and they had three children, Cindy, a pharmacist, married Richard Wansley and had two sons. Sandra, a nurse practitioner, married Peter Brown and had three children. Randy, who is a race car driver and is in the trucking business with his dad, married Stacey and had one daughter. Frank Reuben Brock moved to Westminster where he met and married Betty Freeman.

They had five children, Teresa, Frankie, Marvin, Rosie and Jackie.

Eadie and Sally Farrow Brock

L to R Sue, Mary (Sis), Reese, Ethel, Fred (Berry), J. C. taken about 1920

Marvin & Rosa Brock   J. O., Willie Mae, Frank

J. O. & Sue Brock 1970s   J. O., Willie Mae, Frank
Brock,

Gail, Lynda, Romeo, Jayne 2006

BROWN FAMILY HISTORY

Benjamin Brown

Benjamin Brown was born on February 17, 1763, in Orange, Virginia. He had 10 children: Dozier Thornton 1789; Elizabeth; Jincy 1794; Asa 1796; Lucy 1798; Rosanna 1800; Sara 1802; Nancy 1804; Matilda 1806; and Elbert Jackson 1806, with Nancy Dozier. He then married Prudence on April 8, 1823, in Elbert, Georgia. He died on February 27, 1846, in Elbert, Georgia, having lived a long life of 83 years.

John Elbert, Ella, Sarah Aderhold, Lloyd, Mirtie, Winnie Rebecca Aderhold, Macy, Maggie, John Dozier, Sally, Benjamin, Lucy Iola, Junius

Dozier Thornton Brown

When Dozier Thornton Brown was born on April 13, 1789, in Wilkes, Georgia, his father, Benjamin, was 26 and his mother, Nancy, was 25. He married Mary Gaines Herndon on October 5, 1809. They had seven children during their marriage. Edward Herndon; Sagwell B., 1810; George Washington, 1814; Lucy Ann, 1816; Elbert Jackson, 1817; Sarah Elizabeth, 1822; and Rachel S., 1829. He died on June 18, 1845, in Elbert, Georgia, at the age of 56.

Elbert Jackson Brown

Elbert Jackson Brown was born on August 17, 1817, in Elbert, GA. He married Sarah Pressley McCurry March 27, 1845. They had one child according to Family Tree Maker: John Dozier, January 14, 1846. Elbert Jackson Brown died February 23, 1903 in Hart County, GA.

John Dozier Brown

John Dozier Brown was born January 14, 1846 in Hart County, GA. He married Winnie Rebecca Aderhold on December 12, 1865. They had 12 children: Mary Ella, December 6, 1866; John Elbert, August 30, 1868; James Benjamin, February 6,1871; Junius Washington, December 25,1873; Sallie Ada, September 4,1874; Lucy lola, December 20,1876; Leonard Owen, June 11,1879; Myrtie and Maggie (twins), September 26,1881; Lloyd and Lois (twins), April 8, 1884. John Dozier Brown died in Martin, December 13, 1912 and Winnie Rebecca died October 24 1930.

John Elbert Brown

John Elbert Brown was born August 30, 1868 in Martin, died October 16, 1946. He married Lela Stovall on September 27, 1890. To this marriage was born Herbert Stanton Brown. Herbert Stanton Brown married Gladys
Farmer.

Lloyd Brown

Lloyd Brown lived in the house presently occupied by Sheriff Randy Shirley. He first married Ada Bolding September 2, 1906. Second to Lucille Stephenson date unknown. No children. I remember Lloyd having the first television in Martin. He invited all the local children over to watch television.

Lucy Iola Brown

Lucy lola Brown married Richard Arthur Dean April 11, 1895 in Martin.

Family History of John E. Brown

John E. Brown married Lela Stoval in 1890 in Franklin County. Herbert Stanton Brown, Sr. (he was called Grand Hub), married Gladys Turner Farmer and moved to Martin, GA in the early 1900's. Herbert Stanton Brown, Jr. (Pete) was born in 1918. He attended Georgia Tech and received an aeronautical engineer degree. Pete promptly entered the U.S. Navy as a pilot. He married Ada Louise Wilcox (Nia) of Norfolk, VA, daughter of Judge E. B. Wilcox.

He had a wonderful 20 years in the Navy and retired at the age of 40. His peers said that he was one of the most knowledgeable engineers in helicopter construction in the world. He joined Sikorsky Helicopter in 1958 and retired back to Martin 20 years later.

Pete and Nia had 5 children. They spent their summers in Martin. That was their real home since they moved every two or three years while Pete was in the Navy. The oldest son, Peter, graduated from Emory University Medical School and became a surgical oncologist in Richmond, VA. He was thrilled to be part of the football team at Stephens County that won the state championship in 1958.

He and Judy Lumpton Brown of Atlanta, have three daughters, Charlotte, an MD., Francine and Elizabeth are lawyers, all living in Richmond. Denise, the youngest child attended Hollins College and works in the area of mental health.

Randy attended North Georgia College and is in the construction business. Carter went to the University of Connecticut and is an engineer. Stan attended Georgia Tech. He returned to Martin, where he lived until his untimely death.

Herbert (Pete) Stanton Brown, Jr. fought the Japanese in WWII, which is documented in two books: "Zero and Samurai" by Henry Sanada, who was the Japanese ace that wounded Pete on August 7, 1942, at the Battle of Guadalcanal, along with seven other pilots that encountered eighteen Japanese Zero pilots. Pete survived his wounds and lived to be 86 years of age.

Nathaniel Brown Sr.

Nathaniel was born August 5, 1923 and died August 6, 1987. He is buried in the Full Gospel Baptist Church Cemetery. He was married to Marietta Teasley Brown, who was born in 1921 and died in 2006. She is buried by her husband. They had 3 children: Pricilla Brown Harrison, born in 1942; Nathaniel Brown, Jr., born in 1946 and Earlene Brown Scott. Nathaniel Brown, Sr., served in WWII and Nathaniel Brown, Jr., served in Viet Nam.

Troy Burton Family

Troy was married to Lizzie B. Burton. He served in the U.S. Army in WWII and they had 11 children: Kenneth, T. W., Joe Evelyn, Wanda, Gary, Gloria, Terry, Harrietta, Pennie, Nadine and Robert. Tammie served in the U.S. Navy. Troy and Lizzie are buried in the Hurricane Grove Church cemetery. Troy was a farmer and drove a bus for the Stephens County School system.

Cheek Family

Prior to 1923 Mr. Henry & Mrs. Lillie Pearman Cheek lived in Martin in a house near the Martin School and operated a store in Martin. They moved to the country, Clarks Creek Road, in 1923 and began farming and growing strawberries. Mr. Henry was well known for his excellent quality produce, especially the strawberries he grew. He also had a creamery and sold apple cider. He drove a little Model A automobile until old age, knew everybody, and attended more funerals than anyone else in Northeast Georgia.

Mr. & Mrs. Cheek had a family of seven children. Bill, the youngest son and his wife, Laverne Cash Cheek, moved back to the home place and built a new house in 1997, years after Mr. Henry & Mrs. Lillie had passed away. Mrs. Laverne Cheek says that the family had an old icebox which had been discarded to the back porch in 1975. Mr. Henry promised it to her, and after his death she had it refinished. It is now one of her most precious possessions. Mr. Bill Cheek is now deceased and Mrs. Laverne continues to live on the home place.

Clark Family

Clem Terrell Clark was born April 13, 1868. He was the son of Safronia (Hanks) and Pless Clark. He lacked a formal education, but was self-educated. Clem valued education and served as trustee of Fairview School for 15 years.

Clem and his wife, Fannie Delilah Sanders Clark, had ten children. Fannie gave birth to all of the children at home; the first five without the benefit of a doctor. First were six sons Terrell, who married Sara Wilson; Lon, who married Clovis Christian; Craig, who married Maybelle Vickery; Tom, who married Lula Gilbert; Mark, who never married; George, who married Ina Baker and then four daughters Essie, who married J. C. Herron, Sr.; Sally, who married Sam Hill; Belver, who married Maurice DeFoor; Jewel, who married Floyd Scott. This large family grew up living and working on a large farm in the area near what is now Holcomb's Landing on Lake Hartwell. Fannie was an excellent cook.

With such a large family of her own, and extended family of cousins, nieces, and nephews, she entertained a family reunion every summer and a huge birthday celebration for her husband every April.

Clem was very active in the community and invited friends to have meals with them on short, or no notice. It was often said that Fannie had probably cooked more meals for more people than any other woman in Stephens County at that time. Clem loved politics and enjoyed reading the *Atlanta Constitution*. He was well-known and had many friends. Also very active in the Masons, he was a member for many years. He was a Deacon and active member of Mullins Ford Baptist Church. His home was a gathering place for many friends and a large extended family.

In his later years, he enjoyed sitting on his front porch in his rocker, reading his daily newspaper or visiting with friends. Clem also continued to do odd jobs around the house and farm.

At the age of 87, Clem died, busy on his feet. While reaching for his hammer, a heart attack killed him instantly. He had the type of funeral he had wanted, conducted by the Masons and attended by many friends and relatives.

Tom & Cleave Meaders, Craig, Lon, Terrell

Belver, Sally, Essie & Jewel

Fannie, Jewel & Clem   Sally Hill, Jewel, Terrell
                        Fannie, Jewel & Clem

Dalice Teasley Cowan

Curtis Crawford, Sr. Family

Curtis Crawford, Sr. settled in Martin in 1955. His family lived on Thomas Anderson Rd. Curtis married Lorene, Burton April 24, 1935.

Curtis, Sr., was born July 4, 1917 in Carnesville, GA. Mrs. Burton was born Feb 22, 1922 in Franklin County, GA. Curtis died August 17, 2007 and she died Dec 24, 1999. Both are buried in the Full Gospel Cemetery in Martin.

The Crawford children are: Arlene Frazier (11 – 2 - 1937), Ethel L. Mullins (5 – 12 - 1939), Betty Ann Beasley (10-23-1941), Curtis, Jr., 4 – 24-1943), Annie Sue Crawford (3 -18 -46) deceased, John Arthur Crawford (11-11-1948), Mary Ann Smith (2-12-1950), Shirley Simpson (6-14-1953), Belinda Smith (8-7-1957), Geraldine Crawford (7-14-58).

Niece Sgt. Letisha Sedette Crawford, served in the U. S. Army (1999), highest rank E7, Staff Sgt. Those who were accomplished in sports were Latisha, Raveen and Nikelgha (Owens). Latisha was MVP in 2003 and Raveen went to Breman University in Greenville, GA on an athletic scholarship in basketball. Spouses were: Leslie Frazier, Lamy Mullins, John Beasley, Lorene Teasley, Willie D. Smith, Marvin Simpson and Bobby Smith.

THE MITCHELL/DEAN/MARTIN/CLODFELTER/ STEPHENSON FAMILY

On January 14, 1920, Felix Luther Clodfelter purchased the large two-story house across from the depot from J.R Martin. Felix was married to Sarah Lucy Yow Clodfelter. They had six children who were adults when Felix purchased the house. According to Sarah Stephenson Whittemore, as told to her son Alton D. Whittemore, Jr., prior to this the Clodfelters lived a couple of houses south of the Martin School then bought the "big house" because he wanted a house in town.

Ralph Duncan Clodfelter and his older sister Minnie Lee Clodfelter Stephenson were the only Clodfelter children to live in this house. Ralph Duncan Clodfelter and his wife Julia Bell King Clodfelter lived in an upstairs apartment of the house for several years. Ralph was a merchant and had a pharmacy in Martin before moving to Toccoa and entering the insurance business.

Minnie Lee Clodfelter Stephenson, the oldest child of

Felix and Sarah, and at least eight of her ten children moved in with the Clodfelter's after her husband and youngest son died from the typhoid outbreak in 1921.

After Felix died in 1926, Minnie remained with her mother, acting as companion and caregiver until Sarah died in 1948. The house then passed to the living Clodfelter children (Ortis died in England during World War I of pneumonia). At that time, Minnie's remaining siblings gave her their portion in the house for the years of devoted service to their mother. Sarah had been an invalid for a number of years as a result of complications from breaking her hip.

Marion Morene Stephenson (Moe) Herring returned to Martin to live with her mother, Minnie, when her husband died in 1950. Sometime between the time, Morene returned to Martin and when Minnie suffered her stroke, Hattie Lucile Stephenson Allen Page Fisher returned to live in Martin with Minnie. Lucile lived in the house with Morene and Anne until she married Lloyd Brown.

Annie Leona Stephenson, who never married returned to Martin in 1958 to help Morene care for their mother, Minnie who suffered a stroke in 1956.

After Minnie's death in 1959, Morene's siblings, like Minnie's before her, signed over their portion of the property to Morene. Morene and Anne lived in the house together until Anne's death. After Anne's death, Morene lived there alone until her death.

Morene had deeded the property to her only living sibling, Mary Cannie Stephenson Mulkey and her husband Edwin Hayes Mulkey.

The property remained in the family until the estate of Mary Cannie Stephenson Mulkey sold it to the present owner in 2006.

 Thomas Young Stephenson and Minnie Lee Clodfelter Stephenson lived where the railroad spur crossed highway 17 north of Martin across from the Baptist church. Tom was a farmer. He and Minnie had 11 children all of whom lived in Martin at one time or other. Tom and his son Tommie died from typhoid fever during the outbreak in 1921, leaving Minnie with eight of their 10 living children to raise. Minnie did sewing and took in ironing to earn money to support herself and the remaining children. As mentioned above Minnie moved in with her parents after Tom died in 1921.

Felix Luther Clodfelter (1858-1928) & Sara Lucy Yow Clodfelter (1860-1948).
Children were; Minnie Lee, Thomas Clarence, Glen Marcellus, Ralph Duncan and Madge Carn Otis.

Minnie Lee Clodfelter Stephenson (1883-1959) & Thomas Young Stephenson (1874-1921). Children were; Lucille, Azalee, Luther, Hershel, Morene, Annie, Sarah, Clarence,
Mary, Ben and Tommie Lee.

WEYMAN LEE COMBS

Weyman Lee Combs was the fourth child born to Rev. Theron Combs and Corrie Combs. Weyman Lee's father was a Baptist Minister and Sharecropper. His mother was a homemaker. Weyman Lee's other siblings were Ella, John, George, Emma, and Jude. Rev. Theron Combs was married three times during his life. The children he fathered by his second wife (name unknown) were Ollie Mae, Texas, Glover, Warren and Winfred. He had no children by third wife (name unknown). Corrie Combs, first wife of Rev. Theron Combs died on July 20, 1886 and Rev. Theron Combs died March 24, 1919. They both are buried in the cemetery at Greater Hope Baptist Church, Martin, Georgia. A tombstone marks their graves.

Weyman Lee Combs was born on April 4, 1880 and was married to former Bertha Johnson. The date of their marriage is unknown. Weyman Lee and Bertha Johnson Combs were father and mother to nine children.

The names of their children are; Carl, Nannie, Clarence, Robert, F.B., Claude, Ernelle, Vemice, and Doyle. Weyman Lee Combs and his family sharecropped on several farms around Martin, Georgia, Stephens and Franklin Counties. Weyman Lee Combs was hired by a Veterinarian (name unknown) to assist with the treatment of farm animals. He was employed by him for several years. The Veterinarian died and his widow gave all his Veterinary books to Weyman Lee. Weyman Lee had no formal education. He could not read or write. His wife, Bertha could read and write. His wife would read these books to him. After the death of the Veterinarian, he traveled around the community assisting with the birth of farm animals and treating their illnesses. Weyman Lee and Bertha Johnson Combs were members of the Greater Hope Baptist Church, Martin, Georgia. Weyman Lee was a member of the Deacon Board until his death.

Weyman Lee Combs died on August 3, 1975 and his wife, Bertha died on May 2, 1923 'Her death came 5 months after the birth of her ninth child, Doyle. They both are buried in the cemetery of the Greater Hope Baptist Church, Martin, Georgia.

Ernelle Hughes Combs

Memories of myself go back most vividly to "moving times". I was born June 8, 1918 to Weyman Lee and Bertha Johnson Combs. My mother died in 1923 leaving nine children for my daddy to rear. I was 4yrs 11 months old. I remember moving three times by the time my mother passed away. I did love to move. I recall my father saying that he was moving to one of the Yow boy's farm (Lee, Pope, Hubert). Russell Yow owned much of Martin, Georgia, the small town that I grew up in. My dad left my birthplace at John E. Brown and moved to Lee Yow's farm. "This was a better house", my daddy said. The Yow's kept up their tenant houses well.

We could see the train roll by every day with many rail cars hauling bales and bales of cotton and pulp wood. There was a black fireman on the train named Johnny Williams. It was a pleasure to get a wave from Johnny. These trains were referred to by my father as the Elberton Trains; a freight train and a passenger train would go up to Toccoa daily to meet the main line trains.

My most vivid memory of this farm was a pond below the barn. My older brothers made a pond by damming up the branch. My father would check the depth and on many occasions would let my older brothers walk me around in the water and let me sit down in the cool water.

The water came up around my neck. My brothers taught me how to hold my breath and dive. We stayed a couple of years on Yow Boy # 1 place. One day my father said Mr. Russell Yow said it was time to go on Hubert Yow's place (Yow's place # 2). I couldn't understand the shifting, but I realized that Russell Yow was giving all the boys an equal chance to benefit from sharecroppers.

Hubert Yow was my father's favorite. Everybody called him "Hube", short for Hubert. I remember that Hube would bring his three boys often to look at the farm. Hube's boys, Hugh, Fields, and Ben, loved homemade syrup. My mother made big pones of biscuits called hoecakes. The boys always wanted syrup and bread when they entered the house. My father grew cane and made syrup. So, there was always plenty syrup on hand. It seemed that my mother knew when to expect the boys, she always had plenty hoecakes on hand.

We were living on Yow's place # 2 when my mother passed away. Mother had my baby brother Doyle, January 6, 1923; she had just given birth to a baby girl, February 14, 1921. She seemed to have taken all the affection. She was a fat chubby, yellow baby, adorable but abominable to me.

I recall the cold night my baby brother was born. Grandmother lived just up the road on the same place. My father took me up to her house, when my mother began to feel labor pains.

On the way to grandmother's house he told me that Sister Gibbs had come to bring my mother a little baby and I have to stay with Grandma. My mother was already sick with a heart condition known then as "dropsy". Her arms and legs were swollen to the extent of bursting. I recall that I was lying in the bed with my grandmother, but I couldn't sleep. My father came back to grandmother's house for something and I cried to go home. He wrapped me up and carried me in his arms back home. When we walked in the door, my mother said "turn around and take her right back up to Mama's". Don't think a child's heart can't bleed. Oh, how I suffered that night.

My mother was never well again. She passed away in May 1923 leaving a five month old baby and 8 children ranging in ages 2, 4 1/2, 7, 13, 15, 17, 19 and 21. My father said the Lord would help him rear his children. My oldest brother, Carl had moved to Detroit, Michigan and had a job with Ford Motor Company. My sister, Nannie was just like a mother; she washed, sewed, patched, worked in the field and did everything humanly possible for us.

The next year was moving time. We left (Yow's Place #2) and went to share crop with Bud Crawford. Bud had a family of children with age's equivalent to ours. They were our playmates. We loved each other and that love lasted down through the years to the present moment. All have passed away in that family except three and all of us are gone except four.

Mary and Ned wrote me a sweet letter and sent a clipping from the Toccoa Record when my husband passed away December 25, 1983. I remember going to school one year and it was moving time again. My father's family evidently had lived with the Zeke Thomas family, when he was growing up. We moved on Zeke Thomas' place where we spent the major portion of my childhood and teenage years. My father sharecropped as usual, but he accumulated enough to buy his own stock mules and horses. I remember what a difference it made to be sharing our crops on the half instead of third and fourth. Zeke Thomas owned much land, white and blacks share cropped alike on his place.

Relationships with whites were good. During my growing up years all my playmates were white except the ones I went to school with.

During the Depression years, we fared fairly well. My father had a good relationship with white people and they were always giving us clothes and ham bones with a little meat. Thanks to Dr. Swaim, Henry and Etta Mitchell for leaving some ham on their bones, it made our beans and peas taste delicious. We didn't always wear second hand clothes, my father would buy cloth and my sister Nannie would make clothes for us. When she ran away and got married, the white folks made our dresses.

My father would never plant a whole lot of cotton, but grew corn and wheat. He had a bottom land garden which was always moist and we had fresh vegetables until frost came. My father hired his boys out to white folks and gave the boys just about all the money they made.

My brothers also had cotton patches of their own when they reached a certain age. The bought their own clothes and had money to spend. My father wanted all his children to get an education. All of his children went as far as the public school taught at Martin, Georgia. I was determined not to stop at the seventh grade. I finished the seventh grade and stayed home 3 years before I went to high school.

I was twenty-three years old when I finished high school. I was Valedictorian of my class. I would never tell my age. Only the doctors, Social Security and my family knew my age.

I was determined to go to school. Thanks to Governor Ed Rivers for free books, I entered high school in 1937 at the Toccoa Colored High School. I had to live in Toccoa and pay board. Thanks to Lewis Thomas for giving me wood to pay my room rent and Rev. A.A. Rice who transported me on weekends that he was preaching at Greater Hope Baptist Church. He also inspired me to get an education.

Moving time came again. This time we moved to John Mitchell's place. Later on we moved back to Lewis Thomas's Place. We moved later on to Bartow Crawford's place, brother of Bud Crawford. I was in college when my father lived on Bud Crawford's place. Later, my father moved to the farm of Jimmy Crawford. This was 1945-1946; I came out of school and taught school that year.

In 1946-1947, I went back to Spelman College and receive my degree in English and History. It was several years later, I received my Master's degree from the University of Georgia. **Note:** Ernelle Hughes Combs taught in the public school system of Hart County for 35 years. After her retirement, she served on the Hart County Board of Education for 5 years. The first African-American to serve in this capacity.

After the death of her husband, she moved to Martin, Georgia in 1985. She resided in Martin until her death, September 1985. Ernelle Hughes Combs wrote this autobiography in early 1985, one year prior to her death.

CRAWFORD FAMILY HISTORY

James Harrison Crawford, MD was one of 8 children, descendants of Hugh Crawford (1195 - 1265) who immigrated from Ayrshire, Scotland to the USA. Hugh was the Second Sheriff of Ayrshire, Chief of Clan Crawford, and Lord of Loudon Castle; Hugh's daughter, Margaret, married Sir Malcolm Wallace of Ellerslie in Ayrshire and became the mother of Sir William Wallace, the immortal hero of Scotland. Dr. Crawford's father, William Harrison Crawford, was born Nov 18, 1826 and died May 15, 1917. He was a member of the 3rd Georgia Cavalry State Guards Company E. He is buried at Clark's Creek Baptist Cemetery. His mother was Nancy Elizabeth Shirley, born May 8, 1840 in Hart County, GA.

James Harrison Crawford was born Oct 13, 1873 and died Sept 22, 1923 of appendicitis. He was a prominent practitioner of medicine for the town of Martin and surrounding communities and served in World War 1. He had a fondness for cars, politics, and baseball. Dr. Crawford along with his wife Blanche Ketchersid (born May 19 1884 and died Dee 22, 1985) are buried in the Martin Community Cemetery. (See Ketchersid History).

Dr. Crawford and Blanche raised four children. Annie, born Aug 10 1903 - died Oct 26 1915 in an accident at the age of 12; James Harrison, born Nov 27 1909 in Martin, died June 22001 in College Park, GA.; Mildred Elizabeth Hoke, born Jan 2 1914 in Martin, died Nov 142004 in Toccoa; and Vivian Doris, born Dee 4, 1917 in Martin and lives since 1957 in Marietta GA.

James (Jim) was an aviator and built an airplane at the age of 18; one of 4 he would build in his lifetime. He would take the local townsfolk for rides in his airplane. James married June Rose Schmitt from Wisconsin and had 2 sons (James III and Peter) who made NASCAR history with an upset win at Talladega on Aug. 12, 1973.

The Crawford brothers were pilots for Eastern Airlines at the time; took a car prepared in their parents' basement in College Park, hired a journeyman driver named Dick Brooks and astounded the racing world by winning the Talladega 500. James III started his NASCAR career as a driver, from 1970 to 1974; he made 15 starts in the series now known as the Nextel Cup. His best days as a driver came in February 1974, when he qualified for NASCAR's biggest race, the Daytona 500, and finished 19th.

Mildred was an accomplished pianist and served as the pianist / organist at Martin Baptist Church for over 60 years. She was also a star basketball player for the Martin school. Mildred attended Brenau College where she studied music and spent her career as a teller at the Bank of Toccoa.

Vivian married Lawrence Deweese (aka Pete) McCall (b. May 23.1916 d. August 21.1963) who she had grown up with and gone to school with in Martin. Vivian studied voice at Greenville Woman's College (now merged with Furman). Pete was a gunner in the Air Force during wwn and remained in the Air Force until receiving a medical retirement in 1953. Vivian and Pete had 3 children, James Michael (1942), Andrea Gail (1944), and Dawn Lucinda (1954). Pete and family moved to Marietta GA in 1957 where he worked for Lockheed Aeronautics and Dobbins Air Force Base, always around airplanes.

Son Michael also has spent his career in the aeronautic parts sales business. Michael and wife Ann Harrison from Cornelia married in 1965 and had 2 children, Michael Sean and Elizabeth Ann. Andrea graduated from The Woman's College of Georgia (now Georgia College) and married Charles Thomas Pair born 1944 Ft MacPherson GA in 1966. They have 4 children, Dawn Michele (1970), Jason Thomas (1971), Andrea Nicole (1975), and Joshua Bradley (1977). Dawn is a graduate of University of Georgia, worked on the Carter Campaign after graduating receiving a political appointee position under the Carter Administration, and later served as President International for The Discovery Channel. Dawn also served with the State Department under Hillary Clinton.

James Harrison Crawford

Dr. James H. Crawford with children, Annie, James II and Mildred

Mildred, James II and
Vivian Crawford

Mildred Crawford
Martin School Basketball

Brothers Peter (left) and
Jimmy Crawford (right)
- pilots for Eastern
Airlines at the time - put
together the car, then
Dick Brooks did the
driving to win the 1973
Talladega 500.

DEAN FAMILY HISTORY

The Dean family came to the area of Mullins Ford, Franklin County from South Carolina. 1-1 Samuel Dean born 1751 Cumberland County, PA died May 23, 1836 in Anderson District, SC, where he had come after serving as a Revolutionary soldier in the War for Independence. He married Gwendolyn James and their children were: Miriam; Aron; Thomas; Samuel; John; Joseph; Richard; Griffin; Mary; and Moses.

Richard Dean, son of Samuel and Gwendolyn Dean, born 1791 in Anderson District, SC died June 1864 Oconee County, SC where he owned large tracts of land on both sides of the Tugaloo River. Richard and Cynthia Dean were the parents of 2-1 Emily, 2-2 Russell, 2-3 Melissa Catherine, and 2-4 Elizabeth. **Emily Dean** married Abe Hester of SC.

RUSSELL DEAN, born June 24, 1829 in Pickens District, SC, married Mary Melinda Craig, born August 1, 1824, August 28, 1849 in Pickens District, SC. For a wedding dower Arthur Craig deeded 1287 acres across the Tugaloo River in Franklin County, GA. To this marriage seven children were born: Richard Arthur Dean, Infant Son, Henrietta Catherine Dean, Cynthia Elizabeth Dean, Lucinda Sally Dean, Emily Melissa Dean and Margaret Susan Dean. They lived on the parcel of land on the Tugaloo River. Russell Dean died May 16, 1877 in Oconee County, SC. Buried in Family plot on Black Jack Road, Oconee, SC.

Melissa Catherine Dean, born October 31, 1824 in SC, died January 1902 Martin, GA married Thomas Anderson Yow. Their children were 3-1 Henrietta Catherine Dean born October 13,1852 married Jules Davis and settled in Richland, SC.

Elizabeth Dean married Enoch Breazelle and settled in Westminster, SC. Henrietta Catherine Dean, born October 13, 1852 in Franklin County, GA married Jules Davis and settled in Richland, SC.

Richard Arthur Dean

Richard Arthur Dean, born March 3, 1856 in Franklin County, GA, married Lucy Iola Brown, born December 20, 1876, April 11 , 1895 in Martin, GA. Arthur moved to Martin after his mother died. He worked as Postmaster. He was a progressive farmer in the Martin area. He was active member of Martin Baptist Church, a member of the Martin Board of Education, and a member of the Woodmen of the World. Lived in the little house until he built the Dean Family house in 1904. To this marriage six children were born: 4-1 Winnie Mary (Mae) Dean, 4-2 Russell Yow Dean, 4-3 Margaret Ruth Dean, 4-4 Robert Arthur Dean, 4-5 Sarah Elizabeth Dean and 4-6 Richard Brown Dean, Sr.

During the Great Depression Arthur walked a milk cow to Atlanta because his sister needed the milk for her baby boy. I'm not sure how long many days it took but remember that Highway 123 was our means of travel to Atlanta.

Richard Arthur Dean

Cynthia Elizabeth Dean, born October 13, 1857 in Franklin County, GA, died November 10, 1933 in Martin, GA. Married Thomas Russell Yow. Their children were 4-1 Lee Ray; 4-2 Hubert; 4-3 Pope; 4-4 Flora; 4-5 Grace.

Lucinda Sally Dean born February 6, 1860 in Franklin County, GA married Milton W. Thompson and had one son Von Milton Thompson.

Emily Melissa Dean born February 11, 1862 in Franklin County, GA married James Lawrence of Central, SC. Margaret Susan Dean born December 9, 1864 in Franklin County, GA married James K. Polk of Atlanta, GA.

Winnie Mary Dean born May 7, 1896 in Franklin County, GA. Lived in Erwin TN and worked for Clinchfield Railroad. She returned to the home place at Mullins Ford area where she lived until death. She is buried in the Martin Cemetery.

Russell Yow Dean born December 29, 1898 in Franklin County, GA married Lucille Roark and lived in Atlanta. Yow worked for Sears Roebuck and Company until he died.

Margaret Ruth Dean born December 31, 1900 in Martin, GA married T. Fred Terrell, son of William and Martha Ann Terrell. They are the parents of Marcile and Dean Terrell.

Robert A. Dean born March 27, 1904 in Martin, GA married 1st Margaret Hoff of Madison, WI and had one daughter; 5-1 Mary Dean who married Eddie Oxford and lived in Seneca, SC. 2nd Florence Cox of Belton, SC

Sara Elizabeth Dean born October 2, 1906 in Martin, GA married John Dexter Jones and both taught in the Toccoa School System. They had one son, Thomas Arthur Jones, who served as Southern Baptist Missionary in Nairobi, Kenya with his wife from Toccoa, Nancy Kirk. They had three children, Sara, Thomas and Andrew. Andrew lived in the old Dean Family home on the original tract of land on Lake Hartwell.

Richard Brown Dean, Sr. born October 31, 1914 in Martin, GA married Joan Richardson of Toccoa, GA.

Melinda Dean born May 7, 1941 married Ralph Clifton of Metter, GA. They had two children: 6-1 Leigh Clifton Chambers of Milledgeville, GA and 6-2 Wesley Clifton of Metter, GA.

Rebecca Dean Kennemur born December 3, 1942 married 1st Don Feldman Kesler of Toccoa, GA and had three children: 6-3 Veronica Ann (Vicki) married Oliver Wayne Edwards and had two children: Blake of Reedville, VA. Ashley of Chesterfield, VA; 6-4 Don Steven of Chester, VA and 6-5 Russell Dean of Martin, GA. 2nd John Noah Kennemur of Liberty, SC. While researching our ancestry John and I had 6th generation kinship with John Neon Craig.

Richard Brown Dean, Jr. born September 17, 1945 married Jo Evelyn Whitworth. They live in Martin See their write-up!

Terry Lynn Dean born March 8, 1956 married Dr. Robert Edmonds of Toccoa, GA. They have two boys: Bryan "B-Shoc" Edmonds and Alan Edmonds.

Richard Brown Dean Sr.

Richard Dean was born October 31, 1914 to Richard Arthur Dean and Lucy lola Brown. Richard finished high school at Toccoa City School and attended Presbyterian College in Clinton, SC until his mother became ill and he returned home to work on the farm. He was very active in the community, Martin Lions Club and Martin Baptist Church. For several years he served on the Stephens County Hospital Authority and the Stephens County Tax Assessors Board. Richard B. Dean Sr., one of the oldest lifelong citizens, held the office of Mayor for many years. During his tenure, the water system was built with the aid of Senator Landrum, who was born in Martin.

The town streets were paved and the Martin Fire Department was established, with the assistance of Governor Ernest Vandiver and the Martin Lions Club. The Martin Lions Club and the Martin Woman's Club (originally called Young Matron's Working Club), have long been interested in keeping the town together and have been instrumental in accomplishing many tasks along with the Town Council's assistance. The Martin Community Center and the Martin Town Park are examples of this commitment. He married Joan Richardson of Toccoa, April 25, 1940 and they lived in the little house next door to the Dean house. They moved to the Dean house after Arthur Dean passed away.

Joan Richardson attended Toccoa High School and Georgia State College for Women where she earned a Home Economics Degree with a minor in Art. After her children were all in school she taught school in Stephens County High School in Home Economics. She was a member of the Martin Woman's Club, the "As You Like It Club" and active member of Martin Baptist Church where she taught in many areas during her life. She studied and read the Bible every day. Joan and Richard had four children: Melinda Ann -1941, Lucy Rebecca - 1942, Richard Brown, Jr. -1945 and Terry Lynn 1954. Richard Brown Dean,

Sr., was very resourceful with his farming. He raised crops to feed the cows; He had a garden to feed us with the meat of cows, pigs and chickens. He was very progressive with his cows, milking them two times a day. Daddy and Mama bottled milk for the local families and there was a refrigerator intended just for them. The neighbors paid when they could. Richard Brown Dean, Sr., traded for Melinda's and Rebecca's piano lessons by providing milk to Pastor Herbert Doud's family.

I remember he bought baby chickens for Melinda and me to raise and gather eggs to sell. We had 500 chickens and Melinda and Rebecca slept in the chicken house with the baby chicks the first night we got them. I remember gathering eggs every day after school and we would wash and crate the eggs. One day I remember running into a snake on the path from the chicken house. Several eggs were broken and the broken eggs ran down my legs. What a Mess! I also remember taking eggs to Atlanta to our Aunts and Uncles there and because the road was bumpy some of the eggs broke. We had to sell the car when the smell got so bad.

 When Lake Hartwell was built, it took several large fields. Daddy and Mama built a cabin on Dean Property on the Lake. That cabin made memories for the whole family. Daddy bought a boat; we enjoyed boating, skiing, swimming and just playing in the water. I can go on and on with experiences of living on the farm. Time is short and I want to say I am so happy living in the age I was raised. I had two great parents and I appreciate them.

Richard Brown Dean Junior Family

Known as Brown, since his father was already called Richard. Richard Brown Dean Junior was born September 17, 1945 and spent his early years growing up in Martin, Georgia with his sisters Melinda, Rebecca and Terry. Growing up on a dairy farm instilled in him a strong work ethic but still allowed him ample opportunity to develop lifelong friendships with Martin friends. Some tales of their boyhood adventures still dominated conversations when any of those Martin buddies would see each other.

Brown reluctantly left home to go to North Georgia College in Dahlonega after graduation from Stephens County High School, where his mother taught English and Home Economics during his years there. That was probably reason enough for him to limit the pranks he was known for participating in. After an automobile accident that first year, he didn't return to Dahlonega, but completed the year at Truett McConnell College, in Cleveland and later transferred to THE UNIVERSITY OF GEORGIA, where he received his BS degree upon graduation.

It was during this time, he married Jo Evelyn Whitworth, b. October 8, 1945, at Martin Baptist Church, on September 10, 1966. Jo Evelyn was born in Stephens County to Robert Joel and Donna Blanche Crawford Whitworth. Jo graduated from Woman's College of Georgia in 1966.

She had the distinction of being the last class of all girl graduates, before the school became coed and changed its name to Georgia College, later Georgia College and State University. Brown's Mother, Joan, had graduated from the same school in Milledgeville when it was known as GSCW, Georgia State College for Women.

They shared another common denominator, other than the fact both were named and called Jo, both graduated from the same college in Milledgeville: both had majored in Home Economics Education.

In 1968, Brown partnered with his father on the dairy farm Richard Sr. had begun in the 1940's with 6 cows. It became a business that the family stayed involved in until Brown's retirement in 2005. The herd during that time grew from 25 cows when Brown joined the partnership to over 300 cows in the milking herd and 300 more replacement dairy heifers. Brown's cornfields were legendary over a period of 30 years in and around Martin, as his father's had been the years before that. Those cornfields that were part of the dairy operation were now no longer part of the Martin landscape as were the black and white cows that were seen in the pastures in the middle of Martin for decades, across from the Martin Community Center. Brown, however, did not miss the cows getting out in the middle of the night. Jo Evelyn once had a cartoon on their refrigerator that aptly conveyed that occurrence. The cartoon was a farm wife, asking her husband, "Its 10pm. Do you know where your cows are?"

Their children had the unique opportunity to grow up in Martin on a dairy farm.

Richard Brown Dean Ill, born December 7, 1971 on his great Grandmother Sallie Gray Whitworth's birthday, worked on the dairy farm when growing up as did his dad and after graduation from Stephens County High School, earned an Agricultural Engineering Degree from the University of Georgia. It was there he met his future wife, Monica Fernandez, who had grown up in Florida and later Alpharetta, Georgia. They had a daughter, Sofia Renee Dean, born June 11, 2007. Rich owned and operated Classic Designs in Athens.

Krista Delane Dean, born December 14, 1974, graduated from Stephens County High and received degrees in Fine Arts and Art Education from the University of Georgia and taught Art Education in Clarke County. Krista married John David Marr, who had grown up in Chicago, in 2002.

Brown and Jo Evelyn were members of Martin Baptist Church, where they served as teachers in Sunday school, Vacation Bible School, Mission organizations, as chaperones for Youth functions and RA camping trips. Jo was active in choir, and served on Fellowship committees, while Brown served as Deacon, as Deacon Chairman, was on Pastor Search committees and was active in Van ministry.

Brown has been Stephens County Farm Bureau President, has been active in Georgia Farm Bureau leadership, and has served on the board and as President for Georgia DHIA (Dairy Herd Improvement Association). He represented Georgia for National DHIA, and served on the board of American Dairy Association of Georgia.

Brown and Jo have been recognized as County and District Young Farm Family of the year, Conservation Family of the Year, and Jo as Farm Woman of the Year.

Jo Evelyn retired from the University of Georgia Cooperative Extension Service in 2006, after serving in Clarke, Hart, Banks, Jackson, Stephens, and Franklin Counties. However, she followed her heart and did not return to work until both children were in college. During the time they were in college, she became "mother" to hundreds of 4-H'ers, seeing them through weeks of summer camps at Rock Eagle, coaching them for District and State competitions and providing leadership to District and State officers. Upon retirement, Brown and Jo enjoyed traveling, spending time with family and flying in the airplane Brown built.

Richard Brown Dean, Junior

George Hayden Dean Family History

Robert A. Pinkney Dean, born July 31, 1851 and died January 5, 1930, married Martha McCall, born March 17, 1851 and died September 4, 1908. Children were: John c., James B., Henry Richard, George Hayden, and Ben.

George Hayden, was born November 1, 1874, in his parent's home located at the corner of HWY 17 and Yow Mill Road- between railroad and highway, and died July 12, 1941. He married Martha McCall, who was born March 22, 1877 and died April 6, 1947. Their children were; Beulah, Florence, Carl, William Clyde, Ralph, Leila, Martha, Ruth, Ben, Estelle, Joe McCall, Edna and Fred.

They were born and raised in the home built by George Hayden, on Freeman Road in Martin. Two sons, Carl and Clyde died during the flu epidemic of 1918. George Hayden lived to see his namesake be born. It is said that he saw the baby one time and said "That's a fine boy". He died 10 days later.

Joe McCall was born September 14, 1915 and married Mary Gwendolyn Grimes, who was born December 2, 1923. Their children were: Joe McCall Jr., George Hayden, Carl Grimes, Tamara Romelle. Joe and Gwendolyn lived in the home that his father built and raised their four children. Ten days after George Hayden, Jr. was born his Grandfather, George Hayden, Sr. saw the baby and said "That's a fine boy".

Joe McCall Jr., married Linda, and they have two sons; Kevin and Kendall. Joe Jr. moved back to Martin and lives in the old home place. Jan George Hayden was born July 4, 1941 and married Linda Anne Farmer, born January 2, 1944. They have two daughters; Hayden Romelle, born June 3, 1966; Hayley Noele, born December 25, 1968.

Carl Grimes, born 1948 and died April 19, 1981, married Sara Whitmire, born in 1948. They had three children: Carla, Joe, and Delane.

Tamara Romelle, was born in 1953 and married Bill Eckhart. They had one son, Will and his second marriage was to Wilkie Brown.

George Hayden Dean was the only child of Joe and Gwendolyn to remain in Stephens County. He and his father's brother, Ralph, established Dean's Grocery, a landmark in the community. But this wasn't enough to keep him busy. George and his wife, Linda, became very active in the Young Farmers, the Farm Bureau, and Currahee Saddle Club. Each year their farm is where all the local elementary students want to visit during the Farm Bureau's annual farm tours.

Martha McCall and George Hayden Dean, Sr.

George Sr. & Martha McCall Dean home place 1910

Children of George and Martha McCall Dean; L to R: Fred, Edna, Joe, Estelle, Ben, Martha, Ruth, Leila, Florence, Beulah, and Mattie and George. Two children Carle and Clyde died in the 1918 flu epidemic.

FAGAN FAMILY HISTORY

This story is about Lula Albertson Fagan, William
Tatum Fagan, Ben Fagan and others.

Lulu was a very self-reliant and independent person. She
farmed a 40 plus acre farm by herself. She married Will
Fagan and was reported to have told a friend she knew she
had made a mistake even before they got home. However,
they "made a crop that year, were not getting along well at
all, so Will left. They decided to try one more time though,
and "started another crop" the next spring. Things still were
not going well so Will left saying he would never put his
foot back in the state of Georgia again. (Incidentally, the
farm was about 2 miles from Martin on route 1). True to his
word, Will never came back. However, they not only made
a crop, Lulu's son (Ben) was on the way! Lulu reared Ben,
taught him to farm, etc. by herself. She specifically did not
want him to try to locate his Father.

After Lulu's death in the late 1930's, Ben launched a
search for his Father. With the Assistance of a number of
people, he located his Father in Benton, Arkansas. Will's
Brother Joe moved to Arkansas with him also.

In 1940, Ben took the train to Arkansas hoping to see his
Father. He had several reference letters from Will's old
friends, a few pictures, etc. for identification. Ben went to
Joe's house first and met with him to explain his situation.

Joe fully accepted him and went to Will's house nearby
where Joe introduced them. Ben was 49 years of age when
he met his Father for the first time and Will was 74 years of
age before he knew he had this Son. Ben was treated
extremely well by his Father, Step Mother and his two Half
Brothers. Will and Joe were both Farmers.

Joe had a very nice home but Will's had the look of a true "farm house".

For Christmas in 1941, Ben and his family (Beulah, Floreine, Ben Evelyn and Charles) drove their 1940 Ford to Arkansas as their Christmas gift to each other (Charles wanted a bicycle instead!). Ben's family was warmly welcomed by both Joe and Will's families and the trip was very successful and worthwhile. This was the only time the family ever had an opportunity to visit them. Will passed away in 1946.

BEN F. PAGAN (at right) and his Father, H. F. Pagan

FARROW FAMILY HISTORY

The Martin Branch of the Farrow family emigrated to the U.S. from Hingham, England in 1635, eventually settling in Prince William County, VA. Our great-great-great-great-great grandparents, John and Rosanna Waters Farrow moved to the State of South Carolina around 1765, settling in the Old Ninety-Six District on the north side of the Enoree River.

John Farrow, Jr. (1754-1843) second son of John and Rosanna Farrow served in the Revolutionary War under the command of his uncle Colonel Pwlemon Waters and his brother, Captain Thomas Farrow. He was married to a Miss Brown.

Thomas Farrow (1780-1864) married Mary Ann Harris. Thomas Farrow was the son of John Farrow, Jr. Tombstone inscription reads: "fought in the War of 1812, consistent member of the Baptist church". Firstborn son of Henry Farrow.

Henry Farrow moved to then Franklin County, GA, around 1837. He was married to Martha Richardson. Both are buried in the Liberty Hill Baptist Church cemetery. Records show that he was the first postmaster of the Eastanollee Post Office. He also served in the Confederate War - Co. E 3rd Regiment Calvary, GA State Guards. Eight children were born to this union: Jane, Sarah Ann, Andy, Cecilia, James Perry, Mary, Hannah and Tommy.

James Perry Farrow (1849-1913) married Sophia Catherine Mitchell (1853- 1909). Both are buried in the Martin Cemetery. Perry was a farmer and operated a sawmill. Perry became a student of shaped note singing eventually teaching singing schools. The Toccoa Record (July 1891) records: "Professor Farrow commences a singing school at Liberty, SC, Monday night and the week following he holds one in Cleveland, SC."

Two daughters were born to this union, Rosetta and Beulah. Both are buried in the Martin Cemetery. Five sons were also born: Esty, Eady, Arthur, Raymond, and Roy. Eady was the only son who remained in Ga.

Eady K. Farrow (b. 1-21-1887 d. 8-26-1957) married Sallie
DeFoor (b.4-23-1888 d. 11-17-1959). They are both buried in the
Martin Cemetery. They owned a farm just west of the Town of
Martin. He owned and operated a sawmill. Sallie Farrow was
known for her beautiful flower gardens, her rock walls and a
large display of boxwoods. Recollection is of many visitors
during spring, summer and fall coming to see the lovely display
of blooms and to get a cutting to take home to root. Six children
were born to this union:
Fred (b. 1-18-1911 d. 3-22-1975) married Fay Stancil. Moved
to Broad River Community but owned and operated Farrow's
Grocery in Martin for several years. Both are buried in the
Broad River Church cemetery. Their children: Gwendolyn
(Betty) and Mary. Ethel (b. 5-27-1912 d. 1-28-1981) married
Dante (Dan) Freeman.
They lived in Martin on Freeman Road all of their lives. Both are
buried in the Martin Baptist Church cemetery. Their children:
Gwenelle, Dannie Sue, Stanley and Joy. Mary (b. 2-20-1916 d. 5-8-
1989) married James Mosley. They lived in Gainesville, GA, and
both are buried at Memorial Par~ Cemetery. Their children: James,
Jr., and Daniel. Emma Sue (b. 8-24-1917 **d.** 10-29-1978) married J.
O. Brock. They lived in the Martin community all of their lives and
both are buried in the Martin Baptist Church cemetery. Their children:
Romeo, Jayne, Linda and Gail. Reece (b. 10-4-1914 **d.** 5-9-1964)
married Mozelle Wilson. They moved to Toccoa. Both are buried in
Stephens Memorial Gardens. Their children: Patsy, John Eady and
Peggy.
J. C. Farrow (b. 1-26-1919 **d.** 2-7-2012) married Frances Kirby.
They lived in the Broad River Community. They are buried in the
Broad River Baptist Church cemetery. Their children: Roger and
Donald.

Eady and Sally Farrow   Reece, Mozelle, Patsy & John Farrow

Ethel and Fred Farrow   J. C. Farrow
                              Graduation Toccoa Falls

Sister in law Frances, Mozelle,   C. Ethel, Mary, Fred, Sue,
Daughters Ethel, Mary,   Benny Farrow
Grandchildren Gwenelle,
Dannie Sue, Stanley & Patsy

FREEMAN FAMILY HISTORY

The Freeman family lived in the area before the Town of Martin was established. The known history of the Freeman family dates back to 1853 when John T. Freeman married Rebecca Ann Brock in Franklin County, GA. Their son Samuel Freeman was born in 1854. Samuel married Vandorah (Dora) Dean (b. 1856) in 1874 in Franklin County, GA. Their children were Rasial Mattison Freeman (b. 1875), Tom Gerome Freeman (b. 1879) and Joe Freeman (b. 1881). After the disappearance of Samuel Freeman in 1881, Vandorah married Thomas W. Mitchell and moved to Texas where she is buried in Gregg County, Texas. Tom and Joe Freeman also moved to Texas.

Rasial Mattison (R. M. - better known as "Matt") Freeman remained on the Freeman property which is located on what is now known as Freeman Road, Martin. At one time, the property consisted of a total of approximately 500 acres at several different locations. R. M. (Matt) and his sons farmed the land until sometime after the loss of his barn and livestock by fire. Over the years, the majority of the land was sold.

R. M. Freeman married Maude Thomas (b. 1879). Their children were Elmer (married Julia Garland), Owen married Augusta Luzert), Dora (married Curtis Poole), Dante (Dan) (married Ethel Farrow), Joe (married Jo Rayma "Jody" Pitts), Geraldine "Gerry" (married Miller Stovall) and Merle (married George Pruitt). All are now deceased.

Elmer and Julia Freeman had the following children: Eleanor (Morrow), Harold, R. M., Cerelle (Holcomb), and Celeste (Perry). Born to Owen and Augusta Freeman was one daughter, Marie (Fisher). Curtis and Dora Poole had three sons, Freeman, Joe and Jerry Poole. Dan and Ethel Freeman had four children, Gwenelle (Johnson), Dannie Sue (White), Stanley and Joy (Mitchell). Joe and Jody Freeman had one son, Max.

Two children were born to Miller and Geraldine "Gerry" Stovall, Bryan and Nancy (White).

George and Merle Pruitt had two children, Doug and Debbie (Thomas). Several of R. M. and Maude Freeman's children, grandchildren and great-grandchildren have lived on the original Freeman land near Martin.

Their son, Elmer, and his family lived on a part of the land located on Highway 17. Joe and Jody Freeman also lived on property located on Highway 17. At the present time, George and Merle Pruitt's children, Debbie and husband Harold Thomas, and Doug and wife Lisa, live on part of the original farm land.

After the deaths of R. M. and Maude Freeman, the remaining eighty acres of land located on Freeman Road was owned by Dan and Ethel Freeman. Following their deaths, the land was divided equally between their four children.

At the present time, Dan and Ethel's daughter, Joy and husband David Mitchell, live at the home place in the house built by R. M. Freeman in the early 1930's. This house was built to replace the original house that was destroyed by fire. Another daughter and husband, Howard and Dannie Sue White, also live on the property. Dan and Ethel's son, Stanley and wife Martha Dowis Freeman, live on the Freeman land. Stanley and Martha's son Daryl and wife Judy, live on the family property located on Freeman Road. Stanley and Martha's son Chad and wife Crystal and their sons recently moved away. Chad's sons are the seventh generation known to have lived on the family property.

Over the years, members of the Freeman family have been active in Martin Baptist Church. Several of the R. M. Freeman family have served as deacons. The history of Martin Baptist Church states that among the first deacons were R. M. Freeman and Elmer Freeman. R. M. Freeman also served as a Justice of the Peace and served as the first mayor of the Town of Martin.

Gwenelle, Dannie Sue

Merle Freeman Pruitt

Martin Basketball Dan Freeman, Coach & Teacher Mr. Fisher

Joe, Jody, Max Freeman

Freeman Family: Back – Maude, Elmer, Owen, R. M. (Matt) Front – Dan, Dora & Joe

L to R: R. M. (Matt), Elmer,. Dora, Maude

Max & Barbara Freeman

Freemans: Front LtoR
Celeste, Gwenelle,
Holding Joy, Marie, Cerelle.
Back – Joe, Max & Jerry

Joe & Dan Freeman

THE GOODWINS IN MARTIN AS REMEMBERED
BY GRADY GOODWIN

My dad, John Goodwin, was born and raised in Gillsville, Georgia. After graduating from high school, he went to work for Southern Railway as a depot agent. When World War" came along, he was drafted into the Army. Because he had worked for the railroad, he was assigned to a railroad outfit that was formed and trained at Fort Snelling in St. Paul, Minnesota. It was there that he met Jean. They dated until his outfit was shipped to England in 1944 and then to Normandy, France. His outfit moved trains all over Europe until he was finally shipped home in February 1946. He went back to Gillsville, picked up his mother Lucy and sister Nita and went to Minnesota and married Jean. He had return rights to Southern Railway, but the position available was in Martin, Georgia. He and Jean moved to Martin in March of 1946.

They rented a room from the Mitchells for a time, then moved to a room with Pope and Donna Yow. They next moved to an apartment over the garage of Hub and Gladys Brown where they stayed until the summer of 1955. I am not sure about when they moved to the garage apartment. I think it was sometime around 1948-1950. I was born in 1948 and my sister Jill was born in 1951. I have many fond memories of the apartment and Gran Hub and Gran Gladys. Gran Hub enjoyed getting me all greasy while he was working on his cars much to the chagrin of my mother. My Grandmother Lucy Goodwin lived with us part of the time.

Sometime between 1948 and 1952, Daddy left Southern Railway and became a partner with Dan Matthews in Matthews and Goodwin, the general store in Martin. You could get almost anything there.

During the summer of 1955, John and Jean bought a lot from Miller Stovall on Mitchell Street. Daddy's cousin, Grady Bell (who was like his brother) and wife Wilma bought land next door. Together they built houses that were our homes until they moved to the Lake many years later. These houses stayed in their possession until their deaths.

Sometime after 1955, Dad bought the land across the street and built a house for his mother, my Grandma Lucy, where she lived until her death in 1979. She was a member of Martin Baptist Church and is buried in its cemetery. She was also an active member of the Martin Women's Club.

In 1957 Dan Matthews sold his part of the store and bought a funeral home. Sometime after that Bruce Thomas joined John, and the store became Goodwin and Thomas. Sometime in the 1980's, Daddy retired and sold out to Bruce.

Mom and Dad were very active in the town of Martin. We attended Martin Baptist Church until 1963, when we joined the Presbyterian Church in Toccoa. Later in life, Daddy and Mom would attend morning services at the Presbyterian Church and evening services at Martin Baptist Church. Both are buried in the Martin Baptist Church Cemetery.

Daddy was active in the Lions Club and Mom was in the Women's Club. Dad served on the City Council, county school board, and other functions. He was an assistant scoutmaster with the Martin troop until it was disbanded. They were both active members of the Avalon Grammar School PTA. When I was in eighth grade, Mom went to work for the Department of Family and Children's Services from which she would retire.

After their retirement, my parents moved to their cabin on Lake Hartwell. They rented the house in Martin until Jill and her husband moved into it in 1987. They lived there until Ronald's death in 2010. She now resides at the Wilkerson Center in Toccoa.

I attended Avalon Grammar School and graduated from Stephens County High in 1966. I went to Georgia Tech for a couple of years. 1969 was an eventful year for me. I went to work for Southern Bell in Atlanta. I met my wife Judy at Myrtle Beach and joined the Army. Judy and I were married in 1970 before I was sent to Southeast Asia. After this attitude adjustment I returned to Southern Bell in Atlanta and eventually graduated from Georgia Tech. I worked for the phone company for 43 years and Judy was an elementary teacher. Ma Bell moved me from Atlanta to Rome to Valdosta back to Rome and finally to Cumming. Our two sons Scott and Johnny were born in Atlanta. They are now married and each have two kids. Judy and I are now retired and live in Cumming, Georgia. Jill also attended Avalon Grammar School and graduated from Stephens County High.

Jill's son Ronnie Ivester was born in 1982. He graduated from Stephens County High and worked for Caterpillar before he joined the Army. He has served four tours in Iraq and Afghanistan and is still serving at Fort Stewart, Georgia. While serving in Germany, he met and married. They have a daughter Cattie.

HAYES FAMILY HISTORY

 George W. Hayes was a merchant in Martin. He was a clerk of Court in Stephens County for 8 years and served as Ordinary for the County for 4 years. George and his wife Lula had 4 children: Mary Frances (Miss Cleo), Lena L., Ollie, William and Moses. "Miss" Cleo and Ollie were Martin residents. Fred Lee Hayes Jr., is a descendent of George W. Hayes.

"MISS" CLEO
MARY FRANCES (CLEO) HAYES MITCHELL

Mrs. Cleo Mitchell is one of the most well-known, unforgettable, dear persons who ever lived in the little town of Martin. She was known and loved by everyone from Martin to Toccoa.

She was an employee of the Bank of Toccoa from Sept. 12, 1928 until her last retirement in Sept. 1985 after a total of 57 years of employment.

She retired first at the age of 65 and the bank gave her a big retirement party and a television as a retirement gift. The following Monday morning she was back at the bank and continued to work until the age of 92. She drove herself in her own car up and down highway 17 from Martin to Toccoa each day, and from observing her automobile, she obviously bumped a few along the way.

Mrs. Cleo was lovingly called "Miss Cleo" as she was known before her marriage to Bob Mitchell, the love of her life, at the age of 43. Mr. Mitchell passed away in 1959, so "Miss Cleo" spent much of her life as a single, very independent lady. She had no children of her own, but loved every child she saw.

She taught Junior boys in Sunday School for many years, and always gave each one a silver dollar for Christmas. She always called them her boys, and they never wanted to leave her class! She seldom missed church and attended regularly until just prior to her death, walking with the use of a walker.

In addition to her own automobile parking spot at church, she also had her own church pew. If anyone parked in either of her spaces, she would very politely tell them so.

Mrs. Cleo Mitchell was definitely "one of a kind" and was a legend many years before she passed away.

Mary Frances (Cleo) Hayes Mitchell

THE HILLIARD FAMILY

On November 4, 1950, Cynthia Williams, daughter of Flora Yow Williams and Copland Reah Williams, married John Warren Hilliard, son of Asa Farris and Flora Bowers Hilliard of Bowersville, Georgia.

Our children, Carol Ann, was born October 7, 1959 and Rebecca was born September 15, 1964 in Marietta, Georgia, where John was a design engineer for Lockheed Aircraft. Though we moved to West Palm Beach, Florida, during their childhood, we spent summers at Grandmother, Flora Yow Williams' house in Martin. Carol Ann married Mark

LaRosa and lives in New Smyrna Beach, Florida. Rebecca graduated from Florida State University. She married Charles Curry Isiminger, Sr. They live in North Palm Beach, Florida, where Charles has a costal engineering business.

Cynthia Williams Hilliard

Virginia Perry Howard Born April 26, 1934, Died February 6, 1986

The Hulsey Family

This is a short story of the Joseph Benjamin Hulsey and Bonnie White Hulsey family, who lived on a farm in the Martin community, neighbors of Mr. & Mrs. Henry Cheek, Mr. & Mrs. Albert Carter, Mr. & Mrs. Curt Pitts, and others.

By the end of 1948 there were seven young Hulsey children, with Billy the eldest being 13 years old. In the mid to late 1940's the family was living on a rental farm outside Lavonia, in the Pleasant Hill Community. Mr. Hulsey was employed full time at LeTourneau Company in Toccoa, but farming was necessary to help support the family and he wanted a farm all his own.

The children helped out on the farm, too, learning at an early age to take care of the animals, to produce cotton, and other crops to supplement the income. Mrs. Hulsey took care of the children, the home and assisted in the fields. She preserved the food grown on the farm, sewed clothes for the girls, and made quilts to keep them all warm in the winter.

In 1950, the family moved to the Clarks Creek Community outside Martin. At first they rented the 60+ acre farm known as the "Bailey Place", but soon became the proud owners. It was here the last of the eight children, Marlene, was born. This farm became known as the "Hulsey Home Place", located on what was to later be named, Hulsey Road. The family continued to raise strawberries, cotton and corn to sell; and, animals and vegetables to feed the family.

Bonnie and Joe had married in 1934 and during this decade they had given birth to three of their children; Billy, Sarah Jane and Max. During the forties, along came Betty Jo, Kenneth, Mary and Martha. And, in the fifties Marlene was born. With five daughters and three sons there was always something funny and mischievous happening on the farm. It was a loving, caring, and hardworking family.

Tragedy would strike the family in March of 1961, when Mr. Hulsey, at age 44, passed away after a four-month illness with heart problems. Mrs. Hulsey and the 6 children remaining at home continued to run the farm and make a living for the family. It was a hard, tough road but Mrs. Hulsey was a hardworking woman.

It was later that year, in 1961, the first time I pulled up a chair to the large kitchen table in the big old farmhouse, to have lunch with the Hulsey Family. But after all these years, I can remember it as if it were yesterday. Mrs. Hulsey cooked several bowls of home grown vegetables, big plates of buttermilk biscuits, a bowl of gravy, and the largest platter of fried chicken I had ever seen.

The big platter of chicken started around the table on the opposite side from where I sat. Now, of course my favorite piece of chicken was the pulley bone and I just knew there would be nothing much left on the plate by the time it got passed to my side of the table, much less have my favorite piece of chicken left on it. However, to my amazement there lay the pulley bone when the plate reached me.

I remember thinking to myself, these people are crazy - leaving the best piece of chicken on the plate and eating those wings and thighs. So, of course I took the pulley bone and ate it - most wonderful tasting pulley bone I ever had. Well, after dinner I could not hold back any longer so I said something about their family not liking the pulley bone. Little Marlene was quick to jump in and announced that Kenneth had threatened all of them with their life, if anyone of them took the pulley bone off that plate. Well, after something as sweet as that - how could I not marry him? So, in 1963 Kenneth and I married and this year 2014 we're celebrating our 51st Wedding Anniversary - and, I still think the pulley bone is the best piece of the chicken!

 As the children married, some moved away and others chose to build homes on the Hulsey Home Place. Billy, Kenneth and Martha chose to build houses on the Hulsey farm in the late 60's and early 70's, but only Billy remained there through the years, until his death in 1994. After Mrs. Hulsey passed away in 1985, the children sold the farm to Billy and Clara Andrews Hulsey, where they raised a family: Billy Jr., Gary and Patty.

Their family continues to own the farm in 2014. Gary lives in the spot where the old farm house was tom down; Patty and Billy Jr. own the land across the street and Clara continued to live there until her death.

The Hulsey family has grown over the years, till now it numbers around 100. Gone are Billy, Sarah Jane and Max. But, when the rest of us gather round and talk of the "good old days" the children reminisce of the days when they played outside so as not to mess up Mama's house. They played hopscotch, built playhouses, climbed trees, rode horses, and went swimming in the fish pond or
water hole.

Patty Hulsey Haley tells a story, as told by her Daddy Billy, about how they would go swimming in the water hole - which had snakes. Billy and Kenneth would make Max dive into the water hole so the snakes would pop their heads out at the top - where, Billy and Kenneth would smack them with a stick or board.

Marlene Hulsey Bryant says the thing she remembers most about the farm is how they had strawberries, strawberries and more strawberries and how the children would have strawberry fights while picking to sell, but only when their Daddy was not looking.

I remember: Old John, the mule used for plowing, who was still alive when I moved to the Hulsey Home Place in 1963; and, I remember thinking the woods were on fire early one morning when it turned out only to be a moonshine still on another farm up the road; and,

I remember the dog "Funny Face" that Mr. Henry Cheek gave to Kenneth one year; and, I remember feeding cows for our neighbors Mr. & Mrs. Inman Brown during the winter months because they were old, sick and had no children of their own to help out; and, I remember the wonderful Sunday afternoons when the Hulsey children and their spouses would come home, eat lunch together, sit under the shade trees and talk after church and the little cousins would play with each other and family was family - looking out for each other - and loving one another.

Joseph Johnson Family History

Joseph Johnson was born May 8, 1915 and recently celebrated his 100-year anniversary. He married Agnes Arthur. Agnes is buried in Hurricane Grove Baptist Church in Martin. Mr. Johnson's occupation was farming. The Johnson children are Joe, Jr., Roger. Mrs. Webb, Rosetta, Ablene and Janice Whitworth.

Jack Johnson Family History

Jack Johnson married Madge Johnson. Both are buried at Greater Hope Church in Martin. Their children are Josephine, Joe, Mike, Hilda Davis, (deceased 1996), Douglas and O'Lucious. Mr. Johnson was a builder and dry wall hanger.

Samuel Johnson Family History

Samuel Homer and Eliza Elizabeth Jordan Johnson built their first home in the Avalon area in the early 1830's. When their children had all left home, they decided to build a smaller home just down the road. They started on this home in the early 1950's. Mr. Johnson did not live to see the home completed. He died in 1954. The smaller home is now a brick home, owned by Mr. and Mrs. Charles Morgan.

Samuel, known as Big Daddy, and Eliza had four children, Eddie Victoria born 1904, Ruth Lavonia born 1905, Joseph James Burruss born 1910, and Mallie Fay Johnson born 1913. Joseph, "Joe", married Floy Mae Sheriff of Bowersville, GA, in 1929. They had two children, Samuel Homer, born 1930, and Mae Jo, born 1935. S. Homer, married Annie Ruth Flanigan of Toccoa in 1947. They had two children, Patricia Anne, born 1948 and Roger Dale, born 1949. Most of the family members stayed in the Stephens, Franklin County areas. Patricia, "Tricia", married Walter Michael Kay of Toccoa in 1968. After completing his tour of duty in the military, they lived in Tennessee, until after the birth of their first child, Stephanie Denise, born 1973.

Before she was a year old, they moved home to Stephens County and built a home in Martin. Their second child, Heather Michelle, was born 1978.

Stephanie married Charles L. Shiflet of Toccoa, and they have two children, Carter and Brayden. Heather married R. Brent Brown of Toccoa, and they have two children, Anna Kay and Mallory. Mike and Tricia continue to live in their home in Martin. Week days find them at their business, Industrial Supply Center in Toccoa, and their weekends are devoted to their children and grandchildren and a little bit of golf.

MACK KAY FAMILY HISTORY

Mack Kay was known by everyone for miles around. He broke horses, shoed horses and could make a horse lay down in order for him to climb on him. His son Joe Kay, was also a real horseman. He was always a part of various parades in this area. Mack and his wife, Tommie were well known and loved by many, many people in the Martin area. Both are deceased.

Mack Kay

Mack Kay

Grandparents Wilson

Willie Joe Kay

Tommie Kay

Kay Sisters

KETCHERSIDE FAMILY HISTORY

James Douglas Ketcherside, MD was one of 10 children born to John P Ketcherside and wife Nancy. He was born July 26 1823 in Sparta TN; died Feb 3 1895 in Martin and is buried in the Martin Community Cemetery. In 1876 he married second wife Maude Annie Brown, born Feb 9 1847 and who died in Martin March 6 1928 and is buried in the Martin Community Cemetery.

He was a descendant of Thomas Ketcherside who emigrated from Edinburgh, Scotland to the USA before 1757. The clansmen of the highlands were ardent supporters of Charles Stuart, whom they called "Bonnie Prince Charlie". In 1745 the clansmen overwhelmed English troops in Scotland and marched into England where they were forced to retreat. In a battle on Culloden Moor in 1746, Prince Charles was defeated and fled to France. The English executed several clan leaders. This spat of violence by the English may have precipitated the coming of our ancestors to the US. We have been unable to determine the exact date of their arrival or the ship on which they crossed the Atlantic Ocean and its port of entry.

Dr. Ketchersid was a prominent practitioner of medicine and was an efficient surgeon in the Federal Army during the Civil War. For about 28 years he practiced medicine in Ducktown, TN, married to Ellen Cline (1829 – 1877) with whom he had three children; James Napoleon MD (1850-1934), Josephine (1858-1925), and John Milton (1860-1946). Dr. James Napoleon Ketchersid settled in Kansas.

Dr. Ketchersid came to Martin in 1876 and for about 26 years had an intensive practice up to the time of his death and where he mentored many young physicians. James Douglas is credited with dropping the "e" from the family name because he thought it sounded too flat. He is credited with building the first house in Martin in 1882.

James Douglas and Maude Annie had four children. John Wesley MD (1878-19??) a graduate of Vanderbilt University Medical School in 1898. John Wesley married Hattie Morgan, daughter of W. M. Morgan and Almina (Thomas) Morgan. They had 6 children. He was a graduate of Vanderbilt University 4.1.1898. His first practice was at his homestead in Martin where he remained for six years. Moving to the west he first located at McAlester in Indian Territory, where he remained for three years and from there to Dallas, Texas, in 1906, and a year later went to El Paso, Texas; Thomas Lyon DDS (1880-1977) graduated Atlanta Dental College in 1907, married Tommie Cochran.

He practiced in Martin, then around 1920 in Eatonton, GA before moving to Sarasota FL in 1925. Dr. Tom and Tommie had two daughters (Agnes (Dr Alston Brown); and Louise (Warren Lawrence); Maude (1882-1950) married Tom Freeman and settled in Los Angeles CA.

Youngest child Blanche (May 19 1884 – Dec 21 1985) married Dr James Harrison Crawford (1873-1923) and raised 4 children in Martin while Dr. Crawford practiced medicine for the Town of Martin.   (See Crawford Family)

Dr. John Douglas liked to tell the story of an old lady in Martin who stayed in bed all the time. She was not sick, as Dr. JD examined her and found nothing wrong. The husband was told to get a shotgun and shoot under the bed.

He did, and she jumped several feet high out of the bed, and that was the last of her sickness.

KNOX FAMILY HISTORY

The ancestors of Will Knox lived on a farm containing approximately 1000 acres in the Clarks Creek area. Mr. Knox was born on the Knox farm, grew up and married Eula Martin in 1920. They farmed for a living and reared four children: Mary Ellen White, Thomas, George and William Lewis Knox. All three sons served in the U.S. Military; Son, George, served in WW II, Vietnam & Korean war. He retired from the U. S. Army in 1973. Son, Thomas, served in the Army, and son, William Lewis, served in the Navy.

When they were no longer able to farm the land, Mr. & Mrs. Knox sold the large family farm and moved to Martin. Son, George, continued to own a farm which is located on highway 17 south of Martin.

LAND FAMILY HISTORY

Robert Cooper Land, b. 1-15-1881, married Lillian Sadie Patterson, b.6-4-1884. On May 2, 1909, their only son, Lester Doyle was born, and they lost one daughter at birth. Robert Land was also known as R. C. and "Mr. Robbie". The Lands came from South Carolina, maybe Fairplay. Mr. Robbie had a brother, Farmer Land, who lived to be over 100 years old. They farmed for a living.

Doyle met Miss Thelma Kathryn Brown from Elberton. After meeting they used the railway to "visit". They were married in 1933, and Doyle moved his bride to Martin. They had a family of three children: Jimmy Ronald "Ronnie" b. 1934; Roger Delane, b. 1939 and Robbie Jean, b. 1840. Doyle farmed and worked at WABCO, Toccoa, until he retired. Thelma was a housewife except for a period of time after farming failed, when they moved to Marietta, and she worked on B-52 airplanes. The Lands were all members of Martin Baptist Church where Mr. Robbie and Doyle both served as deacons. Doyle was also a member of Martin Lions Club. Thelma was very active in all areas of church teaching and is lovingly remembered by the many former students she taught in Sunday school and Bible School.

PHILLIP MITCHELL LANDRUM, SR.
FAMILY HISTORY

Phillip Mitchell Landrum was born September 10, 1907, in Martin, Stephens County, Georgia, the oldest son of Phillip Davis Landrum and Blanche Mitchell Landrum. He married the former Laura Brown of Dewy Rose in Elbert County where they taught school for three years. He attended Mercer University and earned a B.A. degree from Piedmont College. Laura earned a B. S. degree from the University of Georgia in 1932. They moved to Nelson to teach and while he was Superintendent of Schools in Nelson, he attended night classes at Atlanta Law School, receiving an LL.B. degree and admission to the Georgia Bar in 1941.

During the Second World War, from 1942 to 1945, he saw active duty as a member of the Ninth Air Force in the European theater of operations. In 1946, just out of the service, Landrum was named Assistant Attorney General of Georgia. Beginning in 1947, he served as executive secretary to Governor M. E. Thompson for two years, then settled down in Jasper and returned to an active law practice until his election to Congress in 1952.

Landrum represented the Ninth Congressional District for 24 years, from January 3, 1953 to January 3, 1977. Only four Georgians served in Congress longer: Carl Vinson (1914- 1965), Edward Cox (1925-1952), Paul Brown (1934-1961), and Alexander Stephens (1843-1882).

During his 24 years in Congress he Wrote and sponsored several major legislative accomplishments: Landrum-Griffin Act of 1959 (Labor Management Reporting and Disclosure Act) amending the Taft-Hartley Act; the 1963 Vocational Educational bill; the 1956 Library Services Act; the 1964 Economic Opportunity Act (which provided funds for Georgia's Appalachian Highway from metro Atlanta to Blairsville); legislation assisting development of Lake Lanier Islands, Unicoi State Park and Brasstown Bald.

An arts and crafts center at Brasstown Bald is named the Phil and Laura Landrum Mountain Interpretive Center. While in Congress he served on the House Education and Labor Committee (1952-1965) and the House Ways and Means Committee (1965-1977). Also while in Congress he was the first Southerner to oppose the Viet-Nam War helping to pass the House Resolution opposing President Nixon's decision to bomb Cambodia. He was Dean of the Georgia Congressional Delegation from 1971 - 1977.

Phillip Mitchell Landrum, Sr. died November 19, 1990 in Jasper, Georgia. His wife Laura died October 22, 2001. They had two children, Phillip Mitchell Landrum, Jr. and Susan Landrum

Phillip Mitchell Landrum, Jr., was born July 23, 1937 in Atlanta, Georgia. He graduated from The Citadel in 1959 and from Emory University School of Law in 1964. Phil, Jr. married the former Elaine Sayers of Columbus, Georgia in 1962. .Elaine is a graduate of Agnes Scott College, received her Master's Degree from the University of Georgia in 1992, and is currently the Adult Literacy Director at Pickens Technical Institute in Jasper. Phil, Jr. and Elaine have two children: Phillip Mitchell Landrum, III and Laura Elaine. Landrum.

Phil III is a 1989 graduate, cum laude, of The Citadel and received his J. D. degree from The University of Georgia School of Law in 1991. Laura received her B.S. degree, cum laude, from Kennesaw College in 1994 and worked at REI in Eugene, Oregon before returning to Jasper, Georgia.

Susan Landrum was born October 6, 1944 in Atlanta, Georgia. She is a 1966 graduate of Agnes Scott College, received her M.A. degree from Emory University in 1968; taught at Gainesville College from 1968-1973; received her J. D. degree, cum laude, in 1975 from The University of Georgia School of Law. Susan had a long illness with cancer and died February 10, 2001.

Phil M. Landrum, Sr., Phil M. Landrum, Jr., Susan Landrum, and Phil M. Landrum, III practiced law in Jasper, Georgia under the firm name of Landrum & Landrum.

THE NINTH SALUTES

II PHIL M. LANDRUM

Our Man For All Seasons

THE FAMILY OF REP. LANDRUM

REP. LANDRUM, MRS. LANDRUM, THEIR DAUGHTER SUSAN, THEIR SON AND HIS WIFE, PHIL JR. AND ELAINE

A MESSAGE TO THE PEOPLE OF THE NINTH DISTRICT

PHIL M. LANDRUM

FRED LOONEY FAMILY HISTORY

Looney is an Irish name. James C. Looney moved to San Francisco, CA. in 1851 from Ireland. A relative (J.M. Looney) donated $1,000 to help build the first brick school in Franklin County (now Stephens) in 1902. Fred Edward Looney, Sr., Born June 28, 1899 and died February 16, 1987, was a son of Mead and Nancy Looney. He married Beulah Medlin, born December 24, 1903 and died May 18, 1992. They married on March 4, 1922. She was the daughter of Foster and Nancy Etta Medlin. Fred Edward Looney, Sr. was a farmer and carpenter. Beulah Looney never worked at public work, as she was a housewife. They were share croppers on the Perkins Place before they moved to Avalon Road about 1940.

Fred and Beulah had 8 children and raised these children in a small 5 room house, with no indoor restroom or running water. They had an outhouse and a well. They did not have a TV or electricity. Washing clothes was done by hand. They had no air conditioning. Doctor visits were limited, so they used home remedies. They slept on wheat stuffed beds that were called wheat straw sticks. This family got their first car in 1950. It was a '28 Model A Ford, with a rumble seat.

Normally, they only had 2 meals a day and ate leftovers for a third meal. Their farm was 60 acres. They had a cow for milk, butter and buttermilk. There were two mules on the farm. The yard was full of chickens that were used for eggs and meat. They grew and canned their own food. Some of the things they grew on their farm were corn, wheat, cotton, vegetables, peanuts, and potatoes. Popcorn was made over an open fire. Their family killed two hogs each year for meat. Beulah played a pump organ which is in Fred, Jr.'s home today. The children went to school at Avalon. They carried their lunch or walked home for lunch and then back to school. They lived one mile from the school house.

Front: Beulah, Betty, Lorene, Madge, Ralph
Back: Harold, Fred, Jr., Swain

The 8 children were as follows: Madge, who married Lynn Morgan. They had no children. Swain married Jean Crunkleton. They had 3 children – Freddie, Thomas and Roger, who had no children. Lorene married Archie Devlin (Scottish). They had 2 girls; Sheila (Dickerson) and Nancy (Tisdale). Ralph never married. Herbert, married Betty Jo Garland.

They had 2 boys, Tony and Richard. Betty (Hornick) had 2 children, LaDonna (Graham) and David. Harold married Catherine Outz. They had 2 girls - Tammay (Gearhart) and Connie (Moore).Fred Edward Looney, Jr., married Annie Mae Addison. They had 2 children, Chris Howard and Susan (Watkins).

The only sibling living in 2014 is Fred Edward Looney, Jr. Three of the boys served in the military. Swain was in the Air Force. Herbert was in the Army and Ralph retired from the Navy.

Swain Looney Family History

Swain Looney was one of eight children born to Fred Looney Sr. and Beulah Medlin. The other children were Harold, Herbert, Ralph, Betty, Lorene, Madge and Fred Jr. All the children are now deceased except Fred. Jr. who continues to live in the Martin area.

Swain Looney married Jean Crumpton and moved from Madison, South Carolina to Martin, Ga. in 1964. He was employed at Coats & Clark for thirty seven years, Patterson Pump for two years and retired from Vermont American. He passed away in 2011. He & Mrs. Looney had a family of three boys - Freddie, Thomas and Roger who all continue to reside in Martin. Freddie continues to live in the house with Mrs. Looney in Martin. Roger and wife, Judy, also live in Martin, and he works at Coats American.

Thomas lives about a block away from the others, on highway 17 in Martin. He does construction work, backhoe service, owns heavy duty equipment and has been very helpful to Martin Baptist Church in the past with water, septic tank and plumbing issues. He has three children - Adam, Christie and Holly; Adam works at Bosal and lives in Lavonia; Christie is married to Scott Lester and works at the Courthouse in Jackson County; Holly works in the bakery at Ingles in Toccoa. She has two children, Mason and Grace.

Thomas served as Mayor of Martin from 1977 until 1989. Thomas enjoys talking about the big rock in his Mother's yard. It has been a curiosity for years among the Martin locals. It is huge, about the size of a car, has strange markings on it, and according to "historians" was used by Indians in making medicines. Geologists have visited many times in an effort to learn more about the mysterious rock. He says that whatever it is, the Looney boys and most of the children in Martin spent lots of fun days, climbing and playing on the big rock. Thomas Looney attends Martin Baptist Church.

K. E. MATHEWS FAMILY HISTORY

Mr. Kay E. Mathews moved from Anderson, SC to the Martin area shortly after the Civil War. He was the son of John H. Mathews and Wildy Barnett Mathews. Kay E. Mathews was born July 24, 1846 and died June 10, 1933 in Franklin County, GA. He was married to Amelia Nnn Smith.Their children were Mary C, John Griffin, Benjamin F, Edward Lee, William P., Mineava J. Martha E. Lula A, George M., Thomas Monroe, Wilda O, Joseph B, and Minnie. Edward Lee, born May 3, 1873 and died October 2, 1938. He married Ethel Iceleen Smith. Edward Lee and his family settled in Martin, GA in the early 1900's. He was a farmer, school trustee, church deacon and member of Tom's Creek Baptist Church. Their 2nd child was Dan Allen Mathews, born January 16, 1913. Dan married Ruth Spearman. Their children were, Martha Jo & Barbara Ann. Dan resided in Martin before moving to Toccoa. He was the owner of a furniture store in Martin & later owned a funeral home in Toccoa.

Martha Jo (Hunt) and her husband Bill live in the old home place and have 4 children.

MCCALL FAMILY HISTORY

John McCall (July 19 1840 – May 19 1930) was the second son of Francis McCall (Jan 4 1804-Oct 28 1895) and Nancy McNeil McCall (June 03, 1815 - February 20, 1897). Francis and Nancy married in May 19, 1831. The McCall family came to USA from Antrim County, IRELAND and located in Mecklenburg County, NC migrating to SC before settling in Franklin County GA.

John's Military Service: 52nd Regiment, Co. K. Private March 4, 1862; appointed 3rd Corporal Dec. 1862. Captured at Baker's Creek, Miss. May 16, 1863. Paroled at Fort Delaware, De. July 3, 1863. Roll for Dec. 31, 1863, last on file, shows him present. Pension records show he was at home on furlough close of war.

In 1880, John was 39 living in Franklin Co with wife Mary A. DEAN (Jan 5 1843 – Dec 3 1881) in Franklin Co GA. He was a farmer and there were six children in the home: George F, 13, John Thomas, 7, William F, 6, Lucy, 4, James B, 3, and Henry, 1. Twenty years later John, age 59 is married to Celia R., 45. He owns his own farm. There are five children at home. Two are from the first marriage, Maggie, 21, and John Thomas, 27; three are from the second marriage, Curtis, 11, Douglas, 8, and Doomas, 4. By 1910 according to the Franklin Co census, John is 69, owns his own farm near Toccoa and Elberton Rd. He has been married to Celia, 55, for 24 years, with this being the second marriage for both. She is the mother of 7 children, 5 of whom are living. Of the 5 children living at home, 2 are from John's first marriage: John Thomas, 37, and Maggie, 27.

Curtis S, 19, Douglas, 16, and Doomas C, 14, are from the second marriage. In 1920, John is 79, owns his own farm mortgage free and is married to Celia, 66. Living at home is John Thomas (JT), 48, a cotton ginner, Maggie, 38, Douglas, 26, Doomas, 24, Racine, 18, and Astor, 8. Racine and Astor are John's grandsons.

From the Lavonia Times and Gauge, dated July 29, 1927: Quite a large crowd of relatives and friends enjoyed the birthday dinner Sunday at the home of Mr. John McCall. The dinner was given to celebrate Mr. McCall's 87th birthday. John McCall made the newspaper again March 16, 1928 with the headline: FIRE BURNS McCALL HOME NEAR MARTIN. During the electrical storm on Wednesday morning of this week, the home of Mr. John McCall near Martin caught fire and was burned to the ground. It is presumed that lightning caused the home to catch and that it had gained considerable headway before being discovered. The home was a large and comfortable one located near Martin. John McCall, died at age 90 (May 19 1930) at his home at Martin. Death came suddenly. He was up and as active as usual till the very day of his death. The remains were interred at Clarkes Creek Baptist Church. Surviving was: George, Thomas. Curtis, and Doomas McCall of Martin; W.P. McCall of New Mexico and Mrs. T. S. Segars of Martin and a number of grandchildren and great grandchildren. John McCall lived practically all his life in the neighborhood where he died. He was one of the fifteen remaining Confederate Veterans in the county at the time of his death. He was honored by the many who had known him.

A large concourse of relatives and friends gathered at the church for the funeral, attesting to the popularity of Mr. John McCall, and many were the beautiful floral offerings.

Mr. McCall was a good man and helpful citizen of his community and his many friends feel a great loss in his death. Dr. W. H. Swaim signed the Death Certificate and the undertakers were Clodfelter and Stovall of Martin, GA.

Samuel Curtis McCall (1889 - 1961) married Addie Gable (12.24.1892 - 2.2.1966). Both are buried in Martin Community Cemetery. There were three surviving sons from the marriage. Lawrence Deweese who late changed his name to Pete (May 23 1916 – Aug 21 1963), John Melvin (1920 – May 25.1990), and Daniel Thomas (Nov 17 1922 – March 11 1974).

Pete married Vivian Crawford (Dec 4 1917 – Living) and had three children (James Michael (1942), Andrea Gail (1944), and Dawn Lucinda (1954). Pete was in the Army/Air Corps during WWII as a gunner. His plane was shot down, they were captured by the Germans and placed in Stalag 17 until the end of the war. (See Crawford Family)

John Melvin married Sara Jordan (1926-1993) and after the WWII, settled in Royston where he had a jewelry store (McCall's Jewelry). John and Sara had one child Tamara Lee (1961-2013). John was in General Patton's Army and was in the group that liberated Stalag 17 and his brother Pete.

Daniel Thomas married Mary Faith Sanders (Jun 26 1925 – Apr 22 2008). Both are buried in the Martin Baptist Cemetery. Dan and Mary's children are Larry Thomas (1942) and Samuel Jerry (Aug 28 1946 – Nov 2 2014) who was killed in an automobile accident.

MEDLIN FAMILY HISTORY

Joe R Medlin, son of Will and Ida Medlin married Dollie Watkins. While serving in the Military during and after World War II, he contracted tuberculosis, and returned home to Martin. He was unable to work for some time. He had served a total of eleven years in the Navy. After his health improved, Mr. Medlin owned and operated a small engine repair shop in Martin for years. Mr. & Mrs. Medlin had three children: Raymond, who, like his father, also served in the Military. He served in the Air Force. He now lives in Lexington, Massachusetts and has three children, Thomas, Wayne, and Brenda and is blessed with eight grandchildren.

The other Medlin son is David, who also served in the military, in the Navy. He retired from the Martin Post Office as a rural mail carrier, and lives in Toccoa. He has one son, Chad who has a daughter.

The third child is Opal Griffin, who lives in Toccoa and is married to Fred Griffin, who is an electrical contractor. They have one daughter, Allison. Both Allison and her husband, Jacob Addison, are employed at Clemson University. She is an event coordinator, and he works with the athletic facilities. Both Mr. and Mrs. Joe Medlin are now deceased.

MELTON – ELROD FAMILY HISTORY

John H. Melton

Corrie Newton Melton

John Hampton Melton married Corrie Newton and in Liberty, SC raised their six children, May, Irene, Ruth, Roy William, born 1915 and died 2000, Clarence and Amanda.

Sylvanus Smith married Bertie Lee Owens and had three children: Marie, Ansel and Edna, born 1919, died 2006.

Rev. Roy & Edna Smith Melton

Roy William Melton married Edna Smith and their children are: Ramah Ellen, who lived only a few weeks, Wayne, Anne, Loyd William, born 1941, and Allen. Roy had had to leave school to work during the depression so he went back to high school after the children were born, and went on to college, all the while pastoring a small church near Greenville to support his family. They moved to the Line Community where he was principal of Line Elementary and was pastor at Pleasant Hill Baptist Church, He knew his bible and was known to quote the book of Revelation, Hebrews and Romans. He was pastor of Martin Baptist Church from 1961-1963. Edna was the life of the party, participating in all the women's activities at the church.

One time a pulpit committee came and said they would like to have Preacher Melton as their next pastor primarily because of Edna!

Loyd Melton, born 1941, married Linda Joyce Elrod, born 1944. Loyd graduated from Southern Technical Institute in Marietta and his 34 year working career was

spent with the GA DOT as a civil engineer. Linda attended Anderson College and graduated from Anderson Memorial Hospital School of Medical Technology. She worked as a medical technologist until her retirement in 2005. They have two children, Ryan William, b. 1968 and Deana Lynn, born 1971.

Loyd & Linda Elrod Melton

Ryan graduated from Piedmont College and was nominated by the college to *Who's Who Among American Colleges and Universities in* 1991. He was also Alpha Chi. He is married to Melissa Abernathy and is employed in Madison County as Family Connection coordinator and also is Minister of Music at Wesley Chapel UMC. Deana graduated from UGA with honors and taught school for 21 years. She is married to Matt Mitchell and is enjoying being full time mom to Lainey and Garrison, who are very active in school and sports.

Linda and Loyd have spent their entire married life on the old Elrod home place and were active in the Martin Baptist Church as deacon, Sunday school teacher and Linda pianist for 36 years.

ELROD – MOSELEY FAMILY HISTORY

Thomas Hayden Elrod, born 1867 and died in 1941, married Leai T. Owens, born 1863 and died in 1925 and they were the parents of five children: Effie, Home, Hayden, William John Richard, born 18912 and died in 1954, and Floyd. Will, my grandfather, first married Janier Pierce and Clarence was their only child. Janier died in a house fire and Will married Sarah Maud Estelle Moseley, born in 1890 and died in 1921, who is a great, great-granddaughter of Revolutionary War soldier Samuel Moseley, who married Susannah Bledsoe in NC in 1786 and later brought his family to SC, then to Franklin County, GA to land that was granted to him for his service. Will's marriage to Maud Moseley was a short one, as she died when her son, Thomas Harold was 3 and son Ollie Chaffin was 14 months old. Will married for the third time to Katy Kay and together they had six children; Leona, who lived only two years, George, Eric,

James, Jean Elrod Outz Frost, and Helen Elrod Adams. All of the boys who were of age would later be found serving their country in the U. S. Armed Forces.

Ollie Chaffin, born 1920 and died 1989, married Blonde Dean Briley, born 1924 and died 1989 and they had three daughters, Linda Joyce Elrod Melton, Elaine Broussard and Pamela Elrod Woodson.

Ollie was a mechanic for most of his life and operated a garage with his brother Harold for years. He was an airplane mechanic in WWII in Europe and was among the many soldiers who suffered frostbite in the trenches near Bastogne, Belgium. He was postmaster at the Martin Post Office and was instrumental in obtaining government approval for the building of the new post office building. He eventually took a rural route and was a mail carrier, retiring in 1983 after serving for 27 years.

Blonde graduated from Toccoa High School in 1941 and worked at Troups, Coats and Clark for a number of years and part time at the Martin Post Office as clerk, while continuing to raise her girls. She retired in 1981 after 19 years at the Post Office. About 1977 Blonde decided that she might want to check out the trout fishing that Ollie kept doing and once she got "hooked" they were fishing and camping all the time.

Their frequent and most loved camping and fishing buddy was Ossie Bell Briley, Blonde's step-mother. They had the best time getting the camper ready and would giggle all the way to Moccasin Creek Campground.

Maude Mosely Elrod   Will and Katie Kaye Elrod

Matt and Deana Mitchell
Garrison & Lainey

DEAN-BRILEY FAMILY HISTORY

Legend has it that the first Eldrod's to arrive in the U.S. was Johan Dider Elroot, our Great-Grandfather, along with

his wife and one child. They were from either Hessen Germany or Switzerland and many people from the Palatinate region of Germany. Many of them sailed from Rotterdam for either Pennsylvania or New York. These Elrods arrived about 1710 and settled in Delaware, Pennsylvania, and Maryland and later in North and South Carolina. The first of our Elrod ancestors to be born on U. S. soil was Christopher Elrod in 1721.

Dr. Robert Pink Dean

In Germany, the Elrods were an educated and accomplished family. The earliest known of our Elrod ancestors was Jacob Elrod I, who was born in Kulmbach, Germany in the late 1500's. His son, Johann Christophorus was our ancestor. Another son, Jacob Elrod II published the Mittle Calendar in 1657. I worked out that differences between the Catholic Gregorian calendar and the Protestant Julian Calendar.

The first of the Dean family to move to the area was PA born Samuel Dean, who had been a Revolutionary War soldier and whose children with Gwendolyn James of MD prospered in NC, SC, TN and GA.

Henry Richard Dean, born 1877 and died 1944, and Lillie Qualls, born 1876 and died 1947 married and had six children.

Henry Richard Dean
& Lillie Qualls

Dean Children
L to R: Lola, Ethel, Myrtie, Maggie

My great-grandfather believed in education and their children became nurses, teachers and a dentist. The children were Paul, Ethel, Lola, Maggie, Pink, and Myrtie Lee, who was my grandmother.

Matt Briley, born 1866 died 1950, and Emma Thomas, born 1868 died 1951, were the parents of four children: Ila Briley Brown, Eulalie Briley Payne, Thomas Carl Briley and Dewey Hobson Briley, my grandfather.

Matt & Emma Thomas Briley   Blonde & Ollie Briley Elrod

Myrtie Dean, born 1899 died 1932, who was a great, great, great-granddaughter of Samuel Dean, married Dewey Hobson Briley, born 1900 died 1973 and they had three

children: Dorothy, Blonde Dean, b. 1924 d. 1989, and Max. During her short life, Myrtie was pianist at Confidence United Methodist Church, a tradition that was carried on by her three Elrod grand-daughters.

Dewey and Ossie Wilbanks Briley

MILLS FAMILY HISTORY

The Mills family has been in Stephens County since 1735 when Lafayette Mills Moved here. The Mills family and the Stowe family are related on both the maternal and paternal sides of the family. Alice Mills married Gibbs Stowe on the paternal side.

Relatives of J. Edwin Stowe married Poole relatives on the maternal side. Tyrus Mills was a long time employee of Trogdon Furniture and worked at Camp Toccoa during World War II. He was known to have one of the oldest cars in Stephens County. Lou Mills worked at Wrights Manufacturing her entire career and actually made the outfit for Paul Anderson to wear in the 1956 Olympics weightlifting event in Russia.

John Frank Mills, Tyrus's brother, served under General George S. Patton in World War II. John was a charter member of the local VFW and was instrumental in importing a herd of deer from Germany to populate the Currahee Mountain area for hunters.

Manley Mills was John and Tyrus's brother. He was a certified genius and designed planes for Lockheed. He drew the blueprints for the C-130 Hercules, the C-5 Galaxy, the C-141 and the SR-71. Rumors were that he was working on the Stealth fighter when he passed away in 1971, but it was a secret project and cannot be confirmed.

Ed Mills is the son of Lou Parker Mills and Tyrus Edward Mills of Toccoa. Ann Mills, his wife of 40 years, was formerly Charlotte Ann Copenhaver from West Virginia. Ed is a 1969 graduate of Stephens County High School, a graduate of Young Harris College, Georgia Southern College twice, and the University of Georgia.

Ann graduated from Bellville High School in Michigan and attended Eastern Michigan, DeKalb College and twice graduated from the University of Georgia. Both Ed and Ann have Specialist Degrees in Education.

Ed and Ann Mills bought their present residence, the Pink Mitchell home on Childs Street in Martin, in the summer of 1978. The home is a two story Victorian constructed in 1908. Ann was the first Stephens County Middle School Counselor in 1974 and held that position for thirty years until her retirement in 2004. Ed was a Social Studies teacher at the same Middle School, the last elected Superintendent of Stephens County Schools and retired in 2003 from the Georgia Department of Education where he served as the State Coordinator for Education Field Services. Ed and Ann have two sons, Jon and Matt. Jon works for Sony Online Entertainment and Matt has a degree in Archaeology and Anthropology from the University of Georgia.

WILEY JACKSON (JACK) MITCHELL FAMILY

Wiley, better known to his family and friends as Jack, was born on May 21, 1868, within the area of what is now known as Martin, Georgia. Martin was then officially recognized as being located in Franklin County. At the time of Jack's death in 1946, a land deed dated in the 1790's was found in his personal papers indicating that the owner of the land was from North Carolina. While that land has been in Franklin County, it would later be a part of the newly created Stephens County.

Jack was the son of Henry Mitchell, born May 1, 1832 and died December 4, 1878 and Rhoda E. Walters, born September 29, 1832 and died November 20, 1907, were farmers who owned land and a small number of slaves. Henry was buried in the family plot in the cemetery at Red Hill and Rhoda was buried in the Martin City Cemetery.

Jack's grandparents (Henry's parents) were Wiley Mitchell, for whom Jack was named, and Martha Wilkerson. Wiley was the Mitchell who came to Martin from North Carolina.

Jack was one of eight children born to Henry and Rhoda. At the time of Jack's death in 1946, all of his siblings had preceded him in death except for Mary Manola Mitchell Owens.

Jack was married to Rilla Estella Sewell on October 16, 1890. She was the daughter of John A. Sewell and Nancy L. Jackson. Rilla was born on September 10, 1868 and died on May 8, 1954. At the time of Jack's death in 1946, they had celebrated fifty-six years of marriage. Jack and Rilla are buried in the family plot in the Martin City Cemetery.

Four children born to Rilla and Jack: Millage Dorcus, August 26, 1891; Flem Goode, April 7, 1895, Isham Goss, December 23, 1902 and Kell Freeman, June 2, 1912. Isham Goss, better known to his parents as Goss, died on November 27, 1906 of meningitis, a disease of fatal consequences at that time.

Jack was reared on a farm in the vicinity of Martin and was a farmer in Martin all of his life. He owned a sawmill and from the timber on the farm he built a home for the family. The family house stood on the hill on the street that is now known as Martin Drive until the 1990's. The farm consisted of approximately one hundred acres of farmland and pasture. The farm produced cotton, corn, wheat and oats as well as fruits and vegetables. There were also animals both for work and food. Basically the farm was self-sustaining. There were two sharecroppers assisting in the farm duties.

Jack and Rilla cared for several members of their families who needed room and board. Jack's mother, Rhoda, lived with them until her death. Jack was the guardian of his nephew, Napolian, whose mother had died shortly after giving birth to her third child. Jack and Rilla also reared Flem's four children, Flem, Jr., Elizabeth, Katherine and Royce after Flem and his wife, Agnes, were separated.

During the depression years, they suffered from the decline of farm prices and the failure of the Bank of Martin where their money had been deposited. Jack was a mild and quiet, but a very stern man, who was respected by not only his family but also the members of his community. He did not talk excessively but spoke quietly and could be assertive in expressing his views and opinions. For many years he served as a deacon in the Martin Baptist Church.

In the printed notice of his death, the "Toccoa Record" said, "His interests centered in his home, church and community, and his character reflected the best and noblest qualities of Christian manhood."

He was a model to those who knew and loved him.

Rilla was the driving force in their marriage. She was an active person who helped to make the decisions concerning the needs of the family. She was much more stern and reserved than Jack, but considerate and thoughtful with regards to the needs of the family, friends and neighbors. Like Jack, she knew the value of an education and they put schooling their children and grandchildren ahead of personal needs.

Jack and Rilla even in their older years could tell you the page and word that they had completed in the "Blue Book Speller" in their own education.

Millage Dorcas Mitchell (1891 - 1969)

Jack and Rilla's oldest son, Millage graduated from Georgia Tech and returned to this area and married Kate Nettie Powers from Toccoa. Millage worked with National Biscuit Company in Atlanta for many years and retired as a master machinist. Millage and Kate had three daughters: Hilda, Celia and Peggy. Millage died in June 1969 and Kate died in July 1970. They are buried in Crestlawn Cemetery in Atlanta.

Flem Goode Mitchell (1895 - 1990)

The next son, Flem was drafted into the Army at the beginning of World War I where he obtained the rank of sergeant. He did not serve overseas. While stationed at Fort McPherson (Atlanta), he met and married Agnes May Holt. After being discharged from the Army, he returned to Atlanta to work as textile engineer for "Texas Oil Company." Early in his employment, he was transferred to Clinton, SC. Flem and Agnes had four children: Flem, Jr., Elizabeth, Katherine and Royce. These children were reared on the Mitchell Family Farm in Martin with their grandparents, Jack and Rilla Mitchell. The marriage of Flem and Agnes was dissolved by a decree of divorce in 1935. Flem married Frances Drury Salmon in 1942 in Columbia, SC. Flem died in 1990 at the age of ninety-five and Frances preceded him in death in 1989. They are buried in Columbia, SC.

Flem, Jr. attended Clemson College and was working at Georgia Power Company in Atlanta when he entered the US Navy during World War II. Flem Jr. returned to Georgia Power Company after his time in the Navy. He graduated from Georgia Tech with a degree in electrical engineering. Flem, Jr. and Dela Head from Atlanta were married in 1947. Flem, Jr. and Dela had four children: Eugenia, Flem III, Miriam and Tyra. After working for Georgia Power for over forty years, Flem, Jr. retired as Vice President of Construction. Flem, Jr. died in 2011 at the age of ninety-two and Dela died at the age of 90 in 2015. Their children and grandchildren continue to reside in the Atlanta area.

Elizabeth completed her college education at Winthrop College, SC. She was teaching in high school in South Carolina when she entered the US Navy Waves in 1944. It was there that she met George Barnes. They were married in 1945 while on duty in California. George and Elizabeth made their home in San Mateo, California. Elizabeth died in 2007 and George died in 2011. Elizabeth and George had four children: Katherine, Lee, Paula and Charles.

Katherine completed here college education at Winthrop College, SC and taught in the public schools in Georgia. She was married to David Payne Jr. at Martin Baptist Church in 1945. Katherine and David had three children. Carolyn, David III and Jackson. David died in 1988. Katherine continues to make her home in Carrollton, Georgia. Her children live in the area.

Royce entered the US Navy in 1943, serving three years, with two years of active sea duty. He graduated from the University of Georgia and from the University of Tennessee in Knoxville where he received his master's degree. After working in the transportation industry in Atlanta, he entered the priesthood of the Catholic Church, serving in the Archdiocese of New Orleans. His ministry has included parish ministry, Administrator of Notre Dame Seminary and both prison and hospital chaplaincy. Royce's home and everything he had was destroyed in Hurricane Katrina in 2004. Royce continued his ministry as chaplain in an assisted living facility in New Orleans until his death in 2015.

Kell Freeman Mitchell (1912 - 1979)

Kell, the youngest son of Jack and Rilla, did not leave home for college or military, as his siblings had done. While he did not work on the family farm, he did stay in Martin. One of his early endeavors was to own and operate a service station in Martin. This was his occupation when he married Emily Evelyn Wilbanks from Carnesville on December 26, 1933. He later owned and operated a general merchandise store serving the needs of the people of Martin and surrounding areas. Kell was mayor of the town of Martin in 1939 and 1940. In the early 1940's Kell and Emily purchased a farm in Martin and when the poultry industry started in the Martin area, they built chicken houses, a hatchery and feed processing mill. Later, they purchased additional farmland and began to raise cattle along with the poultry business.

Kell died suddenly of a massive heart attack in the morning on January 4, 1979 just a few days after their forty-fifth wedding anniversary. Emily had a heart attack that same day in the afternoon. She was in intensive care in the Stephens County Hospital for nine days. Emily continued to live in the family home for almost twenty years after Kell's death. She died on October 16, 1998. Kell and Emily are buried in the family plot in the Martin Town Cemetery.

Kell had many similar ways of his father, Jack, especially his disposition. He was interested in helping those who needed assistance and was greatly respected in the community. He was an active member of the Martin Baptist Church teaching Sunday School, serving on many committees and like his father, a long-time deacon in the church.

Kell and Emily had three children: Kell Freeman, Jr., Jackson David and Sandra Kay. Kell Jr. attended West Georgia College in Carrollton for his two-year degree. That is where he met Mary Joyce Calhoun and they were married in 1956. He then attended the University of Georgia in Athens, where he received his bachelors, masters and doctorate degrees in history. After graduation, he taught for a short period of time at Limestone College in Spartanburg, South Carolina. He then moved to Memphis State University (now University of Memphis) where he taught in the history department until his death in 2010.

Kell Jr. was seventy-four years old at the time of his death and only missed one day of teaching for sickness in over fifty years. Kell and Joyce had two daughters: Katherine Elizabeth and Karen Helena. Kell and Joyce were divorced and he later married Debora Dowda.

David served in the US Air Force after graduation from high school. After his discharge, he moved back to Martin to work with his dad on the family farm. In 1965, David married Eunice Ann Finley from Toccoa. David and Ann purchased their own home and David was a beef and poultry farmer for thirty years. David and Ann have four children: James Cleveland, Randolph David, Susan LeAnn and Amy Elizabeth. David gave up the farm business and drove a truck for Boyd Brothers for a number of years.

, Ann

Front row (I to r): Chad and Gabe Cleveland, Jake Kerwood, Ben Cleveland, Ryan Mitchell, Jackson ~1~welanIO Mitchell, Alex Mitchell, Kay Martz, Kelli Paul, Brett Paul, Katherine Mitchell, Karen Schiebelhoffer, David Schiebelhoffer, Flem Mitchell, Jr.;

Back row (I to r): LeAnn Cleveland, Jeff and Amy Kerwood, Miranda Mitchell, Pat and Randy Mitchell, David Mitchell, Michael Paul, Kristen Paul, Joshua Paul, Kell Mitchell, Jr., Michael Hathaway, Delia Mitchell, Ken Martz.

David purchased the property where his grandparents had lived. The old farmhouse has been torn down and David and Ann have built a beautiful house in the exact locations as the "Old Home Place." David has a beautiful flower and vegetable garden. Ann worked at the Northeast Georgia Bank for over thirty years before her retirement in 2014. David and Ann have been active members of Martin Baptist Church for over forty years, and have raised their children in the church.

Kay was married to James Emory Edwards from Toccoa for four years. They had a daughter, Kassandra Lynn. After the marriage ended in divorce, Kay married Daniel Leon Clements and lived in Lakeland, Florida for almost forty years. Dan and Kay had one daughter, Kelli Adele. Dan adopted Kassandra when she was six years old. Kay worked in the library at a private Christian school while the children were in school, and then was in charge of the accounts receivable department at Southeastern University for fifteen years.

Dan and Kay were instrumental in starting the Lakeland
Drive-In Church and were active there until Dan's death on
November 8 1995 Dan is buried in the Florida National
Cemetery in Bushnell Florida Kay married Kenneth Duane
Martz Sr in February 2004 and in May 2004 they moved to
Martin to live in her parents' home Ken and Kay are active
members of Martin Baptist Church where Kay is the church
secretary Ken enjoys farming and has a small herd of cattle
on the family farm. Kay is an active member of the Martin
Woman's Club.

Jackson David Mitchell Family History

Jackson David Mitchell was born and reared in Martin in
Stephens County. His parents were Kell Freeman Mitchell
and Emily Wilbanks Mitchell. David attended schools in
Franklin and Stephens County and is a graduate of Stephens
County High School in 1958. After high school, he enlisted
in the United States Air Force where he served for four
years. After returning home he was associated with Mitchell
and Son Farms for thirty years. David was actively involved
in the Stephens County Young Farmers serving on the local,
district and state level.

He was also active in the Stephens County Farm Bureau
serving as president and director. David was a charter
member of the Georgia Beef Board representing the
Georgia Farm Bureau. He was also active in the local
chapter of the Georgia Cattlemen's Association serving one
term as president.

David married Eunice Ann Finley on June 19, 1965 at Old
Toccoa Baptist Church. Her parents were William Fred
Finley and Eunice Isabel Sosebee Finley. Ann attended
Lakeview Elementary and Big A Elementary School and
graduated from Stephens County High School in 1962.

She enrolled at North Georgia Technical School where she graduated in Business Education in 1963. After graduation, she worked with Citizens Bank and Toccoa Clinic for several years. She retired from Northeast Georgia Bank after thirty-three years. Ann is an active member of Chapter 1294 of the United Daughters of the Confederacy. David and Ann reside in Martin, Georgia and are members of Martin Baptist Church. They are the parents of four children; James Cleveland was born in September 1962, Randolph David was born December 1967, Susan LeAnn was born July, 1971, and Amy Elizabeth was born December 1973.

James "Jimmy" Cleveland Mitchell

Jimmy lives in Bakersville, CA with his wife, Denise. Jimmy served in the Navy from 1981-1985, was stationed at Oceania Navy Air Station and was on the Aircraft Carrier USS John F. Kennedy. Jimmy is presently employed at Quinn Company in Bakersville. Jimmy has three children. Tiffany lives in Portland, OR and is an author, David lives in Jasper, GA and Amanda lives in Greenville with Jimmy's two grandchildren, Lily and Damion.

Randolph "Randy" David Mitchell

Randy lives with his three children in Salisbury, Maryland, where they moved in 1998. Randy obtained his BS, MS, and PhD degrees from the University of Georgia in Poultry Science and an MBA from Salisbury University. Randy serves as Vice President of Technical Services at Perdue Farms. They are members of Wicomico Presbyterian Church. Maranda was born in April 1994, Alex was born in May 1996, and Ryan was born in May 2001.

Susan LeAnn Mitchell Cleveland

Chad Garrett Cleveland and LeAnn were married on December 30, 1995 at Martin Baptist Church. Chad graduated from UGA in 1994 with a BBA in Accounting. He has worked at the University of Georgia since 1994 and currently serves as the Controller. LeAnn graduated from UGA in 1993 with a B.S.Ed. in Special Education. She received her M.Ed. in Interrelated Special Education in 1999. LeAnn teaches in the Student Learning Center at Prince Avenue Christian School. Chad and LeAnn reside in Athens, Georgia and have three sons. Jackson was born in October 1999, Gabe was born in December 2001, and Benjamin was born in July 2004. They are all active members at Prince Avenue Baptist Church.

Amy Elizabeth Mitchell Kerwood

Jeffrey Nelson Kerwood and Amy were married August 8, 1998 at Martin Baptist Church in Martin, Georgia. Jeff graduated from the University of Georgia in June of 1997 with a B.S. in Agriculture, and is the Atlanta General Manager for Chapel Valley, a private landscaping company. Amy graduated from the State University of West Georgia in December of 1997 with a BS in Education. She is currently a teacher at Mountain Road Elementary in Cherokee County.

Jeff and Amy have two children, Jake was born in October 2001 and Annalyn was born in February 2008. They reside in Canton, Georgia and are active members of North Point Community Church.

Willie Montgomery

Willie was a farmer, who passed away February 2, 1952. He was married to Pecola Arthur Montgomery, born in 1924 and died in 1998. They had 4 children;
Charles, Merlean Montgomery Brown, Inail Montgomery Drinkard, W. C. Montgomery. Willie served in WWII and son W. C. served in Germany.

CHARLES MORGAN FAMILY HISTORY

Tom & Millie Morgan moved from Toccoa to Martin in the late 1960s after son, Charles, moved his family to Martin. They joined Charles and his family at Martin Baptist church, and they all became very active in both church and community. Mr. Tom served as a deacon, and joined the Lions club, and Mrs. Millie was active in church and joined the Martin Woman's club. They had four children: Charles, Carl, Evelyn, and Kathryn. Both Carl and Evelyn are deceased.

Charles married Pauline Bolman from Toccoa, and they lived in Toccoa until the middle 1960s when they moved their family of three daughters, Janet, Peggy and Sherri, to Martin. They purchased a grocery store known as Morgan's Superette, and operated this business until they retired. Charles has also done carpentry work during all these years, and has rental property on which he continues to do the maintenance work with Pauline's assistance.

 Charles & Pauline have served faithfully in the Martin Baptist church. Charles served as a deacon, and he & Pauline both sing in the church choir, and Pauline occasionally sings solos. Their daughters were musically talented and sang in the church choir. Sherri & Peggy were soloists and Sherri choreographed the Martin Youth Choir's version of the musical "Life" in 1981. Daughter, Janet Neal, has two children, Dr. Stephanie Chapman and Barrett Neal.

Peggy Whitfield, has two sons, Adam & Andy and two grandsons, Braxton and Brock. Sherri has two daughters, Morgan and Emily. The Morgan family members have always been known to have lots of family get-togethers and family fun times. They enjoy clowning around, dressing up in strange costumes and making lots of family videos.

All birthdays, Christmases, and any other occasions that can be called "special" are celebrated in a big way with all family members joining in, dressing up and enjoying every minute of time with their hilarious family members!

It has been known by the general public that Pauline has waited for over 40 years for her carpenter husband to build her a carport! It seems that Charles just cannot depart with the big pecan tree which is growing where the carport should be. Pauline's friends have tried to help her by talking to him, but the carpenter just turns a deaf ear. Now Pauline fears time may be running out because they may soon have to give up their car keys!

GLEN MOSLEY FAMILY HISTORY

Glen Mosley, son of William Mosley and Sally Adams Mosley of Martin, married Ollie Sisk of Martin. He served in the Army during World War 11 from 1942 until 1945. After getting out of the Army, Mr. Mosley operated a gas station in the Stovall building which was located on hwy. 17 near the post office. Later he built his own station across the street. He continued to own and operate this station until just prior to his death in 1987.

Mr. and Mrs. Mosley had one daughter, Glenda Ivester, who continues to live in Martin. Glenda has two sons: Richard, who lives in Montgomery, Alabama and has four children: Chad, Lauren, Daniel, and Eric; Bobby, who continues to live in the Martin area. He has two children, Elizabeth and Baylee.

After Mrs. Mosley's death in 1984, Mr. Mosley was lonely and spent much of his time the next few years sitting on the old church pew which was located in front of his station.

 The bench was the gathering place for many people who came by just to chat with him and discuss the latest news. After he passed away in 1987, Glenda intended to take the old bench to her house, but when she was ready to move it, someone had stolen it. Most people who lived in the Martin area will remember the old church bench in front of Glen Mosley's gas station.

THE NUNNALLY FAMILY HISTORY

Howard Nunnally - born 3-08-22, Banks Co., GA
Maxine Carlan - born 5-31-23, Banks Co., GA Married Dec. 20, 1941

Howard served in World War II in the Pacific theatre, and was a recipient of the Purple, Bronze Star and Oak Leaf Cluster. After discharge from the army in 1945, Howard and Maxine made their home in Gainesville, GA, where Howard worked at the Ford dealership.
In 1951, Howard and Maxine, their four children and Howard's father, Calvin Nunnally, moved to the Avalon/Martin area of Stephens Co. when Howard was employed with WABCO. The children born at that time were:

Rita Frances, born 1-14-1943
Sandra Lee, born 5-26-1946
Linda Maxine, born 12-28-47
Jerry Howard, born 8-3-1950

After renting homes for a few years, Howard and Maxine purchased a 50-acre farm on Gumlog Rd. (Hwy. 328) in 1954. They lived on that farm until their deaths (Maxine in March, 2008 and Howard in December, 2009). On the farm, they grew cotton, corn, wheat, and food for the family, along with milk and beef cattle. Calvin operated a chicken (layers) house for a number of years.

Howard worked at WABCO until his retirement when the plant closed in 1983. Later he and son, Jerry, owned and operated Nunnally's Paint and Body Shop, where Howard continued to work until his retirement in 2000. Howard served as mayor of Avalon and as a town councilman for several terms.

Maxine was a homemaker, raising 5 children, helping tend to the farm crops, and milking a cow for many years. She was an excellent seamstress and made most of her and the children's clothing, and made clothing for other people of the community as well.

Their fifth child, Steven Barry was born Jan. 5, 1962.

The children attended Avalon Grammar School. Eastanollee Elementary (Jerry and Steve), and all graduated from Stephens Co. High School. The family were active members of Martin Baptist Church.

Rita first married Charles Cheek in 1963 and John Brazauskas in 1984. She worked at The Citizens Bank. WABCO. and Gilbert and Bennett and was a graduate of Brenau University. In 1984 Rita moved to Connecticut and later to Jacksonville. FL. where she worked for the Jacksonville Jaguars. Rita died in January. 2000. She had two stepchildren, Lynn Brazauskas and John Brazauskas, Jr.

Sandra married Jerry Oliver and worked at 1st Franklin Financial after graduation from Stephens Co. High School until her retirement in 2012. They still live in the Avalon/Martin area. Sandra was very active in leadership of the American Cancer Society Relay for Life for a number of years and served in many positions with Martin Baptist Church. Sandra and Jerry have two daughters. Dawn. who married Todd Broome and Kristi. who married James Moore. Dawn and Todd have two daughters. Heather and Breanna and all live in the Avalon/Martin area. Kristi and James have three daughters, Josie, Kalli and Kasie and live in North Port, Florida.

Linda married William Howard and worked at Coats and Clark. Schokbeton. and Patterson Pump until she retired in 2013. Linda graduated from North Georgia Tech. Linda and William live and Toccoa and have two children. Brad Howard. who married Lori Payne. and Monica. who married Ed Howard. Brad and Lori have 4 children. Crystal Hunt. Tanner. Cooper and Mia. Monica and Ed have 4 children, Ashton, Carlan, Maddie, and Bryson.

Jerry was married to Deborah Whitworth and worked at WABCO for a number of years. Later he was co-owner of Nunnally's Paint and Body shop. Jerry and Deborah had one daughter. Any Lynn Nunnally, who married Henry Bohannon. They have one daughter. Kierstyn. and they live in the Eastanollee area. Jerry died in August, 2009.

Steve was very active in Boy Scouts growing up and achieved the rank of Eagle Scout. He married Crystal Dodd and worked at Gilbert and Bennett and Nunnally's Paint and Body Shop.

They had three children, Barry (1983-1989), Raven and Max. Raven and Max still live in the Avalon/Martin area. Steve died in July, 2000. Pump until she retired in 2013. Linda graduated from North Georgia Tech. Linda and William live and Toccoa and have two children, Brad Howard, who married Lori Payne, and Monica, who married Ed Howard. Brad and Lori have 4 children, Crystal Hunt, Tanner, Cooper and Mia. Monica and Ed have 4 children, Ashton, Carlan, Maddie, and Bryson. Jerry was married to Deborah Whitworth and worked at WABCO for a number of years. Later he was co-owner of Nunnally's Paint and Body shop. Jerry and Deborah had one daughter, Any Lynn Nunnally, who married Henry Bohannon.

They have one daughter, Kierstyn, and they live in the Eastanollee area. Jerry died in August, 2009. Steve was very active in Boy Scouts growing up and achieved the rank of Eagle Scout. He married Crystal Dodd and worked at Gilbert and Bennett and Nunnally's Paint and Body Shop. They had three children, Barry (1983-1989), Raven and Max. Raven and Max still live in the Avalon/Martin area. Steve died in July, 2000.

Howard Nunnally Family

OUTZ FAMILY HISTORY

John Outz and his wife Climelia married on August 29, 1929 in Oconee Co., SC. Their son Homer Outz, moved to Martin in 1941 and worked in the F. C. S. Oil Mill. Later he opened his own saw mill company when he and his family lived in Martin. Their home was located where the David Mitchell home is now on Martin Drive. The house was formerly owned by Mr. Kell Mitchell Sr. Homer worked with Mr. Mitchell on his poultry farm after retiring from the saw mill.

Evelyn married Roy Walters on July 4, 1957. Roy died in 1982. Evelyn married Clarence Davis. Her younger sister married David Sheriff in 1963 and lives in S. C. Evelyn and Clarence live in Martin in one of the historic homes of Martin.

PINKSTON FAMILY HISTORY

The Gus Pinkston family lived on the Clarks Creek Road. Mrs. Pinkston died when the youngest child of seven children, all girls, was four years old. Mrs. Jody Freeman, age 92, recalls how she looked forward to seeing Mr. Pinkston and his daughters traveling by her house faithfully every Sunday morning on their way to church. They rode in a large three seated buggy, and all seven girls always wore beautiful dresses and were never without their hats.

The youngest daughter, M. L., married Jimmy Keels and lived at the same location, where they worked for Mr. & Mrs. Curtis Pitts, until they both became too old to continue working. They raised a family of five girls - Marcille, Alma Lee, Pauline, Lula Mae and Beulah Faye. A sixth child, Virginia Ruth, died in infancy. Mr. Keels died in May, 1989, and Mrs. Keels died in Oct., 2004 at the age of 91. It is well known that she had the happiest, most celebrated funeral that anyone had ever witnessed in this part of the country - just the way she wanted it to be.

PITTS FAMILY HISTORY

Joe & Mable McCay Pitts, their three children, Brinsdon (McCall), now deceased, Jody (Freeman), now deceased, and Curt, also now deceased, and two grandchildren, Glen, and infant, Laura Pitts, moved from Abbeville, Ga. in 1925. The family traveled in a car & stopped along the road to eat, get water and take care of the baby. The trip was a very long day. A relative transported the farming tools in a horse drawn wagon, and the round trip took eight days. He hauled the furniture in a truck.

The family purchased a farm in the Clarks Creek area and always attended Martin School & Martin Baptist Church. The farm was later owned by son, Curtis Pitts, who both tree-farmed and operated a sawmill on approximately 1500 acres of land. He married Geneva Welborn, and they had two daughters, Barbara & Peggy. He passed away in 2003, and Geneva continued to live in the home place for several years until she passed away.

Barbara Bowers and husband, Clayton, live in a house on the farm. Also their daughter, Robin, and her two daughters, Jessica & Erin, and their two children live in houses on the Pitts property.

The other daughter, Peggy Cawthon and husband, Ty, live on a farm near Canon, Ga., and their son, Sam, and wife, Lorie & their two children, live near their home. Their other son, Tim, wife, Lisa, and their three children reside in a home located on the Pitts property.

Jody Freeman, daughter of Joe & Mable Pitts, continued to live in Martin in a house that she had lived in since 1956 until her death in 2010. She & husband, Joe Freeman, (deceased in 1968) had one son, Max. He & wife, Barbara continue to live on highway 17 near Martin. They have one son, Jeff, daughter-in-law, Melanie & one grandson, Beau.

The oldest daughter of Joe & Mable McCay Pitts, Brinsdon McCall, is also now deceased. She and husband, Racine McCall, also deceased, had one son, Braxton who is married to Brenda Meeks. They have two sons, Greg and Michael, and four grandchildren.

Laura Wood, (Ernest Wood, deceased) granddaughter, who was the infant in 1925, also lived in a house located on the original Pitts property until she passed away.

PRICE FAMILY HISTORY

Benjamin & Charlotte Moss Price moved from South Carolina to Franklin County Georgia approximately 1875. They had nine children: Sam, Betty, Maggie, Pearl, Will, Lee, Norman, Oscar, and Henry.

Three of their sons settled in the Martin area: 1. Lee Price married Daisy Pearman about 1902. Their children were Fay, Lallie, Grace, Lottie Ruth (Mrs. Jim Phillips), Lorene (Mrs. Harold Elrod). 2. Norman Price married Essie Stonecyper. Their children were Eleanor (Mrs. Leon Denmon) and Evelyn (Mrs. JulianYuiUe) 3. Henry Price married Roxie Cochran.

Norman & Henry had a lumber business and operated a cotton gin located near the railroad track across from the Martin Baptist Church. All three families attended Pleasant Hill Baptist Church.

PURDY FAMILY HISTORY

The ancestors of Irenus Purdy came from Danville, Virginia. Irenus and Cordie Segars Purdy settled on a farm on the Clarks Creek Road near Highway 17 about 1945. His brother, Oscar, and sister, Myrtle, made their home with them. There were four children - Janalu Crowe, Mary Alice, Curtis, and Dorothy York. Curtis Purdy served in World War 11 and married Miriam Whitlow from Carnesville. Dr. Swain came to the home and delivered three of the Purdy children. All are now deceased. Curtis Purdy recalled happy childhood memories of skinny-dipping in the river near Knox Bridge and good times with George Knox, Bill Cheek, Roscoe Chitwood, and several others.*

A grandson of Mr. & Mrs. Purdy, Bart York & wife Buffy, their three children, Grayson, Olivia and
Sarah, continue to live in a house on the Purdy homeplace.

* (Initial information on the Purdy family was given by Mr. and Mrs. Curtis Purdy. They are both
now deceased).

Grace Ramsey – Born March 17, 1939. Died January 24, 1006

FREEMAN REECE FAMILY HISTORY

Freeman Reece was a farmer and was married to Estie Reece. They are buried in the Greater Hope Baptist Church cemetery in Martin. They had the following children;

Billyk Freeman, Malissie Reese Griffin, Madge Reese Johnson, Ruth Reese Slade, Julia Mae Reese Burruss, Elizabeth Reese Combs, L. T. Reese, Booker T. Reese.

SANDERS FAMILY HISTORY

James Madison Sanders did not know his own birthdate, therefore he declared it as July 4, 1843, because of his strong patriotic beliefs. When the Civil War started, he was one of the first men to enlist. James' three brothers followed suit. He was the only one to see the Civil War end alive. For his gallant fighting in the Civil War, the Daughters of the Confederacy awarded him a medal.

In 1870, James married Matilda Harris in Hart County, however they made their home in Stephens County. The couple had four children. Their names were: Fannie (who married Clem Terrell Clark), Jane (who married William Scott, Luther and Andrew. One day, Andrew was fishing in a boat on the river and had an epileptic seizure. He fell out of the boat and drowned. The family witnessed the entire incident and because they could not swim, could only watch helplessly from the bank.

James received a Civil War veteran check each month in the amount of $25. To receive this check, he had to walk from Martin to Carnesville. For protection, James carried a weighted walking stick with him on these trips.

James Sanders was well-known for his ghost stories and love of buck dancing. He died on August 30, 1928.

Submitted by Betty Sosebee.

THE SHIRLEY FAMILY HISTORY

The Shirley Family moved to Martin in the early fifties from the Line Community in Franklin County and soon joined the Martin Baptist Church.

Maggie Bell Farmer Shirley and Robert Lee Shirley spent their childhood years in the Fairview and Clarks Creek area of Franklin County. Rob Shirley owned a big cotton farm near Townville South Carolina until the great depression, and Mag was a homemaker and the mother of six lovely daughters. She stitched all their beautiful garments by lamplight after she grew a garden, fed the animals and cooked a farmer's size meal.
Her Lady Baltimore cake could not be surpassed. Mag became lunchroom manager of the Eastanollee schools soon after moving to Martin.

The Shirley's oldest daughter, Mary Nell Shirley Meyers became a registered nurse and aided Doctor Bruce Schaefer who delivered both Bob and Sue Stovall in the Stovall House in Martin.

Sarah Bob Shirley Stovall, their second daughter, was born two years later on Nell's birthday, January 6, 1914. Sarah Bob graduated from Rabun Gap Nacoochee School. She soon met Clarence Stovall and married in Clarkesville, Georgia on June 9, 1933. Sarah had two children, Bob and Sue Stovall Morgan. Her work as the director of the hospital auxiliary was a job she thoroughly enjoyed. Myrtice Warrene Shirley Stevens (Jackie), attended business school and worked as a court reporter for DeKalb County. Jack had two children, Shelton and Sally Steele.

Grace Margene Shirley Smith attended business school. She worked at a radio station in Toccoa. She married and became the mother of five children. Tom, Shirley Watson, Katie Morris Rebecca Knapp, and Melissa Wolfe. Grace lived in a home at Lake Hartwell and worked in the Stephens County Tax office until she retired.

Henry Frances (Frank) Shirley Altman became a registered nurse and worked in Anderson and Columbia, South Carolina. She was the Mother of three children, Tucker, Michael and Patsy Altman Smith.

Betty Ann Shirley Lawson attended Anderson College and worked in Toccoa law offices of Gross and Stowe until she married Howell Lawson at the Martin Baptist Church, December twenty seventh 1953. She is the mother of two children, William Howell Lawson, Jr. (Billy), and Laura Lee Worthy.

Great celebrations were held every holiday and special birthdays at Granny Mag's and Daddy Bob's home located next to the Martin School, now the Martin community center. Daddy Bob named his daughters boys names since he had no sons. The final resting place of Mr. and Mrs. R. L Shirley is the Martin Baptist Church Cemetery.

The Shirley Family

Thomas Henry Stovall, January 19, 1876 - July 23, 1931
Elizabeth Eugenia (Lizzy) Miller Stovall

Thomas Henry Stovall owned property in Martin, and had interests in many businesses. He and Ralph Clodfelter had a drug store. He also owned an embalming parlor, a bank, a filling station and an oil mill. Sadly, most of this was lost during the depression.

Elizabeth Eugenia Stovall was from a devout Presbyterian family from the Red Hill community in Franklin County, Georgia.

Her siblings include missionaries to Korea and Africa, a minister in Druid Hills, Georgia, and an orthopedic doctor in Charlotte, North Carolina.

Thomas Henry and Lizzy were parents of five children, four of whom grew up in Martin. They are William Henry, who died in infancy, Alpha Elizabeth, George Miller, Leonard Clarence and Sara Christine.

Lizzy loved playing games with her children and grandchildren. Carrom, Parcheesi, Dominos and Rook were a few that she loved. She walked to the schoolhouse every week to have her blood pressure checked by the traveling nurse. She was a fixture at Martin Baptist Church, and to her, attendance was mandatory. She also belonged to the Martin Women's Club and the Home Demonstration Club.

George N. Stovall & Aunt Virginia, Will Stovall & Aunt Nestie, Mr. & Mrs. Tom Clarke Rev. Farmer Stovall and Wife, Joseph Stovall and wife, Thomas Stovall and wife, James Oliver Hix and wife.

Alpha Elizabeth Stovall Sale

Alpha Elizabeth Stovall is the third child of Thomas Henry and Lizzy Stovall, and was married to William Lyman Sale of North Carolina. They had two children.

William Lyman Sale, Jr. was born January 21, 1936, and lives in Sarasota, Florida. He has two children, Eddie and Anita, who live in Maryland.

Betty Jean Sale Strange was born May 18, 1932. She married Dick Strange, and they had three children, Pete, Julie and Craig.

Betty Sale and Lyman Sale, Jr. lived in the Stovall House during the years of their education, and graduated from Stephens County High School, then attended college at the University of Maryland.

Betty was an educator, and Lyman, Jr. attended
seminary in Louisville and became a chaplain in the
United States Army. He married Ferrell and Sue
Morgan at Martin Baptist Church.

George Miller Stovall

Miller Stovall served in World War II, and received the
Bronze Star for bravery. He is a Martin "Hometown Hero!"

After the war, he married Geraldine Freeman, and they had
two children, Bryan and Nancy. Miller worked for R. G.
Letourneau, demonstrating the earth moving equipment
being manufactured at the Letourneau factory in Toccoa.
Miller helped to build Lake Louise, as well as the Toccoa-
Stephens County Airport.

Miller could fix anything, and did so for anyone who
needed his help. The Stovall House yard was the
neighborhood playground, while Miller helped build the
Martin Community Center.

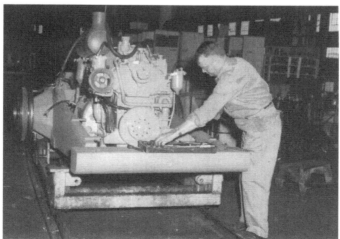

Miller Stovall

Geraldine (Gerry) Freeman Stovall

Gerry Stovall was a native of Martin, and was a lovely and talented lady. She had a nice voice, and sang in the church choir. Her talent as a pianist was shared with family and friends, as well as the members of Martin Baptist Church.

Sewing was a talent shared by many in her family. Gerry loved to decorate and create beautiful things. During her career, Gerry worked at the Letourneau plant, as well as the Citizen's bank. Gerry was married to Miller Stovall. Their two children are Bryan and Nancy Stovall.

William Bryan Stovall, January 13, 1947 – present

William "Bryan" Stovall is the son of Gerry Freeman Stovall and Miller Stovall, and was born in Stephens County. He is a graduate of the University of Georgia, with a degree in Photography.

He was married to Patricia Anne Ryals, and they had two sons. Mattison Bleckley was born September 30, 1973, and Christopher Brent (Kip) was born November 10, 1976. Both sons served in the United States Marine Corp. Bryan later married Carol Ann McLeod. They had one child, Camden Caroline, born December 3, 1984. Bryan currently lives in Savannah, Georgia.

Nancy Jean Stovall White, June 12, 1951- Present

Nancy Jean Stovall White is the daughter of Gerry Freeman Stovall and Miller Stovall, and was born in Stephens County. She graduated from the University of Georgia, and worked as a flight attendant until she retired.

Nancy married John White on July 16, 1978, at the Stovall House in Martin, Georgia. They had one son, Matthew Alan, born September 19, 1983. They live in Fayetteville, Georgia.

Leonard Clarence Stovall, January 28, 1905 - November 21, 1987
"Pop"

Clarence Stovall, the oldest child of Tom and Lizzy, was a real outdoorsman, as well as a talented athlete. He took his dog and shotgun to school every day and hid them behind a terrace until recess, when he would leave school and go hunting for the rest of the day. His dad sent him to a preparatory school for high school, where he excelled in athletics and received a scholarship to Mercer University. At Mercer, he lettered in sports, playing basketball, baseball and football. One of his football teammates and lifelong friends, Wally Butts, went on to become a coach at the University of Georgia.

There are many newspaper articles about Clarence's performance in basketball, but he went to a professional farm league to play baseball.

In 1933, Clarence married Sarah Shirley. They went on to have two children, Shirley Sue Stovall (Morgan), and Robert Thomas Stovall. To provide for his family, Clarence gardened, and raised hogs and beef cattle. For fun, he fox and rabbit hunted.

R. G. Letourneau opened a heavy earth moving equipment factory in Toccoa, and he hired Clarence. Clarence worked there until he retired after 30 years with the company. After his first retirement, Tom Williams hired him to help move tires in his warehouse. Clarence enjoyed his time at the tire store, but eventually retired again.

Clarence was a member of the Martin Baptist Church, and a charter member of the Martin Lions Club. He is buried in the Martin Baptist Cemetery.

Sarah Shirley Stovall,
January 6, 1914 - September 30, 2001
"Nana"

Sarah Shirley Stovall was a graduate of Rabun Gap Nachoochee School. She came to Martin, Georgia, in 1933, when she married Clarence Stovall. They lived in the cream brick two-story house with Mrs. T.H. Stovall.

Their two children, Shirley Sue Stovall (Morgan) and Robert Thomas Stovall, were born to Sarah and Clarence while they lived in the Stovall House. Later, the couple built their own house next door, which was Sarah's pride and joy.

Sarah was a housewife and a member of the Martin Women's Club. As an active member of Martin Baptist Church, she loved singing in the choir, as well as working with the youth. She was director of the Ladies Hospital Auxiliary at Stephens County Hospital, and enjoyed that work very much.

Sarah was very dedicated to her neighbors in the Martin Community and the surrounding area, and when the need arose, she was always there to help in every way possible.

Sara Christine Stovall Garland, December 25, 1921-
February 19, 2010
Jesse lee Garland, October 12, 1920 - January 14, 1991

Sara "Christine" Stovall Garland is the fourth child of Thomas Henry and Elizabeth "Lizzy" Stovall. She graduated from Rabun Gap Nachoochee School, and went on to work at Coats and Clark until her retirement. She was married to Jesse Lee Garland. He also worked at Coats and Clark until he retired, and was a farmer, as well as an employee of the Martin Post Office. He served as Sunday School Superintendent at Martin Baptist Church. The couple adopted two sons, Thomas Lawrence and James Riley. Both are now deceased.

Robert Thomas Stovall, March 5, 1934 - Present
Sandra Frankum Stovall

Bob Stovall is the son of Clarence and Sarah Stovall, and was delivered by Dr. Bruce Schaefer and Mary Nell Shirley Myers at Stovall House in Martin.

Bob is a graduate of the University of Georgia with a degree in Engineering. He was employed by the United States government with the Soil Conservation Engineering Department. He designed and supervised the construction of many watershed dams in Northeast Georgia. He retired in 1994.

Since retirement, Bob has been employed by the Town of Martin as Clerk and Water Department Supervisor.

Bob's wife is Sandra (Sandi) Frankum Stovall. Sandi has been a member of the Martin Town Council for twenty years. Sandi and Bob have three children.

Robert Lee Stovall was born January 11, 1968, and is a graduate of Toccoa Falls College. He married Rebecca Rorabaugh on August 8, 1992. They have four children.

William Andrew Stovall was born February 28, 1970, and is a graduate of Emmanuel College. He is an associate pastor in North Carolina. He married Kirsten Cullum on October 8, 1994, and they have four children.

Leonard Matthew Stovall was born September 17, 1972. He is married to Sonja Whitfield Stovall, and they have one son, Logan. Len is employed as a Field Man with Fielddale Corporation. Len, Sonja and Logan live in Martin.

Bob Stovall & Sister Sue

OTTO TEASLEY FAMILY HISTORY

Otto Teasley was married to Annie Mae Dye Teasley. He was a farmer and worked at the Old Mill in Martin. They are buried in the Greater Hope Baptist Church cemetery in Martin, GA. They had the following children;

Homer Teasley, Roscoe Teasley, Mariette Teasley Brown, Ruby Teasley, Margaret Teasley, Carruth Teasley. Turner Teasley and Roscoe Teasley were in World War II.

Hugh Dorsey Teasley Family (5 Generations of Teasleys)

Hugh Dorsey Teasley was born May 16, 1915 and died in 1957. He was a truck driver for the Yow family of Martin. He is buried in the Greater Hope Baptist Church cemetery. He was married to Alma Grant Teasley October 28, 1933. Alma was born February 5, 1915.

They had the following children;

Eugene Dorsey Teasley born May 26, 1934, Christine Viela Teasley Born December 2, 1936 and died July 11, 1998, Jimmy Lee Teasley born June 11, 1938 and died August 11, 2008, William Sammy Teasley, born July 8, 1940 and died June 14, 2015, Lorene Teasley Crawford, born September 8, 1942, Mary Lou Teasley Oglesby, born September 8, 1946, Joseph B. Teasley, born December 16, 1948, Thelma Denise Teasley, born May 21, 1951 and died May 10, 2004.

Joseph served in the 101st Airborne in Viet Nam and retired in 1975.

Diane Yow & Lorene Teasley

Jim Grant (Alma'sFther), Mary Lou, Alma, Christine, Eugene, Lorene, Charlie, Sammy

Robert Lee Teasley

Robert Lee Teasley was born April 15. 1915 in Martin, GA and died February 15. 1988. He was married to Louise Brown Teasley. born December 20. 1916 and died December 1. 1981. They are buried in the Martin Grove Baptist Church cemetery Martin. Robert was a farmer and worked for the Stephens County School Board.

They had the following children: Marvin G. Teasley. born January 6. 1934 and died March. 14. 1987. Annie E. Teasley. born August 1. 1936. James Teasley. born March 25. 1938. Walter C. Teasley. born March 20, 1942 and died April 6. 1997. Maeunice Teasley. born December 12. 1946 and died February 13. 2013. Ann ie L. Teasley Johnson. born August 3, 1948, Joyce Teasley Pierre, born November 14, 1957.

Turner Teasley Family

Turner Teasley was born in Franklin County, GA and was married to Leila Montgomery Teasley. They are buried in Greater Hope Baptist Church cemetery.

They had the following children: Annie B. Teasley Wiley, died September 6, 1976, Elzora Teasley Rice, Lizzie Teasley, Robert L. Teasley, born April 15, 1915 and died February 15, 1988, Fannie Teasley Jones, born August 12, 1916 and died January 7, 2003, Bessie Teasley Pendleton, born March 12, 1913 and died December 4, 1997, Dessie Teasley Brown, March 13, 1913 and died January 21, 1994, Winnie M. Teasley Carter, Maeola Teasley Walker and Mozell Teasley Pratt.

June Teasley was in the U. S. Army.

Dallas Teasley Cowan
Alice Teasley Earle
James L. Teasley
Floyd Teasley

Thomas family (Howard & Lois) History
Howard Thomas 7-14-10 - 1-6-89 - Lois Thomas 10-26-14 -3-8-95

Howard Thomas and Lois Perkins both grew up in Stephens County. They married and continued to live in the Martin area. Howard farmed, had a fertilizer business in Avalon and drove a school bus. Lois worked at Coats & Clark in Toccoa for more than 35 years. They had one son, Bruce, and attended Martin Baptist Church. There was another family who attended Martin Baptist Church, who had a daughter. Bruce must have thought she was very special because in 1958, he married Robbie Jean Land, daughter of Doyle & Thelma Land. Bruce & Robbie Jean Thomas had four children: William Gregory, b.2-2-62; Kenneth Delane, b. 1- 4-64; Christopher Lee, b.8-23-65; and Stacey Kathryn, b. 2-25-68. Bruce worked as farmer, merchant, assistant mail carrier, worked in Matthews and Goodwin Furniture store, and then purchased as co-owner with John Goodwin in 1958. Later, he became a cattle and chicken farmer, and at one time operated a total of 22 chicken houses. He was also a member of the Martin Lions Club. He retired as furniture store owner in 1990. Bruce and Robbie Jean are lifetime members of Martin Baptist Church where their four children were always involved in church activities, and Bruce served as a deacon.

MOSE & MILDRED THOMAS

Mose Thomas was one of nine children born to William Anderson Thomas and Lou Crawford Thomas. The family lived in Martin and farmed for a living. All of the children moved away from Martin as they became adults except Mose who lived in Martin is entire life.

Mose married Mildred Smith, daughter of Isom Smith and Annie Jones Brock, who were also Martin residents. Mr. Smith owned a mule barn in Lavonia and traded mules for a living. They had one son, Dan, who married Ann Wooten from Ringgold, Ga. Dan & Ann had three children: Lisa Ann, Melinda Jean, and Samuel Brian, all of whom are now married and have children of their own. Dan is now deceased, and Ann lives in Toccoa

Mose and Mildred had no children of their own. Mose worked for Jesse Jewell Co. and later for Coats & Clark from where he retired. At the age of 18 Mildred began working for Coats & Clark and continued until she retired after working for 42 years. They were always faithful members of Martin Baptist Church where Mose served as deacon. They lived directly across highway 17 from the church, and for years he opened the church doors before services and stayed to lock up.

He was also a charter member of the Martin Lions Club and always helped with the chickenques, and any other projects. He enjoyed gardening and each year he grew vegetables in two gardens, giving vegetables to anyone who needed or wanted vegetables. He also cut grass for some of the elderly as long as his health permitted him to do so and furnished transportation for several different people for their medical appointments. His sister-in-law, Ann Smith, says he "had the patience of Job" and recalls that he would sit in the mall or in the car in the parking lot for hours, waiting for Mildred to shop. He always managed to find someone to talk to and would learn as much as possible about them. It is not unusual to hear people referring to Mose as "Good old Mose". He was certainly one you could depend on.

Both Mose & Mildred are now deceased.

CHARLES AND MINNIE ANDREWS TURNER
FAMILY HISTORY

William Harper Turner was born May 26, 1847 in Oglethorpe, GA. He moved to the Franklin County, GA, in 1870. He met Mary A. L. Molly Goolsby born April 24, 1853, of Franklin County, GA. She was the daughter of William Judge Anderson and Louise Catherine Adams Goolsby. Will and Molly were married in Franklin County, GA, and built a home in the Fairview Community. They had 10 children: Charles Alexander, Ila Drucilla, Dewitt Talmadge, John William, James Thomas, Addie Ora, Frank E., Nora Lee, Emma Kate, and Elizabeth Lizzie.

Charles Alexander, known as Charlie, b: 05/07/1876 d: 04/26/1964. On April 17, 1901, Charlie married Minnie Lee Andrews b: *10/19/1883*; d. 03/23/1952. She was the daughter of Jesse Messer and Frances Jane Caudell Andrews of Stephens County. Charlie and Minnie had eleven children: Aussie Lee, Ella Lou, Mildred Loraine, Paul Edward, William Jackson, Charles Dean Harris, Mollie Frances, Sara Evelyn, Fred Heller, Joe Frank, and Jimmy Everett. They lived at the Fairview home place until the 1940's, when they moved to the Chaffin home on Red Hollow Road in Martin, GA.

Jimmy Everett, b: 05/04/1923; d: 10101/1989. On April 23, 1949, Jimmy married Mary Ann Higgins, b: 09/19/1930; d: 12/23/2005. She was the daughter of Wayne and Myrtie Eliza Rumsey Higgins of Franklin County, GA. They lived in Martin in the Walters home place on Walters Road.

They had six children: James Richard (Dicky), Paul Allen, Jimmie Ann, Charles Steven, June Alyson, Susan Nevada Jenkins (niece raised as a daughter).

James Richard, known as Dicky, b: 1/8/1950; d. 11/17/2012. On October 9, 1971, married Laura Kay, b: 01/26/1953, the daughter of Fred W. and Ruth Whitmire Kay of Toccoa, Stephens County, GA. They build their home where Charlie and Minnie's home was on Red Hollow Road, Martin, GA. They have two children: Chad Everett and Carole Ann. Chad Everett, b: 05/03/1973, lives in Atlanta, GA.

Carole Ann, b: 06/05/1974. Carole joined the United States Air Force and met Aron Paul Mitchell. They were married June 5, 1996. Carole left the military after 12 years to present us with grandsons. Aron retired from the United States Air Force after 20 years of service in 2014. Carole and Aron have four boys: Aron Paul Mitchell Jr.

(2005), Marlon James Mitchell (2008), Remington Allen Mitchell (2010), and Ty Turner Mitchell (2011). They live in Colorado at this time.

Photo made in 1941 with Charlie and Minnie Turner in front and their home with 10 of their 11 children (Jimmie E. is in insert). L to R: Jack, Joe Frank, Paul E, Mollie F, M. Loraine, Ella Lou, S. Evelyn, C. Dean H., Fred H. and Aussie L

Sarah Webb
Michael Webb (deceased)
Annie R. Webb
George Webb
T. P. & Lillian Webb

ROY WHITWORTH FAMILY HISTORY

Roy Whitworth, born 01-12-1891, deceased, 10-8-1969, son of Henry Robert Whitworth & Kathryn Roberson Whitworth Sallie Gray Whitworth, born 12-07-1902, deceased 04-04-1988, daughter of Nazareth Gray and Mattie Alewine Gray.

Roy and Sallie Whitworth, along with their 12 children moved from Hart County Georgia to the Martin area about 1942. They soon purchased a large farm house with 100-acre tract of land near Martin. The house had six bedrooms and sufficient space for fourteen people. Parents and children settled into a farming operation that granted the family a good livelihood.

They grew hogs, a large vegetable garden, fruit trees which included apples, cherries, plums, and peach trees, and cows for milk. Hams were always hung in the smokehouse to cure. They also owned horses for the purpose of cultivating the land. Mr. Whitworth and the older boys farmed the land, and Mrs. Whitworth and the other children canned vegetables, fruits, and jars upon jars of jellies and jams.

Nona Freeman, daughter, recalls that even though times were difficult, the fun times were many. There was so much love and happiness in the family, and there was always plenty of food on the table. Neighborhood children gathered at the Whitworth house frequently and entertained themselves with softball games, horseshoes, basketball Sunday afternoon walks, wading in a nearby branch, and any games they could think of.

Even though Mrs. Sallie cared for a family of 12 children she still found time to read the Bible to them and to attend Martin Baptist Church every Sunday and revival services twice a year. The revivals were considered the big events of the year. There would be a road full of people walking to revival meeting. Each of the twelve Whitworth children joined the Martin Baptist Church.

After years of walking to church, Martin Church bought a bus, so then the family rode to church. One of the bus drivers was Harold Freeman, a local young man. Nona stood at the front of the bus to assist him in opening the door. They must have eyed each other many times because years later they married!

Mrs. Whitworth and her daughters enjoyed quilting and the socializing with friends and neighbors when they had quilting parties. She even found time to sew for her children. She used many flour sacks to make pretty articles of clothing. She even made bonnets for each of the girls and made sure they always had them on when they were in the sun. Of course the children could always pass their clothes to the next child, and they didn't mind wearing hand me downs. She sewed for her daughters until they were grown, and they all wore beautiful clothes.

Both Mr. & Mrs. Whitworth were very faithful, active Martin Baptist church members. Mrs. Whitworth belonged to the TEL Sunday school class and the WMU. Mr. Whitworth was a member of the Men's Sunday school class and also served as a deacon.

They were blessed with the following children:

Freeman - married Lorene Hayes. Both are deceased. Children and grandchildren are: Judy, who has one son, William, who is father to Benjamin & Elizabeth; Peggy, who has one son, Todd, who has two children; Betty, who has one daughter, Angie.

Loyd - married Ila Hayes. Both are deceased

Joel - married Blanch Crawford. Both are deceased. They had two daughters: Jo Evelyn Dean is married to Brown Dean and has one son, Rich, who has one daughter, Sofia. Jo Evelyn & Brown also have one daughter, Krista, who has one daughter, Sallie Grey. The other daughter is Faye who is married to Richard Segars and has two sons and four grandchildren.

Gartrell- married Mary Phillips. Both are deceased.
Children & Grandchildren are: Joyce Weaver, married
to Grant Weaver. They have four boys - Andy, Geoff, Alex
& Matthew; Mark is married to Marcie. They
have two sons, Josh and Jacob.

Sara - married Frank Holland. Both are deceased. Children
are: Mike and Tim, who have families of their
own.

James - married Margie Mathews. James is deceased.
Margie lives in Toccoa. Children are: Kenneth, who
has two children; Lynn, who has one child; and Debbie
who recently married.

Brebson - married Polly Owens. Both are deceased.
Children are: Kay who has two children; Karen, three
children; Roger, two children; Sandy, two children; and
Ronnie.

Nona - married Harold Freeman who passed away on July
21, 2014 at the age of 88. Children and
grandchildren are: Their son, Gerald is married to Jane
Harper and they have a daughter, Kelly Mateos who
has one daughter, Lola. Gerald & Jane have a son, Scott,
who has Kaitlyn, Calie, Ella, Connor. Harold &
Nona's daughter, Susan, is married to Ray Strickland, and
has two daughters, Brook Whittle, who has
Jackson & Lilli, and Lauren Moavero, who has Lizzie.

Dwight - married Carrine Simmons, who is now
deceased. Children are: Jerry, who has two children;
Danny, who has one child; and Gail.

Virginia - married James Thomason. Virginia is now
deceased. James lives near Carnesville. One son, Kent.
He and his wife have two children, Kyle and Karley.

Floy Jean - deceased at age of three. Tragedy struck this happy family in 1942 when an accident took the life of three-year-old Floy Jean. She was severely burned when her dress caught fire when she was standing near an open fire. She lived for a few hours and passed away in the hospital. For days following this accident wonderful friends and neighbors came to the Whitworth home and helped the family members to recover from this horrible event.

Maxine - married Bill Thomason. She was a bank employee for many years until her health failed. She also played both the piano and organ at Martin Baptist Church for many years. At the present time she is in extremely poor health.

Much musical talent has come from the Whitworth Family - children, grandchildren, great grandchildren and great-great grandchildren have displayed their talent, especially in the Martin Baptist Church. Daughter, Maxine, played the piano and organ for years, and Nona and Virginia sang in the choir. Granddaughter, Jo Evelyn Dean is a soloist, singing at many weddings and other special occasions. Grandson, Kenneth, has served as a choir director, soloist, and guitarist and has made several CDs. All ofBrebson's children were talented singers and sang in the choirs, both adult and youth, at Martin Baptist Church. Ronnie is also a church choir director. Grandson, Gerald Freeman, as made many CDs, sings in church and also sings in a Southern gospel quartet, The King's Messengers. His granddaughter, Lola, sings solos in church.

Many of the other family members also sing or play musical instruments.

Mr. Roy & Mrs. Sallie and many of their children have now passed away. They would be so proud of the generations that have followed - of their happy, talented family!

THE WILLIAMS FAMILY HISTORY

Flora Yow, daughter of Thomas Russell and Cynthia Elizabeth Dean Yow, married Copeland Rhea Williams, son of Thomas Humes and Annie Copeland Rhea Williams.

Flora was a member of the Toccoa chapter of DAR. It was because of her that much of the area and history has been preserved.

On March 21, 1929, Flora and Copeland had Cynthia Elizabeth. On January 27, 1934 Thomas Russell Yow Williams was born. Tommie graduated from Stephens County High and after graduating from Georgia Tech, went into the army. When he got out of the army, Tommie and his wife, Jean Fackler Williams, moved back to Martin, after living in Columbus, Georgia. Their children, Thomas Russell, Jr., Pamela Ruth and Margaret Elizabeth attended Stephens County Schools.

Russell, Jr., called Rusty, married Mary Hamilton. He was a High Schoiol teacher in Atlanta. They had a daughter, Patricia Jean, born November 25, 1990.

Ruth married Wayne Strickland and had Jennifer Elzabeth, born Februaary 16, 1985 and Jason Thomas, born July 14, 1987.

Betsy graduated from St. John's College and studied pottery making in Japan. Betsy now has her own business in New Mexico.

When Tommie moved to Martin, he opened Magnum Tire Company in the original T. R. Yow and Sons store building. As the business prospered, he built a new warehouse on Highway 17. Tommie has also been active in politics, having served as mayor of Martin twice. One of his many philanthropic projects was the donation of land for the Memorial Park in Martin. He is a member of St. Michael's Episcopal Church in Toccoa. Tommie is married to Margie Cheek of Turnerville, GA.

Cynthia & Tom Williams   Copeland Williams & Flora Yow

Copeland Williams & Cynthia   Tom & Cynthia Williams

Margie & Tom Williams

Geneva Perry Wilson – Born August 29, 1937, died August 4, 2002

THE YOW FAMILY HISTORY

The Martin YOW'S descended from John Yow of Germany and Anne Sutton of England around 1600. Hans Yow came to American on the Ship Molly, around 1727 from Germany. He died in 1741 in Newburn, NC. Hans YOW'S son was Christopher Columbus YOW Sr. His son was Christopher Columbus YOW Jr., who settled in Cumberland County, NC and died in 1814 in Grassy Creek, Moore County, NC. Christopher Columbus junior's son, was Dempsey Yow.

Dempsey YOW born in 1786, in New Burn, Moore County, NC and died in 1862 in Walhalla, Sc. Dempsey YOW'S son was Thomas Anderson YOW (born 1820 and died 1861), who was a Civil War Veteran, and died of typhoid in Richmond, VA in 1861, and is one of several YOW'S buried in the Martin cemetery. Thomas Anderson did not believe in slavery, so he sold his slaves and bought land before the Civil War. Thomas Anderson YOW'S son was Thomas Russell YOW born 1855 in Martin, GA and died in 1922 in Martin, GA.

Thomas Russell did not attend school until he was nine years old; he was in a wagon accident and broke both legs. His teacher, Judge Estes, thought he had great potential so he took him to live with his family in Gainesville, GA. He graduated from Gainesville High School, then went to the University of Georgia for two years. He roomed with Judge Russell (father of Senator Richard Russell). Thomas Russell came back to the Martin area (Goodwill). There he met Cynthia Elizabeth Dean (she was born in 1857 and died in 1933), and married her in 1878.

In 1882, they moved to what was to become Martin, Georgia. Thomas Russell rented a store in Martin, where the post office is now and built a house across the street. Soon he built a brick store in the downtown Martin area and in 1895, he built a house on Red Hollow Road.

In 1902, Thomas Russell formed a stock company and built the Martin Cotton Seed Oil Mill. He also was president of what was later to become the Bank of Toccoa. Thomas Russell Yow had two brothers, Richard Dempsey and Eppe Morris. Richard Dempsey Yow (born 1844 and died in 1899). He married Mary Elizabeth Aderhold (1852-1937). Richard Dempsey Yow was a merchant, farmer and banker. He purchased Whispering Pines Plantation. He owned about 3,000 acres. Later he served as a County School Commissioner, State Representative and State Senator. They had five children.

Their oldest, Samuel Benjamin YOW born 1872 worked on his father's farm in Martin. He attended school in Martin and afterwards in 1894, graduated first honor at the University of Georgia.

Later Samuel attended New York University and Bellevue Hospital Medical College, where he graduated with his MD in 1898. The death of his father, Richard Dempsey Yow caused him to return home and take over the estate. Samuel's business prospered and he branched out into Banking, Oil and Cotton. He was president of the Toccoa Banking Company in Toccoa, Georgia from 1899 to 1904. In 1903 he was elected President of Martin Oil Mill and in 1904 he became President of the Bank of Lavonia, President of Lavonia Publishing Company, and served on the Lavonia Board of Trade, and was Vice President of the Toccoa Cotton Mill and the Lavonia Cotton Mill.

Samuel Benjamin married Mary Faith Dorsey, a daughter of Judge Rufus Dorsey, of Atlanta. They had two children.

The advice given to young men, ambitions to succeed in life, was "avoid idleness above all things, do that which you can do best and stick to it. Don't get excited, it will wear you out. Be confident and move ahead."

Another son was Jones du Bignon Yow Sr. (born June 1882 and died 1959). His son, Jones du Bignon, Jr. was born in 1917 and died 1981. His children were Jones du Bignon III, Phyllis Hayden and Mary Orme.

Eppe Morris, born 1859 and died in 1930, moved to Atlanta, Georgia. He had four children, Claude.Edwin, Lillian and Phillip.

Thomas Russell Yow's children were Leroy Yow, Pope Yow, Hubert Yow, Flora and Grace Yow, all in Martin GA. Pope Yow, the 3rd son of Thomas Russell Yow and Cynthia Elizabeth Dean Yow, was born in Martin, Ga. January 6th, 1890. He was educated at Georgia Tech in Atlanta, Ga. Pope returned home to Martin where he helped his Father run his business as a Merchant and Cotton Broker.

Pope married Donnah Williford from Lavonia, Ga. February 14, 1914. Donnah was the daughter of Judge Luther O. Williford and Kelso Gilmer, a descendent of the SC Calhouns.

MICHAEL McCALL

Dawn McCall

Mike,

pls send check

for $ 17.12

Andrea

"You make a living by
what you get. You make
a life by what you give."
~ Winston Churchill

Pope and Donnah were the parents of Richard Russell (Dick) Yow, Sr. (July 27, 1915) and Pope Yow, Jr. (1923) who died at age 4. Pope contracted with Mr. O. Kelley to build a "Craftsman style" house in 1920-21 on Red Hollow Rd., for Donnah who was only 28. The house was designed by a woman architect in Atlanta. This home remains in the Yow family today by their granddaughter, Diane Yow Cole.

Richard Russell (Dick) Yow was born at his grandmother Williford's home in Lavonia, Ga.

After graduating from Lavonia High School, he was off to Presbyterian College in Clinton, S.C. and graduated there with a degree in Math and Physics. Dick participated in sports at Presbyterian College as a baseball pitcher. His roommate was Kirby Higby, who later played professional ball.

Dick was a better pitcher, but due to a knee injury, he was unable to play with the pros. Dick taught Math at various High Schools in S. C., N.C. and GA. where he coached Football, Baseball and Basketball. He returned home to Martin in 1948 to go into business with his Father, Pope.

Dick married Marion Sharpton from Atlanta in 1939 after dating only 6 weeks. Dick was inducted into the Army and served until the war ended. Dick was involved in Politics in Martin and Stephens Co. He served as the Mayor of Martin, the City Council, the Stephens Co. Board of Education, and later served on Gov. Earnest Vandiver's staff in Atlanta. Dick and Earnest were classmates at Lavonia High School. Dick and Marion had three children, Martha Diane, born May 7th, 1942, Richard Russell (Russ) Jr., born April 27, 1949, and Robert Scott, born December 12, 1958.

Diane married Mike Cole from Austell, Ga. in 1964 after graduating from the University of Ga. with a teaching degree. Mike was a Ga. Football player and Diane, a cheerleader for the Bulldogs. Their children are Michael Derreck Cole and Kerry Diane Cole Vice, both are married and have children. Russ served in the Navy right out of High School and later after receiving a Master's Degree, he taught High School History and coached sports. He and his wife, Wanda, are retired from teaching and live in Murphy, N.C. Russ's children are Richard Russell, III (Richie), Kevin Rolin, and Melanie Lamberson.

Scott attended Anderson College in Anderson, S.C., is married and works for Pepsi Bottling Co. in Anderson. Scott spends his spare time bowling. His children are Ryan, Jamie Yow Davis and Hannah Grace.

In 2008 Diane Yow Cole married Dr. Joe Thomas White from Louisville, KY.

Grsce and Flora Yow

Pope, Donna, Richard & Pope, Jr.

Thomas Anderson Yow Thelma Hood Sharpton Donna Williford
Yow

Richard Russell (Dick), Marion Sharpton,   Cynthia E. Dean Yow
 Diane

Thomas Russell Yow   Cynthia E. Dean Yow

Donnah Williford Yow   Diane Yow Cole

CHAPTER THIRTEEN

OUR MILITARY HERITAGE
HONOR TO THOSE WHO SERVED

Grady Jackson Bell
U. S. Army enlisted Jan 14, 1942 and was assigned to 17th
Calvary Reconnaissance Squadron. He received the Bronze
Star

Grady Jackson Bell
U. S. Army enlisted Jan 14, 1942 and was assigned to 17th
Calvary Reconnaissance Squadron.

Carl Briley in France WW1

Lt. Max D. Briley Korea 1951-53

Chester B. Brock
U. S. Air Force. Jan 30, 1946 – Dec 21, 1946. U. S. Army
Oct 16, 1950 – Aug 8, 1952.

Romeo Brock. U. S. Army. WWII

Rex Brock - Veteran

Herbert Stanton Brown, Jr. (Pete). U.
S. Navy Pilot.
Served 20 years. Shot down 4 enemy
fighters.

Nathaniel Brown Sr. – U. S. Army WWI
Nathaniel Brown, Jr. – Son of Nathanial – U. S. Army –
Vietnam – Reserves

Troy Burton – U. S. Army – WWII
Tammie Burton – Daughter of Troy – U. S. Navy 12 years

George Chaffin, Revolutionary War
Verner Chaffin, Naval Reserve

L. C. Carter – U. S. Army

Lon Clark 1917 WWI Army

George Clark –
U. S. Navy WWII

Mark Clark (R), George
Wharton (L) Navy

Baxter Conwell – WWII

Doyle Combs U. S. Army 1943
Received Purple Heart & other
awards

Claude Davis   Clarence Davis U. S. Army
                      WW II

SSTt. Letisha S. Crawford U. S. Army

James Harrison Crawford Sr., M. D. WW1   Linda Dean
James Harrison Crawford, Jr. WWII   Navy Wave

Samuel Dean – Revolutionary War

Cpl. Ollie Elrod – U. S. Army WWII
Belgium

Ollie C. Elrod 1941-45 Belgium

Cpl. Eric Elrod U.S. Army

S7 2C Thomas Harold Elrod, WWII.
Breckenridge 1944-45
Awarded American Area Medal,
Victory Medal

SN James Alvin ElrodUSS
U. S. Navy Korea

Funeral of James Alvin Elrod

Sgt. George E. Elrod – U. S. Air Force

John Farrow, Jr. Revolutionary War
Capt. Thomas Farrow. Revolutionary War and War of 1812
Henry Farrow. Civil War. Company E. 3rd Reg. Calvary,
Georgia State Gards

Sgt. J. C. Farrow.
U. S. Army July 1941.

Max Freeman U. S. Army
Retired

Dennis Fergerson – U. S. Air Force

Jeff Freeman
U. S. Army (active)

Harold Freeman, Navy WWII
Radar operator, gun captain
On the bow of U. S. LST #122
Seaman 1st Class, Fire Control
Range finder.

Dante Freeman – WWII

Gerald Freeman U. S. Air Force
1970 – 1990

Scott Freeman
Marines 1997 -2001

Donald Foster – National Guard

John Goodwin Army WWII

Ronnie Ivester

Grady Goodwin – U. S. Army – 1969

Charles Gober – U. S. Army – Vietnam

Robert Harrison – U. S. Army - WWII

Max Hipp – U. S. Army

William O. Hunt, Ltc Us Army, Retired After 22 Years Of Service. Training included Infantry Basic, Armor Advanced, Artillery OCS, Airborne, Jungle operations, Field Artillery Advance course and Command and General Staff College. Serviced in Vietnam 1966-67 and South Korea 1970-71. Commands: Infantry Basic Training Company Fort Gordon, GA 2 yrs, 105 FA Battery S. Korea 6 months, and Data Processing Field Office, TRADOC HQS, Fort Monroe, VA 2 years. Retired as Deputy Director of the U.S. Army Computer Science School, Fort Benjamin Harrison, IN, 1986. Decorations: Silver Star, Distinguished Flying Cross, Bronze Star-2, Air Medal W/V-3rd Oak Leaf Cluster, Air Medal- 33 and Other Badges, Citations and Campaign Ribbons.

Joseph J. Johnson
U. S. Army WWII

Walter Mike Kay
U. S. Air Force 1968-1969
Viet Nam

Paul Juday, Jr. – U. S. Marine Corps
Ralph Looney – U. S. Navy

Phil Landrum – U. S. Air Corps WWII

James (Mike) Landrum – Viet Nam
James (Mike) Landrum, Jr. – Marine Corps

Ken Martz – U. S. Air Force

John McCall – Civil War – Georgia Company K – 52 GA
Regiment Infantry

Pete McCall U. S. Army Air Corps Gunner, captured by Germans and
placed in Stalag 17 B located in Braunau Gneikendorf, near Kerms,
Austria. Liberated May 1945

John Melvin McCall – WWII – U. S. Army. Member of General
Patton's Army that liberated prisoners (including his brother Pete).

Kay Mathews – Civil War

Dan McCall – U. S. Navy – WWII

Joe R. Medlin – WWII – U. S. Navy

Dan D. Medlin

David Mitchell
U. S. Air Force

Raymond Medlin – U. S. Air Force
David Medlin – U. S. Navy

Sgt. Flem Goode Mitchell – WWI Army
Flem Mitchell, Jr. U. S. Navy – WWII
Royce Mitchell – U. S. Navy – WWII
Elizabeth Mitchell – U. S. Navy - Wave

Willie Montgomery – WWII – U.S. Army
W. C. Montgomery – Son of Willie – U.S. Army Germany
Keith Montgomery – Grandson of Willie – U. S. Army 4 yrs
– Secret Service

Glen Mosley
U. S. Army
1942 – 1945

Howard Nunnally
U. S. Army. Company M
32nd Infantry. Bronze Star
Purple Heart

James Pless – Viet Nam & National Guard

William H. Payne – Revolutionary War
Michael A. Pressely – Army Career Officer

Curtis Purdy – WWII

Ira W. Randall – Civil War – Captain Mosley's 24th GA
Regiment

Lt. Reese – U. S. Army
James Madison Sanders – Civil War
Edwin Sheriff – National Guard

Cpl. James Alvin (Jimmy) Shore – U. S. Army WWII, 551st Transportation Company – P.O.W. War Command 2 Bronze Service stars – U. N. Service Medal – National Defense Service medal Republic of Korea Presidential Unit Citation.

Tommie Lee Stephenson died as an infant in the same typhoid outbreak of 1921. Hattie Lucile Stephenson Allen Page Fisher Brown married the last time to Lloyd Brown of Martin. Azalee Madge Stephenson Morris, Luther Alexander Stephenson, Hershel Byron Stephenson, Marion Morene Stephenson Herring, Annie Leona Stephenson, Sarah Elizabeth Stephenson Whittemore, Clarence Young Stephenson, Mary Cannie Stephenson Mulkey and Ben Yow Stephenson. Hershel, Clarence and Ben served in World War II. All three had married and moved away from Martin by the time WW II started.

William B. Stovall

Billy Stovall

Jack Stovall – U. S. Navy
1954 – 1958

George Miller Stovall
U. S. Army WWII
Bronze Star

Jimmy E. Turner

While serving in the United States Marine Corp, Jimmy
Turner arrived in Nagasaki, Japan, where the 2nd atom bomb
was dropped by the United States. He received permission
to bring several items home with him. One item was a
Nagasaki car tag that he put on the front of his car. The area
newspaper took a picture and ran it in their paper. His oldest
son, Dicky, now displays the tag on the wall, not his car.

Never Far from Family

L. Cpl. Paul A. Turner & Cpl. James R. (Dicky) Turner
U. S. Marines– HQ Company – 7th Marines

Jimmy and Mary Turner worried about their son, Dicky while he was serving in Vietnam. In 1970, their worries doubled. Dickey was standing in line at the PX to purchase some items and someone hit him on the arm and asked "Where the heck are we?" Dickey turned around and there stood his brother, Paul. They were stationed within 5 minutes of each other for a year until Dickey came home to the States in January 1971. Paul came home in March 1971. They were both glad to be home in Martin GA.

Okinawa was home to several family members while serving in the military. The daughter of Dicky and Laura K. Turner, Carole and her husband Aron Paul Mitchell were stationed in Okinawa for several years in the early 2000's. They thought this was unique until they talked with Dicky and Laura. Carole learned that both of her grandfathers, Fred Kay and Jimmy Turner were stationed in Okinawa for a short time during WWII. Also, her uncles, Leon Kay, Mike Kay, Paul Turner and her dad, Dicky Turner stayed in Okinawa for a short time during the Vietnam War in the 1960's and 1970's Dicky and Laura went to visit Carole and Aron in Okinawa. Dicky visited some of the old places and saw a lot of changes.

One of the most surprising changes was the runway all the planes used in the 1960 – 70's was now part of the main highway in Okinawa. After 12 years in the U.S. Air Force, Carole came out of the military when she and her husband were stationed back in the U.S. Carole gave birth to Dicky and Laura's first grandchild in October 2005. Aron Paul Mitchell, Jr. After three more grandsons, Marlon Remington and Ty, Her husband Aron retired after 20 in the U. S. Air Force. Her husband Aron is still serving in the U. S. Air Force. They are stationed in Tucson, AZ.

James Madison Sanders – Civil War

Junior Teasley – U. S. Army

Turner Teasley – U. S. Army
Roscoe Teasley – Brother of Turner – U. S. Army
Joseph Teasley – U. S. Army – 101st Airborne Vietman –
Honorable Discharge

Anton Thompson – U. S. Army – 1970 – 1999

Henry G. Watkins

Tom Williams U. S. Army

Jack Watkins

Howard White – National Guard

Thomas Anderson Yow –
Civil War – Company H.
5th GA Volunteer Infantry

Richard Dempsey Yow
Civil War – Company B
First GA Voluntary Regiment

Richard (Dick) Russell Yow, Sr.
WWII U. S. Army (with Diane)

Richard (Russ) Russell Yow
U. S. Navy

CHAPTER FOURTEEN

NATIVE SONS

To have been such a small town from its inception, Martin has produced so many Native Sons.

Some of these are R. D. Yow, Senator; Dr. S. B. Yow, Senator, First Editor of "Red and Black" UGA newspaper in 1893; Phil Landrum, U.S. Congressman; Gordon Walters, Director of U. S. Postal Service Rural Route Carriers; Doyle Combs, President of the local chapter of the NAACP; Herbert S. Brown, Jr., helped design the U. S. President's helicopter and decorated WWII Hero;

Jimmy Crawford, Eastern Airlines pilot and airplane builder; Verner Chaffin, Attorney, Edward Brown, surveyor/engineer, Hugh Stovall, Photographer for the Atlanta Journal & Constitution;

Dr. Kell Mitchell, history professor at University of Memphis; Dr. O. C. Aderhold, President University of Georgia; Dr. Thomas S. Yow, President of Young Harris College (1991) and Robert Harrison, who gave his life in WWII.

CHAPTER FIFTEEN

AVALON GEORGIA

The tiny towns of Avalon and Martin are like Siamese twins - inseparable. Located in beautiful Stephens County, Georgia, Avalon (Means Peaceful), lies along Highway 17. It was named after an island in California. When the railroad from Elberton to Toccoa was finished, Richard Dempsey Vow decided to go to California. While there he visited an island named Avalon. On his return home he named the little town Avalon, which it remains today.

The little town really had its beginning when T. R. Yow and E. M. Yow came to that vicinity in 1882. They started a mercantile business and some years later another store was opened by R. A. P. Dean.

The first Post Office was located behind what is now Dean's Grocery (Ralph Dean). The first mail carrier was Johnson Perkins. Avalon also had a Depot and the first agent was J. F. Cooper, who was succeeded by his brother Paul Cooper.

The first school was started in 1925 and finished in 1927. There are several houses left in the city limits of Avalon, which were built in the late 1800's or early 1900's. The Cooper House, built in 1895 by Epp Morris Vow, McBath House, built by Jim McBath, Epp Morris Vow House, built in 1895, Lillie B. Dean House, built by J. F. Cooper, Farmer Land House, Johnson Fuller House and the Tom Morgan House.

Early residents, Mrs. Lillie Belle Dean, Pink Mitchell, George Cooper, Paul Cooper, Farmer Land, W. L. McBath, Jones Kellar, the Browns, Van Crawford R. A. P. Dean, Johnson Perkins and Johnson Fuller

Avalon Post Office in 1918. Left to Right:
Paul Cooper, 4th from left Rev. William Arminus Cooper

CHAPTER SIXTEEN

QUIPS AND QUOTES

"BANG" ENDED HORSE, BUGGY ERA

One of the most exciting things that ever happened in Martin has remained an unsolved mystery for over half a century. A person now probably would wonder why such a minor but noisy incident was the talk of the town. I suspect most haven't even heard the tale about that memorable afternoon.

Made the town drunk, if there was one, think his world was coming to an end. Waked up many a person taking a Sunday afternoon nap after eating too much fried chicken, rice and gravy and string beans. Caused lots of farmers and mules alike to "bring your own water" before heading to town on a hot day.

The ones who lived in Martin in the 1920s will remember the day the horse and buggy era virtually ended with a bang. Imagine the incident:

 What on earth happened? Some mischievous teen-aged boys, who otherwise were "good at heart," inadvertently blew to smithereens an old well in the middle of Martin. The old well in Martin was located in the center of town and served many a trader coming to Martin to sell his chickens, cotton, etc.

The well was hand dug as all wells were at that time, had a wooden structure with a rope attached to a bucket that could be lowered into the well until it hit water.

After filling with water the rope was then wound around a log as you turned the handle until it came to the top of the well. There were troughs where animals could drink.

This well was not far from the gasoline pumps where folks stopped to fill up their Model- T and Model-A horseless carriage.

Reminiscing with Jody & J. C.

No one who worked on the Martin History Book had more enthusiasm and fun that Jody Freeman, age 92, and J. C. Farrow, age 89. They reminisced about school days, Saturday 'night life' in Martin and numerous funny happenings.

Jody and J. C. recalled the names of many school teachers, commented about many of them, including their well-loved principal, Mr. C. F. Fischer. J. C. remembers that Mr. Fischer would put $1.00 bills on top of a greased pole, and the young boys would work hard to climb the poles to retrieve the money.

They recalled Mrs. Mary Mitchell, who was a most unforgettable tough teacher. It seems that she enjoyed using the paddle, especially on Jute McCall, Joseph Landrum, Fred Dean and J. C. Farrow. They were all in the same third through fifth grade room. Seems she just "picked" on them and did her job well, using the paddle on a regular schedule

They talked about Mrs. Hubert Yow. Her husband operated a variety store and had a large glass-covered counter filled with peppermint candy sticks.

The children would give him a nickel, and he would give them about a quarter's worth of candy. Mrs. Yow also had a millinery shop in the store and created beautiful hats for the "fashionable' ladies in Martin.

J. C. and Jody talked about "Miss" West. She began teaching at Martin while she was very young and also very pretty. (Jody says that Joe Freeman thought she was pretty too). She never had to ask any of the bigger, older boys to bring in wood or build fires. In fact, they stood in line waiting for a chance to help her. Older boys were never tardy!

They recalled Miss Madge Land also being single, and Mr. Herschel Crump who paid J.C. quarters to build fires. Other teachers remembered were Sam Crawford, Harold Higgins, Ethel Haynie, Tom McCall, Miss Vera Bagwell, Julia Bell Clodfelter, Lucille Dean, Mrs. Donnah Yow, Mrs. Rossie Harrison, Ben Burkette and Ruth Crawford.

J. C. and Jody talked at length about the MARTIN WELL. It is amazing how many different versions are being told about the destruction of the Martin well. According to them, there was a large square rock well right in the middle of town with watering tubs for travelers to use for watering their horses.

Seems it was the also the town gathering place for the young crowd (boys), especially on Saturday and Sunday afternoons and evenings.

One evening some of the young crowd had gathered for fun and decided to drop a kerosene soaked bag (maybe several) in the well to "kill the mosquitoes".????

Anyway, the well was blown up, making such an explosion, church turned out and people ran for their lives. The young men who remembered this happening were Joe Freeman, Kell Mitchell, England Sisk, & R. M. Walters. Each had his own version of exactly what happened, but never seemed to remember exactly who did it!

The Wheelbarrow Lady.

Most people know that she was Grace Yow. She grew seeds and herbs and shipped them mainly to Europe. She was seen around town pushing her wheelbarrow filled with seeds and herbs.

BANK ROBBERY!

The Bank of Martin was going broke! The word was out that a big robbery was going to take place while there was still money left. However, the person who was staged to make the big haul went to sleep (or drank too much white lightening), and the robbery never happened.

SATURDAY AFTERNOON FUN

J. C. recalls that the young people in Martin had lots of fun on Saturday afternoons. The Martin Woman's Club Members sold cups of ice cream for 5 cents a cup. Then they would have games, foot races, greased pig contests, and horseshoe games. There was very little crime back then, just lots of fun and mischief! They fished lots, went possum hunting, rabbit & squirrel hunting & turtle hunting.

He remembers that once he, his brothers, Reece and Fred, and Curt Pitts had caught lots of fish and decided to play ball for a while before they cleaned the fish.

They put the string on the well and told Jody Pitts to keep an eye on the fish while they played ball. When they were ready to clean their catch, there were no fish because the cats had carried them all off.

J. C. also recalls that someone in town made a banjo from cat skins and taught lots of the boys how to play the banjo. (He didn't say if skins were from the cats that ate their fish).

A not so nice gentleman lived near the depot, and he was known to dislike the young active boys in the community. One evening he had said some very harsh words to some of the teenagers who were in town having a good time. Later that night they turned his outhouse upside down. It is not known who the young men were however.

It was well known that there were certain "out of town" boyfriends of some of the local girls who would gather around the well and hide their white lightening in various places in town so they wouldn't be caught with it in their pockets. Some of the young Martin guys discovered what the boyfriends were doing, so they started finding their bottles, disposing of the booze and urinating into the bottles. What a surprise!

Those to attend the Georgia - Tech game in Athens Saturday were, Mr. and Mrs. H. S. Brown and son, Pete, Mr. and Mrs. Pope Yow, Dick Yow, Misses Marguerite and Ruth Yow, Miss Sarah Dean, Mr. Robert Dean, Mr. Clarence Stovall, Mr. Edge Thomas and Mr. Goss Thomas. Quoted from The Toccoa Record December 12, 1929.

Miss Ann Stephenson spent the week-end with her sister, Mrs. Will Page in Hartwell and attended the Georgia - Tech game in Athens on Saturday. Miss Ruth Yow had as weekend guests, Misses Susie Nell, Julia Crawford and Miss Mary Bailey of Toccoa. These girls were guests of Miss Yow at the game in Athens Saturday. Quoted from the Toccoa Record December 12, 1929

"The play, "A Silver Lining" given at the School House last Friday night was attended by a good crowd. Proceeds to be used for school equipment." This is a quote from "Martin Local News" in *The Toccoa Record* December 12, 1929.

Work has begun on the electric line to Avalon. A crew of the Georgia Power Company came to Martin the first of the week to extend the line from Martin on to Avalon. Quoted from the *Toccoa Record* December 12, 1929

There were Star Routes. Mr. Rip Burress had a contract to pick up mail and deliver mail at the post offices along his Star Route. Martin was on the Star Route that ran from Toccoa to Elberton, stopping at all the post offices between to deliver and pick up mail. The Star Route driver furnished his own truck or whatever vehicle he used and he was paid by some kind of contract to carry that mail. He owned his truck and he might have had a chance to make a little extra money by picking up someone who needed a ride from Eastanollee to Lavonia or even to Elberton. These people would flag him down along the route or wait for him at the post office. He may have carried other light freight in addition to the mail.

Mr. Hansel Miller worked the Star Route in later years. He lived across the street from me (Lamar Davis) when I moved here in 1959. He had already been the Star Route mailman for a long time. He had a Ford van (we sometimes referred to it as a panel truck).

I had an uncle that worked as a mail clerk on the Seaboard Railroad that ran from Washington D. C. to Atlanta, passing through Elberton. He lived at Winston Salem, North Carolina. Sometimes he would take a vacation, getting off the train at Elberton, catch the Star Route mailman and ride to the crossing of Rumsey Road and Highway 17 over to our house and spend a few days with us. I even helped him gather some vegetables from our garden; we took them to the Cannery at Eastanollee.

When the Star Route mail truck came to the post office at Eastanollee, he loaded the canned goods on the mail truck and took them to Elberton, where he transferred them to his mail car on the railroad and took them back with him to Winston Salem. I guess you could call that a working vacation, but he did enjoy the vegetables the next winter.

Hansel Miller was a good neighbor, sharing anything he had with you if you needed it. When the jet planes were placed in service by the U.S. Postal Service, they started flying the mail across the country and cut out all the little Star Routes and the mail car on the train. One big truck started picking up all the mail and carried it to the regional post office and sorted it for the different destinations. I guess that was when zip codes came into being. Contributed by *Lamar Davis*

Judy Medlin rode with Mr. Miler to help him and keep him company. This was scandalous at the time. Mr. Miller's daughter, Rosemary taught at Big A School and advanced students. The fare was fifteen cents to ride on the Star Route. Contributed by *Tom Williams*.

Did you know some of the old store buildings were originally frame. When Grandfather's (T. R. Yow) store was built it was two story frame and there were bedrooms upstairs. Uncle Arthur first moved to Martin to night watch the store because his sister Betty (my Mammy) was upset about him being at the farm alone when our great grandmother had died.

After he married, Mothers brothers Lee and Hubert slept there. One night after Grandmother wouldn't let them do that anymore, the store caught fire. I don't know whether it was the other stores connected to it but all of the stores burned at one time or another.

The bank closed the same year (1929) I was born so the savings account 3.50 that someone gave me was lost. Mother said they knew something important was happening the night before the bank crash. The three men who were officers were at the bank, the lights were on in the wee hours of the night. One could see them counting the money. The next day the bank was closed and the money wasn't there.

The hitching posts were over in front of the first warehouse at the crossing blinking light).

Well, let me see. We also had the train of course. Mother said when she was a little girl the train brought up hot bread in baskets from Elberton and it smelled so good. Everything came by train. In the 30s and early 40s there were the chicken cars that stayed in town before and people loaded them with chickens before they left. When relatives had our trunks taken to the depot and shipped on the train. Even in the late 40s people still rode in buggies and wagons to Martin to catch the one passenger car or freight train. Mother and Winnie May went to Brenau in or about 1914.

Now about the mail bus. It was not a bus.

It was a van type truck and when the mailman carne to town twice a day (once north, once south) people would give him a quarter and he would let them ride in this van-type truck, no windows, with benches on each side. Very uncomfortable but it got you there. One would meet him at the post office and return there. Contributed by *Cynthia Williams Hilliard*.

I wish I had a picture of the cotton days in Martin. I remember as a boy I would go with my dad to the Gin at the old oil mill at Martin, where the scrap metal business is now. Henry Price ran the Gin plus the sawmill and a planer mill, all at that location. When we got to the cotton gin, we went on down to Martin to sell the cotton to Pope Yow, who had advanced the fertilizer to my dad in the spring. Mr. Pope would pull out hands full of cotton from the bale, examine it and tell my dad how much he could pay him for it. Some people took their bale of cotton home and warehoused it themselves until prices were higher.

My dad always needed the money, so if there was any money left over after the fertilizer and whatever else he had bought on credit. Anyway, there would be trucks and mule drawn wagons on both sides of the street, all the way through Martin, from the gin down to the railroad crossing at the school, during the peak of the cotton harvesting season on Saturdays. I don't know about the week days. Daddy would usually settle up with Pope, then go to the barbershop in Martin, where Clarence Thomas was cutting hair.

Being the one barber in Martin, on a busy Saturday like that, there would be men lined up all around the room, waiting for their turn for a haircut. I don't know what the haircut cost then, but I remember the "shave and a haircut…two bits" line that must have come from a song or something. Just another thought. Contributed by *Lamar Davis.*

Dean Terrell remembers that in the 1930's, continuing into the 1940's as a child, his parents would take him to the Toccoa depot and he would ride to Martin on what was referred to as the "Little Elberton Train." (It had one passenger car and three or four freight cars). The engine was put on a round table in Elberton and it would come back that day. He would get off at the Martin Depot and walk over to Cousin Pope Yow's general store (groceries, clothes, plow lines, etc. and one-gallon pump that was manually operated.). The store had one of the few phones in the Martin area and dad would call his mother, Ruth Dean Terrell.

Then he would walk over to his grandparents' house and stay a few days.

Pope Yow had a warehouse directly across the highway where he had fertilizer for the farmers. Pope also bought baled cotton when it was harvested, then would resell it to somebody. The space between his warehouse and the depot was referred to as "The Chicken Car" would come once a week, or once every two weeks.

People who had chickens to sell brought them there and the man on the truck would buy them and put them into chicken crates. Contributed by *Dean Terrell.*

Mary Dean Oxford remembers the phone system. Her granddaddy's number was three longs and a short ring. My dad drank his first Coke at Pope Yow's store and said it blew steam out of his nose.

Pete Brown, daddy, Robert Dean, and others were at the pig pen teasing Pete into biting the pig's tail. It pulled his tooth out. Guess they didn't have much to do back then. I remember at Christmas, they lighted rags with kerosene and used these balls to throw for their fireworks. We always shot fireworks at Christmas on the road in front of granddaddies. We were allowed to wave the sparklers. Santa Clause was put out in MeMamma's bedroom, where we spent many hours by the fire, popping corn and peeling grapefruit.
Submitted by *Mary Dean Oxford.*

When I was about 11 thru 15 I rode the mail truck, which came through Martin probably twice a day. It was driven then by Hansel Miller, who was my Dad's first cousin. I think he went from Toccoa to Elberton, with all the stops in between. I rode with him to baseball practice and games in Toccoa. I think other people did this as well. He never charged me anything

We have lots of checks, stationery, etc. from the Bank of Martin, because my grandfather T. H. Stovall was the President of the bank. I also have some ledger sheets, and a good bit of correspondence between him and his brother, who was president of the Empire Trust Company in Atlanta. They were discussing (this was pre depression era) all of the banks going under in Atlanta, and that they were trying to get the banks as liquid as possible, because times were already hard.

There was no safety net for banks in those days, no Federal Reserve or anything, so when depositors made a run, or debtors couldn't pay, the banks were forced to close, which the Bank of Martin did after the depression hit. I don't have any pictures, but the vault is still in Martha's store, on the side where the Post Office used to be. It says "Bank of Martin" on it.

My grandfather Stovall also ran the Cotton Seed Oil Mill, and I do have a picture of him along with all the employees standing in front of it. I think Nancy also has pictures I took of them dynamiting the oil mill tower. I think someone in our family, maybe Joy, has the standing desk out of the oil mill.

My mother said that her brothers Joe and Dan, and maybe some of the other town boys, blew up the well in the middle of town by draining gas out of the old fashioned pumps in town onto feed sacks, throwing them down the well, and dropping a match down the well. This was during church, and you could hear the explosion all over town. I think it blew off the well shelter. I don't know if the well was used again or not. When you get my mind started, I can remember quite a bit of stuff that probably no one else paid attention to, or can remember. Submitted by *Bryan Stovall*

Bread used to be delivered from Elberton in baskets via the train. (Vivian Crawford has one of the original baskets. It belonged to one of the merchants in town, Dr. Crawford asked to buy one of the baskets; the store owner gave it to him.

Downtown activity in the late 20's included a contest for the men of climbing a greased pole. There were many activities for the Martin residents. Everyone gathered in the downtown area for games.

Schools: The Martin school was grades 1 through 10. After the 10th grade, the students went either to Eastanollee or Toccoa for grade 11. One of the teachers was Mrs. Mary Mitchell whose mode of discipline was to rap you on the fingers with a ruler.

Parties: In the 20 and 30s residents would have taffy pulls and ice cream parties. They also liked to talk about wars and the military.

When the theater opened in Toccoa, some of the Martin children would drive to Toccoa to attend. The movies were silent and during the movie, a man would play the piano along with the silent movie script. The piano player was always a man. After the movie, everyone would go to Wright's Ice Cream in Toccoa where you could get a very generous amount (multiple scoops) of delicious ice cream for a nickel.

Mr. Chappelear and Mr. Bagwell that ran the blacksmith shop would sit downtown and if the children got too close to them, they would pinch the children. Submitted by *Vivian Crawford McCall*.

The largest land owner in the area was Richard Dempsey Yow: He had way over 10,000 acres. Mr. Yow ran a store in Avalon. He made his own electric generating plant and he and his brother Thomas Russell Yow ran a wire from Avalon to Martin and played checkers. His brother Epp MorrisYow also lived in Avalon and built a house that was later lived in by Paul Cooper and Mr. and Mrs. Gus Gonzales.

 The house later burned. Richard Dempsey was a bugler boy at 15 in the Civil War and was captured by the North. His dad died in Richmond, VA and is buried at Stumpy's store on Highway 328.

Richard Dempsey made millions during hard times. He was a member of the legislature and upon his death a train ran from Toccoa to his funeral. He was buried in a homemade suit in a pine box.

Two of his children were Myrtle Yow Davis and Dr. S. B. Yow. Dr. S. B. Yow finished first in his class at seven universities, including University of Georgia, Harvard and Oxford. Even though Mr. Yow was a medical doctor, he could not make a living in medicine. He married the governor's daughter and opened a store in Lavonia, with his first cousin, Edward McMurry.

Uncle Arthur Dean lived on the river with his mom and dad. He moved to Martin and lived in the Thomas Russell store. It burned and Betty Dean Yow would not allow him to be exposed to such after that. He married Lloyd Brown's sister when he was 40 and she was 17 and they had 5 children.

Mrs. Ketcherside did not have a babysitter for Blanche, so she nailed her daughter's dress to the floor to keep her out of the fire.

Russ Mitchell was found dead at the corn mill with no clothes on.

Henry Price and his wife Roxie, lived in the oil mill. Mose and Homer Outz and Elias Collier worked at the oil mill.

Mable Verner married Dr. Chaffin and lived in the Verner House, which is now the home of Laura Turner.

Mack Knox owned all the land where John Goodwin, Grady Bell and Joe Day built homes.

The railroad was maintained by a section foreman and laborers that he hired.

Does anyone remember the 7' black man that lived with his mother on Cliff Mitchell's property?

W. A. Mitchell was the largest merchant in Martin. He moved to Gainesville in about 1900 and his family gave the 40 acres to Martin Baptist Church.

Matt Freeman was mayor for a long time, although he lived outside the town of Martin.

Mr. Lillenthal came through Martin riding the train as all of the drummers (drummers were salesmen) did. He sold lace and was put in jail because he did not have a license. He hollered all night and kept the town up. Behind Lloyd Brown's house was a swimming hole.

Submitted by *Thomas Russell Yow Williams.*

Martha Jo Matthews Hunt interviewed James "Sneck" Landrum. She asked Sneck was the name "Bank" ever on the front of the building? He said the name "Bank" was on the front of the building next to the house that was the Clodfelter House. The Clodfelter House once had the Post Office; caskets and funeral parlor were also inside the house.

The house of the corner where the Mosley's service station was located was where Jolynn Mosley lived. Submitted by *Martha Hunt.*

Clarence Elrod and Joe Cash ran the movie above the Stovall Building. Grace Yow grew herbs which were sold as far away as Germany. Submitted by the *Yow Family.*

Mot Sorrells remembers Dick Yow and Richard Dean sending in answers to a contest on the "Hit Parade", a radio program that was on every Saturday night. Several times they won prizes of Lucky Strike cigarettes. Neither of these men smoked, so they would either sell or give away the prizes.

There were also Eskimo Pie eating contests. Submitted by *Ruth Dean Terrell*

A few years ago I was interested in the large rock in Swain Looney's yard. It had engraving from sometime in the distant past. I had the State archaeologist come up and check it out. He couldn't explain it. Possibly it was from pioneer's burning the rich pine for the pitch. The rock has never been made public because of the danger of vandalism. Submitted by *Walter.*

In the 1950's cotton was brought to Martin to sell. My dad, Dick and Grandad Pope, could not put it all in their warehouses, so they hired a night watchman, Claude and Jackie Lecroy, to watch over the cotton outside on the street.

Mr. Charles Fagan is quite a story teller, and remembers lots of happenings. In July, 1932 when he was two years old, he had a very serious case of the deadly disease, diphtheria. The family contacted Dr. Swaim, who came to the house and recommended the following treatment: Build a large fire in the fireplace, heat a black kettle of water to a rolling boil, add all medicines in the house that might be available - ointments, Watkins Liniment, watermelon seeds, Vicks Salve, and pine needles. Cover the spout of the kettle with a guano horn. Sit with head over Guano Horn, inhale the steam until able to breathe. This treatment worked for Charles. He soon recovered from the dread disease.

Mr. Fagan enjoys telling about Minnie, the family mule. Minnie fit the description of "stubborn as a mule". Mr. Ben would tie Minnie to a tree while he went to the creek to check his traps.

She would always figure a way to get loose and go home before Mr. Ben. After many times of having to walk home, Mr. Ben decided he would outsmart Minnie, so he tied her to a fence post.

However, again she beat him home and took the fence post with her. He also says he remembers the first time he attended church at Martin. He says Mr. Ben and Mrs. Beulah were miserable until after the plate was passed because they feared Charles would take the money. They were very relieved that he didn't! There were five generations of Fagans who lived on the Fagan farm. The property has however been sold. Charles and his wife, Susan Gilbert reside in Pendleton, S. C. and they have two married daughters who have children of their own. Submitted by *Charles Fagan.*

Quilt to Socialize

In the early 1940's, Minnie Andrews Turner and other ladies of the community gathered together to socialize and quilt. At one such meeting they made a friendship quilt. Each lady embroiders their family members' names on the quilt. Minnie was given the quilt and passed it down to her children and grandchildren. One of her grandsons, Dicky Turner, son of Jimmy Turner, now owns the quilt and hopes to pass it to his children one day.

We have listed each name as it appears on the quilt. There are over 314 names - counting Mr. and Mrs. as one name. (Note the underlined name - did he live in the community? Are they showing their pride in their country?)

We have listed the names in alphabetically order for your convenience: Mrs. P. S. Adair, Dwight Adams, Mr. and Mrs. W. A. Adams, Mary Lou Adams, Walter Adams, Mr. Doyle Addison, Mrs. L. T. Addison, Mr. and Mrs. Charles Addison, Mr. Joe Aderhold, Mr. and Mrs. C. B. Akin, Thomas Akin, Bill Allen, Mr. and Mrs. Hoyt Andrews, Preston Andres, Mr. and Mrs. A. G. Andrews, Mr. and Mrs. H. M. Andrews, Mrs. B. C. Arial, Mrs. J. W. Ayers, Mrs. W. P. Ayers, Vera Bagwell, Mrs. Inez Bagwell, Mrs. J. M. Batson, Turner Beasley, Mr. and Mrs. A. B. Beeca, Morris Blair, Mrs. Jack Bond, Mrs. C. D. Bowen, J. C. Breedlove, Rev. E. R. Broadwell, Mrs. Lent Brock, Mildred Brooks, Mr. A. M. Brown, Mrs. A. M. Brown, Mary Stewart Brown, Dr. and Mrs. Stewart Brown, Stewart Brown Jr., Sarah Frances Brown, Doris Brown, Dr. and Mrs. J. R. Brown, Sarah Burroughs, Mr. and Mrs. Tom Burroughs, Mr. and Mrs. Jim Burton, Mr. and Mrs. Rush Burton, Steve Busha, Frank Byrd, Joe

Stewart Byrd, Frances Byrd, Mrs. S. W. Cannon, Mr. and Mrs. Ralph Cannon, Mr. and Mrs. O. D. Cannon, Mrs. and Mrs. Grady Carroll, J. B. Casey, Dr. and Mrs. R. R. Cason, Mrs. M. C. Cawthon, Mr. and Mrs. Herschel Cheek, Mrs. and Mrs. Dwain Cheek, Ralph Cheek, Mrs. and Mrs. W. D. Cheek, Mrs. and Mrs. B. F. Cheek, Morene Cheek, Mr. and Mrs. B. F. Cheek, Mrs. and Mrs. W. T. Cheek, Mr. Hall Chitwood, Winton Chitwood, Mr. and Mrs. Ides Chitwood, Carolyn Clarke, Mr. and Mrs. Ezra Clarke, Mr. and Mrs. Bethel Clarke, Essie Clarke, Mayna Clarke, Mrs. J. C. Clarke, Willard Clarke, Mr. and Mrs. Roy Clarke, James Conley, Mr. and Mrs. W. H. Conwell, Mr. and Mrs. L. T. Cox, Mrs. W. A. Crawford, E. K. Davis, A. L. Decker, Croff Decker, Mrs. Ella Lou Turner Dickson, Jim Elrod, Mr. D. T. Ertzberger, Mrs. G. G. Fanning, Joe Ferguson, Mr. R. Finley, L. E. Fisher, King Edd Floyd, Jacquelyn Floyd, Mrs. Alton Floyd, Mr. and Mrs. Ernest Floyd, Mr. and Mrs. Y. M. Ford, T. W. Freeman, Mrs. Ola Fulghum, Mr. and Mrs. Fred J. Fulghum, Freddie and Mark Fulghum, Noah Fulghum, Mozella Fulghum, Mr. and Mrs. P. E. Fulghum, Jean and Katherine Gard, Mrs. and Mrs. Guy Gard, Mr. and Mrs. Swift Gilmer, John R. Goolsby, Mrs. J. N. Goolsby, W. S. Hale, Grady Haley Jr., Mrs. Grady Haley, Mrs. Alton Haley, Mrs. Julia Hall, Roy Hamby, Mary Lou Hamby, Mr. and Mrs. Lee Hamby, Mr. and Mrs. W. A. Hamby, Mr. W. N. Harrison, Mrs. Horace Harrison, Robbie Ray Harrison, Mr. and Mrs. G. R. Harrison, Marene Harrison, Jack Haynie, Virgie Haynie, Phil Haynie, Ethel Haynie, Mr. and Mrs. Higginbotham, Harold Higgins, Mrs. M. R. Hilliard, Mr. and Mrs. M. G. Hilliard, Carl Holbrook, Mrs. W. L. Holcomb, Roy Holcomb, Ouzie Holcomb, Mr. W. L. Holcomb, Mrs. Chas. Hubbard, Mrs. W. S. Humphreys, Mrs. Ila Isbell, Lucy Phoene Isbelle, Mr. and Mrs. Andy Ivester, Mrs. Jim Jones, H. M. Jones, B. F. Keese, Miss Mary Lou Keesler, T. A. Kelley, Hubert

Kesler, Mrs. H. E. Kesler, Billy Knox, Jr., Mr. and Mrs. Will Knox, George Lankford, Margaret Ledbetter, Hudma Ledbetter, Leon Ledbetter, Johnnie Sue Ledbetter, Tootsie Lenhardt, Mr. and Mrs. Clarence Leverette, R. L. Little, Mrs. J. C. Little, Mrs. W. C. Lolhr, Mrs. A. L. Mabry, Gladys Mason, Lillian Mason, J. O. Mauldin, Z. H. McCall, Hoke McClain, Salon McClain, Ellen Dean McClain, Emma McClesky, Mr. Henty McCollum, Mrs. G. L. McConnell, Mrs. E. Z. McDuffie, George McDuffie, Mrs. E. Z. McDuffie, J. B. McEntire, Mrs. D. H. McGee, W. M. McGee, Mr. E. R. McMurray, M. H. McCurray, E. R. McMurry, Mr. and Mrs. Hugh McMurry, Mr. and Mrs. L. F. McWhorter, Faith McWhorter, Mrs. E. E. McWhorter, Patsy McWhorter, Grace McWhorter, Eddy McWhorter, Mr. and Mrs. C. T. Miller, Mrs. C. C. Miller, Mrs. C. T. Miller, Mr. and Mrs. J. R. Morgan, Mr. and Mrs. T. H. Moss, Helen McDuffie, E. T. Mullinix, Helen Mullinix, Mr. and Mrs. Willis Mullinix, Mr. and Mrs. J. J. Mullinix, Mr. and Mrs. Robert Myers, Mr. and Mrs. J. L. Odom, Mrs. Van Parker, Mrs. Johnson Perkins, Mrs. E. A. Philips, Mr. and Mrs. Floyd Poole, Mr. and Mrs. Odom Purcell, Mrs. Parker Purcell, Charlie Purcell, Martha Louise Rampley, Franklin D. Roosevelt, Allen Roper, H. J. Rumsey, Mrs. R. N> Schaffer, Marjorie Sewell, Mr. Henry Sewell, Mrs. Will Sewell, Bonnie Sewell, Swinton Sewell, Mr. and Mrs. R. H. Sewell, Mrs. Dona Sewell, Mr. and Mrs. M. L. Sewell, Miss Kathleen Sewell, Mr. and Mrs. A. B. Sewell, Mary Nell Sewell, Hubert Sewell, Dr. M. R. Sewell, P. J. Sewell, Mrs. Anna Sewell, Hoke Sewell, T. A. Shelton, Carolyn and Louise Shiflet, Freddie Shiflet, Duard Shirley, Mrs. M. C. Short, W. A. Simpson, Cleo Simpson, Mrs. B. R. Simpson, Mrs. Arad Smith, Mr. and Mrs. Erastus Smith, Ernest H. Smith, Mr. Will Smith, Mr. and Mrw. Wayne Smith, Irvin Smith, Mr. and Mrs. John Smith, J. H. Smith, Mr.

and Mrs. A. D. Smith, Hoyt A. Smith, J. B. Smith, Chief Smith, Mrs. C. R. Spears, Winnie Stephens, Mr. and Mrs. John Stephenson, Mrs.W. E. Stevenson, Gladys Strickland, Judyth Ann Strickland, Clyde Sullivan, Eugene Talmadge, C. C. Thomsa, Hoyt Thomsa, Roy Thomason, Mr. Burie Thomason, Mr. and Mrs. C. L. Tomey, Lorraine Turner Tomlinson, Robert Orr Tribble, Mrs. W. C. Tribble, Dean Turner, Jimmy Turner, Joe Frank Turner, Mr. and Mrs. Charley Turner, Fred Turner, Evelyn Turner, Ausey Turner, Jack Turner, Paul Turner, Mollie Turner, Mrs. J. B. Tyler, J. B. Tyler, George Tyler, Dr. R. L. Vandiver, Lillian Vandiver, Mr. and Mrs. S. E. Vandiver, Mrs. Rebe Vaughan, Prof. and Mrs. J. C. Vaughan, James Vaughan, Mr. and Mrs. H. F. Vaughan, Mrs. Fred Vaughan, Baxter Vaughan, Mary Vaughan, Mr. Fred Vaughan, Mr. and Mrs. W. O. Vaughan, Gloria Walters, Mr. and Mrs. E. S. Walters, Jim Walters, Mr. and Mrs. Jim Walters, Mr. Coyt Walters, Mrs. H. G. Wansley, C. T. Ware, L. P. Webb, Mr. and Mrs. F. N. Weldon, Jane Weldon, Fred Weldon Jr., Mr. and Mrs. G. S. Weldon, Ann Weldon, Dennis Weldon Jr., Dr. and Mrs. D. E. Weldon, Mr. and Mrs. F. N. Weldon, Mr. and Mrs. J. T. Whitfield, Grace Whiting, George Whiting, Miriam Whitlow, Rosetta Whitworth, New Wier, Mrs. Laura Wilder, Jamie Ruth Wilder, Bernice Wilder, Mr. W. M. Williams, Mrs. W. M. Willians, Maxine Williamsn, Mrs. N. R. Wilson, Mrs. Joe Wright, Dr. S. B. Yow. **Submitted by:** *Laura Kay Turner*

THE WEDDING DAY

On Feb. 2, 1957 the marriage of Barbara Williams, daughter of Mr. & Mrs. Pope Williams of Lavonia, and Max Freeman, son of Mr. & Mrs. Joe Freeman of Martin had the first wedding that had ever taken place in Fairview Baptist Church, Lavonia, Ga. After several weeks of miserable weather, rain, sleet and lots of prayers by the bride, the sky opened up, the sun came out, and Feb.2, 1957 was a beautiful day.

Everything about the wedding went smoothly until the newlyweds exited the church. "Where is the car?" asks the bride. "I hid it in Papa Freeman's front yard," says the groom. "You what!! How stupid can you be? You know it will be a mess." Parked in front of the church was a brand new Buick the groom had borrowed from his cousin, Freeman Poole, just for the trip from the church to the bride's parent's house and then to Martin to get the '55 Chevy. The bride had always imagined how exciting it would be to leave the church in a "just married" car with tin cans tied to the back. Now, in addition to her disappointment, she had to worry about what damage their "friends" would do to a borrowed car - a brand new car!

Fortunately, after the reception, the new Buick was still in the yard, waiting to take the couple to Martin, nothing written on it, no tin cans. Up highway 17 the new Buick led the motorcade, maybe breaking the speed limit somewhat. Suddenly, there were blue lights everywhere, and the groom pulled the car over to the side of the road, got out, and faced the Franklin County Sheriff and Deputy.

The borrowed car seemed to be surrounded by people. "Put him in jail." "Make him spend the night in jail." As the groom tried to get his driver's license out of his wallet, the wind blew all of his papers, license, and pictures down the highway. No one offered to help him, so he had to get down on all fours in the middle of highway 17 to retrieve his valuables. (Remember, this was 1957.) The Sheriff didn't even mention that he was speeding, only that he was "weaving" a little in the road, patted him on the back, and told him to have a good evening.

On up the road to Papa Freeman's house. "Just as I expected," said the bride. The '55 Chevy was a mess! - Shaving cream, paint, AND tin cans. The rear tires were jacked up because the rear of the car was sitting on large blocks of wood. The couple finally got in their car but went nowhere. The car just sat there spinning and slinging mud everywhere. The groom got out to look the situation over while the bride sat in the car. The crowd surrounding the car had no suggestions as to how to get the car moving, so both bride and groom sat in the car. After deciding that nobody was going to do anything, someone in the crowd suggested that they might lift the car off the blocks.

Some of the kind friends and relatives came to the rescue, and the newlyweds journeyed on up the road in their car, tin cans and all to the Walhalla Steak House which was famous for steak & grits. Curtis & Miriam Whitlow Purdy of Martin were finishing their dinner and greeted the couple when they entered.

After a very enjoyable dinner, the bride was in a better humor, and they journeyed on down the road. After a few miles there was a strange, horrible odor in the car which seemed to get worse fast, so the groom stopped at a gas station to check out the problem.

Several men who were outside the station held their noses and ran into the station. The source of the horrible smell was a large frozen mullet fish that had been placed on the Chevy's manifold! After the groom took care of the fish, the couple continued on their journey.

There are still unanswered questions. Why was the Sheriff's Department so well represented on highway 17?? How did the big fish get under the hood of the car? Why did the groom think he could "hide" the car in his Grandfather's yard when Charles Fagan had to pass by on his way to the wedding?

The bride's anger didn't last long. In 1960 the couple purchased the Ivan Thomas located on highway 17 south of Martin. Their driveway is the exact spot on the highway that they parked their borrowed car when the Sheriff stopped them on Feb. 2, 1957. After 57 years, the marriage is still lasting. Submitted by *Barbara Freeman.*

Ice-from-sky preserved for eyes of smithsonian
By Mike Edwards
Pieces of the 30-40 pound chunk of ice said to have fallen from the clear blue sky near Toccoa Monday evening were being preserved Thursday in hope that the Smithsonian Institution in Washington would be interested in examining them.

In Atlanta, Dr. William A. Calder, professor of physics and astronomy at Agnes Scott College, said the ice, if the story of its falling isn't a hoax, "might be of great scientific interest."

REMEMBERING THE celebrated man from Mars hoax of 1953, which turned out to be a shaved, bob-tailed monkey planted on a highway, Dr. Calder reserved judgment on the ice chunk. But he said he is greatly interested in it, nonetheless

.

The only possible astronomical explanation. he said. is that the ice-and a chuck reported to have fallen near Acaia, Italy, hours before the one fell near Toccoa-is a "straggling particle" of a comet. Possibly. he said. Giacobini's Comet, whose orbit intersected the orbit of Earth on Oct. 9.

He pointed out that Dr. Fred Whipple. director of the Smithsonian Astrophysical Observatory at Cambridge. Mass.. has advanced the theory that comets are by and large composed of "dirty ices." It was in the backyard of Claud J. Lecroy at Martin. Ga. (a community of perhaps 200), south of Toccoa, that the ice is said to have fallen.

Mr. Lecroy. a milk-truck driver, said he was in the back yard when the ice fell.

"It made a noise like a jet." he said. "and 1 could feel it was fixing to hit something because it was getting louder. It hit in the garden. about 11 or 12 feet from me." The Ice carved a hole about a foot deep and two feet wide in the earth. The ice shattered on impact.

One of the first persons to view it was Roy E. Gaines. co-owner of radio station WNEG at Toccoa. He took home several chunks of the ice. put some in a neighbor's freezer and turned some over to the Toccoa High School science teacher, Joe Vaughn.

MR. VAUGHN SAID he analyzed the water from some of it with assistance from a treadmill chemist and the Toccoa Water Works. The water was found to be soft and not chlorinated. he said. When it was boiled, he said, there was no odor. It was not radioactive.

"But I'm not capable of making the analyses that should be made." he said. "for lack of equipment and lack of knowledge. I hope the Smithsonian will want to check it. Both Mr. Vaughn and Mr. Gaines still have some of the ice in freezers. Mr. Gaines said it had a milky cast. Pieces that appeared to have been on the outside of the chunk were pitted and scarred like the surface of a meteor, he said.

SO FAR AS was known. there were no airplanes overhead when the ice fell. The largest authenticated hailstone weighed 1.213 pounds. The largest hailstones ever reported weighed 4 pounds and supposedly crushed rooftops when they fell on the town of Cazoria. Spain. on June 15. 1829. The United States Weather Bureau in Atlanta said it never heard of ice chunks as large as the one reported in Toccoa. There are no winds aloft capable of supporting such a large chunk. a spokesman said. A Georgia Tech physicist said: "The only explanation 1 can offer is that the iceman cometh:

Two Smyrna men said they found two chunks of ice beside W. Paces Ferry road near the bridge over the Chattahoochee River Saturday morning.

Charles Black of Rte. 1. Smyrna. said he didn't see the ice falling from the sky. as ice is reported to have fallen recently near Toccoa. He and a friend Jim Presslev. also of Smyrna. were driving home from work when they saw the ice on the right-hand side of the road just before they reached the bridge. Mr. Black said. Mr. Black described the bigger of the two pieces as "12 to 14 inches long and eight inches wide."

"IT WAS white and looked like a piece of a snowman.' he said. "The smaller piece was about the size of two hands. It may have broken off the larger piece."

The two men left the ice on the side of the road. where presumably it melted away-but not before a newspaper photographer got a picture of it. Asked for an opinion on how the ice got beside the road. Ed Smith. meteorologist with the Atlanta Weather Bureau. suggested that it might have been dumped from a milk truck. I've seen the drivers of milk trucks remove the ice from the trucks after they've delivered the milk,' he said.

FROM MR. BLACK'S description of the ice and considering the time and place it was found. I'd say it might have gotten there that way." Meanwhile. two chunks of ice each the size of a basketball-were reported to have fallen from the sky over Beachwood, a suburb of Cleveland, Friday.

One chunk tour a 15-inch hold in the roof of a home and a gaping hole in the upstairs' ceiling.

THE OTHER fell on the fairwav of the Highland Park Golf course. about 100 vards from two golfers. Loretta Bray Moody emailed this information on Jan 29, 2007.

How many of y'all remember the Goat Man?

I was reminded of the Goat Man when a little old lady stopped me outside a fast-food restaurant the other day and wanted to talk about some of the columns I have written in the past.

She asked me to guess her favorite, but since I am not clairvoyant and since I have written well over a thousand, I couldn't begin to fathom a guess - although my ego hoped that she would enlighten me. And she did.

She told me that her very favorite column was one I wrote a few years back about the Goat Man, whose real name, I believe, was Charles McCartney - but he was often known as Chas or Ches.

If you remember the Goat Man, then you already know ll about him, but for those of you who don't, he was quite a remarkable fellow who traveled all across the United States - and I am talking for decades now - walking beside a little wooden wagon, accompanied by a herd of goats, thus his name. He really was a goat man and had dozens of goats to prove it.

Life was a lot simpler back in the 1950s, understand, and there wasn't a lot of excitement, usually. But that all changed when the news began to spread through the community - always by word of mouth, of course - that the Goat Man had been spotted in the area.

Everyone would start driving around the county, trying to be the first to locate him. And on one grand day I actually sat on my front porch and watched the Goat Man and his entire herd walking right through the center of Porterdale. It remains one of the highlights of my life.

I am not sure how often the Goat Man passed our way, but it was probably every three or four years. It must take a while to walk to Walla Walla, Washington. The Goat Man always would camp out on the edge of town and seldom stayed in one place more than a day. He was the last of the nomads, I suppose, and it was real treat to get to go out to his campsite and visit with him.
His little wagon was covered from stem to stem with pots and pans and old license plates - souvenirs of his decades of travel across this great land.

I have heard that he visited every state in the lower 48 with his goats, and I know for a fact that he once camped out on the White House lawn in Washington, because I saw the photographs to prove it.

Something tells me they w ouldn't let him do that today. McCartney was something of an evangelist and would sit around his campfire as long as anyone wanted to listen, discussing religion and politics, quoting the King James Bible and playing with his goats.
He was a part of a bygone era and wouldn't be allowed to have the run of the country today. There are too many laws and ordinances today to allow for a character as colorful as him.

Besides, with so much meanness in the world, he wouldn't be safe, anyway. I heard that the Goat Man spent his last days in a nursing home, I want to say down around Macon, and is dead now. But he won't be forgotten - until my generation is all dead and gone. He was a part of the fabric of my youth and I am glad that at least one little old lady remembers him as favorably as I do.

* Darrell Huckaby is an educator, author and public speaker.

THINGS YOU DON'T HEAR ANYMORE

Be sure and refill the ice trays, we are going to have company after a while.

Watch for the postman, I want to get this letter in the mail today.

Quit slamming that screen door!

Be sure to pull the windows down when you leave, it looks like it might rain ... and bring in the clothes from the line.

Don't forget to wind the clock before you go to bed.

Wash your feet before you go to bed, they are nasty from playing bare footed outside all day.

Why can't you remember to roll up your pants legs? Getting them caught in the bicycle chain so many times is tearing them up.

You have torn the knees out of that pair of pants so many times there is nothing left to put a patch on.

Don't you go outside with your good school clothes on!

Hang up your Sunday School clothes; you know you need to pass them down to your brother in good condition.

Go comb your hair. It looks like the rats have nested in it all night.

Be sure and pour the cream off the top of the milk when you open the new bottle. I need it for baking.

Take that empty bottle to the store with you so you won't have to pay a deposit on another one.

Put a dish towel over the cake so the flies won't get on it.

Quit jumping on the floor. I have a cake in the oven and you are going to make it fall!

Let me know when the Fuller Brush man comes by, I need to get a few things from him.

You boys stay close by, the car may not start and I will need you to help push it off.

There is a dollar in my purse, go by the service station on the way to town and get five gallons of gas.

Open the back door and see if we can get a breeze through here. It's getting hot in here.

You can walk to the store; it won't hurt you to get some exercise. Maybe you will learn to be more careful with your bicycle next time.

Don't sit too close to the TV, it's hard on your eyes.

If you pull that stunt again, I am going to wear you out; you hear that?

Don't lose that button; I need to sew it back on after a while.

Wash under your neck before you come to the table, you have beads of dirt and sweat all under there.

Get out from under that sewing machine; pumping it messes up the thread.

Do you want me to go get me a switch?

Be sure and fill the lamps this morning so we don't have to do that tonight in the dark.

Here, take this old magazine to the outhouse (toilet) when you *go,* we're almost out of paper out there.

Go out to the well and draw a bucket of water for me to wash dishes in.

Don't turn the radio on now; I want the battery to be up when the Grand Ole Opry comes on.

Not I don't have five cents for you to go to the show; do you think money grows on trees?

Eat those vegetables; they will make you big and strong like your daddy.

That dog is NOT coming in this house! I don't care how cold it is out there, dogs just don't belong in the house.

Sit still! I am trying to get your hair cut straight and you keep moving and it's getting botched up.
Hush your mouth! I don't want to hear any more words like that, or I'll wash your mouth out with soap again.

It is time for your system to be cleaned out. I'm going to give you a dose of Castor Oil in the morning.

If you get a spanking in school and I find out about it, you will get another one when you get home.

I don't know who wrote the following, but they make you show your age if you are like me and can relate to most if not all of the quotes.
Quit crossing your eyes! They will get stuck that way!

Soak your foot in this pan of coal oil so that cut won't get infected.

When you take your driving test don't forget your hand signals for each turn: left arm straight out the window for a left turn; left arm bent up to the sky at the elbow for a right turn; and straight down to the side of the door when you are going to stop.

Don't forget!   It is *'Yes* sir!' and 'No, sir' to me and your elders young man, and don't you forget it!

While we are at Aunt Mary's and Uncle John's you kids eat when the adults get through and I don't want to hear "I don't like this stuff". You'd better keep your mouth shut and eat everything on your plate.

Bring back memories? It sure did for me.

CHAPTER SEVENTEEN
RAMBLINGS
See how many people you can recognize in these photos.
Enjoy.

The Martin Fall Festival sponsored by the Martin Woman's Club was held Oct. 27, on a beautiful, cool day.

Louise Wilson, the coordinator for the festival, was pleased with the number of vendors and all the folks who came out to support the festival. The Gospel Relations entertained most of the day and the Currahee Squares were out in the morning square dancing.

The Brotherhood from Martin Baptist Church had a tractor parade with Tommy Williams leading the parade with an old retired fire truck from the Martin Volunteer Fire Department.

There were cakewalks every two hours with lots of folks winning beautiful, tasty cakes made by the ladies at the Martin Woman's Club. Raffle tickets were sold for a $150 WalMart gift card and the winner of that card was Dale Davis.

Photos submitted

Martin...
means
History

Driving/
Walking Tour

Town of Martin, Georgia

Established September 7, 1891

Placed on the Register of
National Historic Places
July 7, 1995